MORE ADVANCE PRAISE FOR *MAXIMUM SUCCESS*

"A clear picture of what it takes to be successful . . . The authors take us from theory to practice, never leaning too heavily on one or the other. By the end of the book the reader will have a clear road map for the journey and the set of experiences we call a career."

—THOMAS DELONG, PROFESSOR OF MANAGEMENT,
HARVARD BUSINESS SCHOOL

"Finally, a book that goes beyond the 'keys to success' books that only state the obvious. *Maximum Success* is really about the 'twelve habits of highly ineffective people' and how to change them. It's the most practical, useful book I've read in years."

—JOHN PATTERSON, VICE PRESIDENT FOR TALENT, PRICELINE.COM

"No other business book better helps you understand yourself and your co-workers or provides specific ways to inspire your performance and that of your organization. Ignore Waldroop and Butler's insights at your peril."

—JAMES BIOLOS, VICE PRESIDENT,
HUMAN RESOURCE COMMUNICATIONS, CITIGROUP

"I spend most of my time dealing with difficult people, but nothing had ever prepared me for handling truly challenging personalities, until now. Everyone who manages people should be required to read this book."

—RAYMOND B. RUDDY, CHAIRMAN OF THE BOARD, MAXIMUS

"If you spend a great deal of your time helping your organization attract, grow, and keep great talent, *Maximum Success* should be your bedside and deskside reading material. Filled with straight talk and smart advice, it is a must read for anyone interested in real lessons for real life."

—ANGELA SCALPELLO, SENIOR VICE PRESIDENT
FOR EMPLOYEE DEVELOPMENT, OGILVY PUBLIC RELATIONS

MAXIMUM
SUCCESS

MAXIMUM
SUCCESS

CHANGING THE
12 BEHAVIOR PATTERNS
THAT KEEP YOU FROM GETTING AHEAD

JAMES WALDROOP, PH.D.,
AND
TIMOTHY BUTLER, PH.D.

CURRENCY/DOUBLEDAY

NEW YORK   LONDON   TORONTO   SYDNEY   AUCKLAND

A CURRENCY BOOK
Published by Doubleday
a division of Random House, Inc.
1540 Broadway, New York, New York, 10036

CURRENCY and DOUBLEDAY
are trademarks of Doubleday, a division of Random House, Inc.

Book design by Carol Malcolm Russo / Signet M Design, Inc.

Library of Congress Cataloging-in-Publication Data
Waldroop, James.
Maximum success : changing the 12 behavior patterns
that keep you from getting ahead
/ James Waldroop, Timothy Butler.
p.   cm.
Includes index.
1. Vocational guidance. I. Butler, Timothy.
HF5381 . W348 2000
650.14—dc21   00-034614
ISBN 0-385-49849-7

FOR MY FAMILY,
VALERIE, MAX, AND DANIEL,
AND FOR MY FRIENDS
STEVE AND TIM.

J.W.

ONCE AGAIN,
FOR LINDA AND KIERA,
AND FOR MY PARENTS.

T.B.

CONTENTS

CONTENTS

ACKNOWLEDGMENTS

Our first thanks go to the clients we have worked with over the years. Whatever insights are present in this work are largely born of our experience with those individuals. Certainly our clarity regarding the twelve patterns we've written about here emerged from the time we spent working with them. In a very real sense our clients were there at the beginning of this project—before any of us knew where it would lead.

We want to thank Roger Scholl at Currency for his vision, his faith, and his investment in the project; his enthusiasm, and his encouragement. His questions forced us to think more deeply about what we *really* meant at numerous points of semiobscurity. Most of all we appreciate his many hours making our words "sing" as well as they can. At every stage of the process his input has made this a better book.

Likewise, Lee Smith's creativity and assistance when the book was still in its most germinal stage was invaluable. Our conversations helped to clarify and deepen our thinking about the various behavior patterns, and were a pleasure as well! Truly, without him this book would not have been possible. Thanks and a tip of the Panama hat.

We are enormously grateful to Kris Dahl of International Creative Management for her encouragement in the evolution of this material from a posting on our Website to an article in *Fortune* to its current form. If not for her extra push to overcome our inertia, these pages would likely be blank. And thanks also to *Fortune*'s Geoff Colvin, who was responsible for the first of those evolutionary steps.

We are indebted to our colleagues, present and past, at MBA Career Services at the Harvard Business School, as well as to a multitude of other members of the HBS community, for their support over the many years of our work at the school. And we are indebted as well to Dave LeLacheur, our partner and friend, for juggling even more balls than usual, allowing us to put our hands to our keyboards.

Thanks go to Jacqui Archer for her amazingly accurate translation of our edits (and for catching other errors along the way) and to Stephanie Land for her grace and graciousness, good humor, and for filling in our deficiencies with her organizational ability.

Finally, thanks to our families for their encouragement, understanding, and love; and thanks especially to our wives, Valerie and Linda, for their loving support. They, too, kept more balls in the air while we talked, typed, then talked and typed some more. Without them we would not be who, or where, we are today. Thanks and all our love to Danny, Max, and Valerie, and to Kiera and Linda.

INTRODUCTION

J_ACK HAD EVERYTHING GOING FOR HIM. HE WAS HIGHLY_ intelligent, well educated (with a top school MBA and a master's degree in biological sciences from MIT), articulate, attractive, polished, and knowledgeable in the field of biotechnology. He was happily married with two young sons and a lovely home. At age thirty-three he was the head of a small but promising and growing biotech firm, was earning a high salary, and held stock that was likely to be worth several million dollars when the company went public. In short, Jack had—or was on the way to getting—it all.

Then he began to make a series of baffling management and political mistakes. They were the kinds of errors you might expect from someone in his first job out of college or in his first management position—not from someone with the amount of training, experience, and business savvy that Jack had. He took control away from people on projects in which they had invested a great deal of time, energy, and emotion (nitpicking on which exact shade of red should be used on a sales brochure, for example). He made arbitrary decisions (such as assigning new office spaces to people without their input) that, while not bad choices *per se,* were tremendously annoying to other people in the firm just because of their arbitrariness. He made statements and decisions (such as declining to hire the niece of a board member for a summer internship) that needlessly offended important investors in the company. The result was that Jack went into a tailspin from which he couldn't recover, and ultimately he was forced to resign from his position.

Suzanne was an excellent salesperson, regularly exceeding her sales targets, winning awards, and outselling the competition even when they had arguably superior products. She loved her work, and to a great extent her work was her life—possibly too much so. And she was a superstar when it came to selling ("someone who could talk a dog off a meat truck," as one of her Texas-based customers put it).

Some fourteen years into her career (all spent with the same employer) things started to go wrong for Suzanne. Certain bad habits—expressing her annoyance at company policies too vocally and too often and being overly self-disclosing—that she had had for many years began to show themselves to a much greater degree than ever before. When a new contact tracking system was installed, allowing both managers and other salespeople to easily view critical information via the Internet, Suzanne complained bitterly to her manager, to *his* manager, all the way up to the vice president for worldwide sales. She talked too openly, too loudly, and too often about her personal life (whom she was dating, how it was going, where she was considering moving, and how much it was going to cost her); and about her personal feelings about other people ("I love your tie," "I hate your tie," "That skirt and blouse don't go together," "The car you just bought has lots of problems," "You really should stop smoking," and so on). Warnings from management only made matters worse, further infuriating her. After a protracted and bitter struggle she left the company, ostensibly voluntarily but in fact having been "managed out."

ABOUT OUR WORK

Why *do* talented people fail? And why do talented people fail to be as good (as successful and effective) as they could be? These are questions we have grappled with for many years. As business psychologists and as directors of the Harvard Business School MBA Career Development Program, we've worked with thousands of professionals and students over the years in helping them to choose the right careers and to make their way down the paths they have chosen without falling along the way—or at least with as few slips as possible. Moreover, as consultants and coaches, we are brought in by many Fortune 500 companies to work with highly valued employees who are failing—employees and managers on the verge of being fired—as well as with those who are high benefit but "high maintenance." These are the people who are sometimes described as "95 percent brilliant, a superstar—but 5 percent disaster, someone I spend a huge amount of time taking care of." We are also called on to work with people who are succeeding in their positions but who clearly could be more effective in those positions—and who may need to make that step in order to be promoted. And we work with people who are being groomed for positions at the very highest levels and need to go from grade "A minus" to "A plus."

Our charge in all of these cases is to help the people we are working with become more effective. We do not promise to make them more "right" (that is to say, smarter); if we could do that, we would have already received patents on the procedure (and our Nobel Prizes). As we say to the executives who hire us, "Let's hope Laura is smart and making good business decisions, because if we succeed in this coaching process and she makes bad decisions, they'll be even *bigger* and *more effective* bad decisions!"

In our role as management development coaches, our focus is purely on helping individuals work to their highest level of potential. Does the person need to be a better listener? To be more aggressive? To talk less? To be more direct? To own up to his or her mistakes? To share information more freely? To delegate more? To take more risks? To be more flexible? We are also concerned, regardless of the specific behavioral changes that are needed for the person to be more effective, with why the person exhibits these particular deficits, in order to try to help them achieve insight into themselves and learn effective techniques for behavior modification.

INTRODUCTION

This book is the result of our many hours of thinking and talking together about the question "Why do good people fail or fall short of their potential?"

WHO WE ARE

We came together through our work at the Harvard Business School. Since the early 1980s we have helped thousands of MBA students make their career decisions. Trained as Ph.D. psychologists, we look beneath the surface in trying to understand how and why people act the way they do. Both of us have had extensive training in psychoanalytic psychology, which we feel enriches the way we think about people and organizations as well as about people's relationships with their peers and managers. Our research and our consulting work led to an interactive Internet-based career self-assessment program, called *CareerLeader*, which has been adopted by over one-hundred business schools and corporations. *CareerLeader* acts to help users determine the best career direction for them, assessing their interests, values, and abilities. The program also helps the user to think about what kind of organizational culture (the tone, attitude, and atmosphere) would be the best match for them. For example, would they fit better in a high-change culture or one that is more stable? One that is very team oriented or more of a "star" culture?

Our expertise in formal psychological assessment has been vital in coming to understand "what makes people tick" at work—as well as why some people's clocks run fast and others' run slow—while still others' stop entirely. In *Maximum Success* we're going to share with you what we've learned through our research and work as executive coaches about the *practical psychology* of being effective at work. In our work with clients we gather enormous amounts of information: lengthy life history interviews; comprehensive assessments of their personality traits, abilities, and values (more than a dozen tests in all); colleagues' comments on their strengths, weaknesses, passions, and blind spots; interviews with eight to ten co-workers (including managers, peers, and subordinates). One client half-jokingly asked if we wanted a blood sample to do DNA testing! (We declined.) We then put that information to use in recommending career directions and developing personal development plans for coaching. That experience provides us with a context, a background, that makes our psychological insights more useful to people in their actual working lives.

In our work as executive coaches there often is a great deal of urgency involved. There is also a great deal on the line: whether the client keeps his or her job or is terminated; or whether the client keeps his or her job or is promoted to a level of much greater responsibility. In all cases, though, the emphasis is on immediate action and early results. As you read about the twelve behavior patterns that hinder people's success, then, you will find that our focus is on changing what the person *does,* on a very concrete level. Our training and experience as psychologists informs our work, but our goal is to help people change *now.* We provide the same sort of pragmatic advice in those chapters that we give to our clients.

WHY FOCUS ON HOW PEOPLE FAIL?

We first discussed what we called people's "career Achilles' heels" in a piece we wrote for *CareerLeader* in the summer of 1998 and later published in *Fortune.* What do we mean by this term? Sometimes we use an analogy to driving down the highway in a car. To get to where you are going, it's important to be on the right road, in the right lane, *and* to have your car in good running order. It doesn't do you much good to have charted the right path and pulled into the correct lane if your car then proceeds to break down over and over. And that is what happens to some people's careers. Their "car" breaks down. The desire to help fix such career breakdowns was what motivated us to write a fuller book about people's career Achilles' heels. There are dozens of career success books on the market, some good, some not. Most of them follow a tried-and-true formula, presenting rules by which to live, communicate, work, and manage. Such books, however, suffer from one of two flaws (and sometimes both): they present either advice that applies only to the "lowest common denominator"—that is to say, advice that is so general as to be of limited help—or very specific advice that contradicts other advice presented in the very same book.

There is a reason for these problems. The fact is, the "formula for success" in a Wall Street law firm is not the same "formula" that works in a paper mill in Georgia or at a software company in Redmond, Washington. In fact, the elements of success at one Wall Street law firm may not even hold true at another Wall Street firm! Many of the really important "rules" that make for success in one setting are not transferable to other organizations. People succeed for many different reasons, depending on the job, company, or industry they work in. As a result, authors are forced in such books to give very general, generic advice ("make sure that you build and maintain good relationships with people and customers") in order for it to apply across the broad spectrum of industries and functions, from paper mills, software companies, and music studios to banks, hospitals, auto factories, and government agencies. It's difficult to say anything very fresh or insightful that will apply to all situations.

Alternately, when those kinds of books *do* try to get specific, they often contradict themselves. On page 37 you may read that you should be subtle in your use of power, only to read on page 92 that you should come out with guns blazing, to show people that you are a person to be respected and feared. Of course, you *should* employ subtlety and finesse in using power (sometimes), and you *should* come in with guns *and* an iron fist (sometimes). The trick, of course, is knowing where and when to use each, and these books are usually of little help in making those distinctions. Because success is situation-specific, the overwhelming majority of those books that try to offer a formula for success are either too general or too contradictory to be genuinely useful.

Moreover, each person's experiences of work, and effectiveness at the work they do, are affected to a large extent by core beliefs about the world and other people. These beliefs are created by an individual's genetic disposition (being an introvert, or psychologically resilient, or prone to depression, for example); by relationships with family members, friends, and teachers (being the firstborn or the last of twelve; being extraordinarily bright, attractive, or athletic; having a dysfunctional parent; being independently wealthy; having a wonderful teacher at a critical developmental moment; and so on); and by larger, impersonal, psychological and social forces (being a member of a racial minority, being raised in a large cosmopolitan city or a small town in Montana, or growing up during an economic depression). As a result, each person's experience of work is unique. No formula or list of "rules to live by" or "desired behaviors" can possibly apply to everyone in the same way.

The ways people *fail* in their careers, however, are quite limited. People fail in the same ways, for the same reasons, over and over again, from one industry to another, from the lowest levels to the highest. We have found that whether you work in a law firm or a paper mill or a software firm or a music studio, the patterns of behavior that will get you fired (or stalled) in one are precisely the patterns that will get you fired in another. As a result, we can be far more specific in our advice on how to break those patterns. Moreover, we find that many—if not most—people are amazingly unaware of the patterns of behavior they exhibit that are resulting in their failure.

For example, one client we worked with, whom we will refer to simply as Paula, was perceived by almost everyone she worked with as condescending and a busybody. Paula was eager to rise within her company (a medical device manufacturer), and these reactions from her coworkers were acting as an anchor. What's important to note, however, is that this "Achilles' heel" of Paula's would be a problem whether she was working in a law firm, a paper mill, a software company, or virtually anywhere. Nobody likes to work with a busybody; nobody enjoys being condescended to. Yet her pattern of behavior was not in the least obvious to Paula—in fact, she was shocked and dismayed to get this feedback.

BUILDING STRENGTH FROM WEAKNESS

A few years ago we were talking with the highly successful director of a large, complex organization in a well-known corporation. Martha was not only a star at her organization, but a leader in her profession. She is known as a superb planner and organizer who knows how to get things done, even when they involve large numbers of people and complicated logistics. Our conversation turned to her style as a manager and how it was related to her own personality type. We remarked that we were sure our testing would reveal that she was naturally inclined to focus on details. Martha laughed. She assured us that the testing would indicate precisely the opposite. Martha went on to tell us how she is a highly intuitive, "fly by the seat of your pants" person who found herself, as her career progressed, in a high-level job that demanded exquisite attention to detail and follow-through. Where others with similar traits would have failed, Martha came armed with psychological insight and a will to act on her self-knowledge.

"I knew from previous testing that I was definitely not the detail-oriented type," she told us. "I knew that if I was going to succeed, I would have to focus squarely on this issue. I was so afraid of slipping up that I deliberately checked and rechecked all plans, lists, and schedules. I became so afraid of letting the details slip that I developed an unusual vigilance for planning and checking. Today, I have 'compensated' and almost automatically ask the questions and do the extra checks that spell the difference between success and failure in planning big events. By knowing my devil, I was able to overcome it."

Martha's story is not surprising. Psychological development typically proceeds, not from a building on known strengths, but from an honest recognition and response to what psychologist Carl Jung calls our "shadow," all that is underdeveloped, rejected, suppressed, or experienced as shameful in our individual personalities. We all have traits, tendencies, and weaknesses that we have long ago labeled "not me," because they were unacceptable, or because we were afraid they would be unacceptable, to parents or other important people in our lives. By extension they became unacceptable to ourselves. By cutting off these parts of ourselves, however, we cut off important sources of psychological energy and avenues for growth. By recognizing her weakness—rather than denying it—Martha could then confront and correct it.

Many of the martial arts employ the principle of using your opponent's attack and strength to your advantage. It is the same with our inner battles to be more aware and effective, where the "attack" on "us" comes not from outside, but from another part of ourselves. Change begins with insight into an aspect of our personality that is affecting us in a negative way, that may have been denied and suppressed. It is our hope that by recognizing which of the patterns of behavior described in Part I best describe those that might be limiting your career, you too will be able to change and break those patterns. Of course, behaviors associated with deep-set personality patterns do not change easily. But recognizing those behaviors can serve as a "warning bell" that alerts us that we need to change. For Martha, whenever she experiences her instinct to "wing it," she understands that instinct as a message saying, "It's time to sit down and work this out carefully."

ACHILLES' HEELS IN THOSE AROUND YOU

While our primary goal in writing this book was to help people recognize the behavior patterns that hold them back, we believe the twelve patterns of failure described in Part I can also be a useful tool in understanding those under or above you as well. And understanding the Achilles' heels of the people you work with can make *you* even more effective and more successful in your work.

For example, recently the success of one of our clients, a software company, was being impaired by the bullying behavior of one of its senior managers—a fact not being addressed by the president. By helping the president see this as the manager's Achilles' heel, and working with the manager to correct his behavior, the organization was able to hire and keep more talented people in the manager's department. Or take the case of an employee who works under someone who is threatened by more talented employees and applicants. Recognizing this as the manager's Achilles' heel could help that individual better to "manage his boss," to hire better people and hold on to the talented people already there.

Or suppose one of your colleagues works wonderfully with some people but collapses when a manager, customer, or colleague pushes on them hard. Again, by seeing this as the individual's Achilles' heel, you might be able to help that person in his or her dealings with people who are more aggressive.

We believe *Maximum Success* will also be a useful tool for managers to better understand and work with those under them. As you read through the twelve patterns of career failure, you may find yourself saying, "That sounds a lot like [Tom, Dick, or Mary], who reports to me." Understanding a subordinate's disabling behavior pattern may help you to adapt your management style to get the best from those under you. This requires you to be a bit of a psychologist, but that's part of what being a manager requires. It certainly will help you to think about the people who report to you in a different way.

HOW SUCCESS CAN BEGET FAILURE

One of the most perplexing and frustrating things many people face is that sometimes the very behaviors that helped them achieve the level of success they enjoy are now the very habits that either are preventing them from becoming even more successful or are causing them to fail. It feels as if the rules have changed. And they have!

One of our clients, whom we'll refer to as Ted, was sent to us because he was failing spectacularly. And he was *furious.* "I'm only doing my job!" he said. "And that's why they hired me. That's what they've paid me to do for the last ten years. Now they tell me that I'm too aggressive. They want me to use more *finesse.* Well, forget about finesse! I am who I am. I work hard to get results for this business, and I get them. If they want finesse, let them hire a nursery school teacher."

Think of the company as a pyramid, and Ted as one point in it, well on the inside of the outer "skin" of the pyramid. As long as he remains where he is, he's fine. But if he moves up in the organization, he becomes less and less insulated and closer and closer to upper management and outside scrutiny. His flaws become more visible. In Ted's case, he was promoted several levels and thus became more visible to top management and to the outside world; and then the company he worked for was bought, with the result that its culture changed to one in which Ted's kind of aggressive behavior was neither rewarded nor accepted.

Not surprisingly, the behaviors that may make someone a terrific supervisor on an auto assembly line (or a midlevel manager in a sales organization) may not make for a successful upper-echelon manager or

CEO, even within the same company. But to the person whose career is stymied, this change in attitude can be baffling and infuriating. What was yesterday's asset has become today's liability.

Sometimes a person like Ted, having been told repeatedly how terrific his gung ho, aggressive, results-oriented approach is, becomes even more gung ho and aggressive and results oriented. Ted, figuring that if a little of something is good, a lot must be even better, turns it up another notch or two. This kind of transformation can take on a life of its own. At some point, somebody decides that Ted has gone too far—but only after Ted's behavior is so far beyond the pale that he may be fatally marked.

HOW TO READ THIS BOOK

If you're like most people, you may want to go straight to the twelve Achilles' heels in Part 1 and read through them, looking for those patterns that best reflect aspects of yourself, your friends, and your coworkers. But we also urge you to read Part II, in which we discuss the four essential developmental issues people need to resolve or come to terms with in order to be successful. In both sections we use real-life case examples to help bring to life the concepts we are talking about.

Because many of the stories deal with clients or associates who have suffered career missteps, we have gone to great pains to disguise the identities of the people whose situations we use to illustrate various points we are making. What remain unaltered are those elements of their work situations that are essential to understanding the "teaching point."

Each of the patterns includes the story of one individual, a sort of "pure case" of that particular behavior. We chose each of these people to use as examples because they provide very clear illustrations of each of the patterns. They show what this sort of person looks like, sounds like, and feels like. But it's important that you *not* make the mistake of comparing yourself to those case examples—which are anchor points of 100 on a scale of 1-100—and saying, "Well, I'm not like that, I'm only an 85! I don't have to worry about that one." Remember that even the occasional display of these behaviors (or somewhat milder levels of them operating over a long period of time) can do substantial damage to your progression and success. Also, take time to consider what impact any of these behaviors may be having on your nonwork life—social relationships, marriage, and family. Most of them continue "working" even when you're not, so it's useful to think about how they're affecting you in your private life.

In essence, the twelve Achilles' heels we discuss are the result of not having come to terms with one or more of the four developmental issues described in Part II. To go back to our "right highway/correct lane/well-serviced car" analogy, the *outcomes* are the overheated engine, frozen piston, blown-out tire; the *causes* are lack of coolant, an oil leak, and overinflation. You can let the car cool down, but unless you address the coolant issue, you still aren't going to travel very far. And while you can add oil, unless you fix the leak, you'll run low again very soon. Because of this, when we describe the twelve Achilles' heels—the outcomes—and what you can do about them, we'll refer from time to time to the four developmental issues—their psychological ingredients.

In the cases of Jack and Suzanne, whom we read about at the beginning of the introduction, their Achilles' heels were their undoing. But having *potentially* fatal flaws, as they did, does not necessarily result in career stagnation or termination. In fact, we could argue that we *all* have Achilles' heels of one sort or another. It's just that some of us have learned to manage them successfully while others of us allow them to hold us down. In writing this book, we wanted to provide readers with the tools Jack and Suzanne didn't have. We believe that learning to recognize the ways you—and all of us—engage in behaviors that create your own "glass ceilings" will enable you to break through them and achieve the success you deserve.

PART
I

THE 12 BEHAVIORS
THAT CAN
HOLD YOU BACK

INTRODUCTION

BEFORE YOU BEGIN READING ABOUT THE TWELVE PATTERNS, we want to say just a couple of things to help you get the most from them. We introduced these behavior patterns as Achilles' heels, referring to the hero of Homer's *Iliad*. As an infant, Achilles had been dipped in the river Styx by his mother, making him invulnerable—except for the heel by which she had held him in the process. This heel was where he suffered a mortal wound during the Greeks' battle with Troy. Our Achilles' heels are *our* weaknesses, those parts of us that can be our undoing, *regardless of how strong we are or how well we are doing in every other way*. Many of the people we have consulted with over the years in fact had been doing very well in every way except for that one disabling (and sometimes potentially fatal) flaw. The fact is we all have strengths, and we all have weaknesses—every one of us. Those who are supremely successful have simply managed to find a way to compensate for their weaknesses, either by hiring people to their teams who have strengths in areas where they are weak or by working on strengthening those areas they are weak in and being ever vigilant to what their weaknesses are. That is ultimately what we hope this book will accomplish for you—identify the area or areas you are weak in and allow you to strengthen that weakness so that you can maximize your success.

Many readers will see one *or two* patterns that seem to apply to them. In most cases one pattern is dominant in holding you back, while the other has a much milder impact. So if you see aspects of yourself in two or even three patterns, make note of it, and after you've finished reading Part I, think about which pattern is most central in impeding your success. This prioritizing is important, because you want to make efforts to change your old habits, and you need to put your limited energy, time, and efforts in the places that will be most effective in helping you get ahead.

That said, even if you read one of the chapters and think, "That's me to a 'T,'" we encourage you to read about all of the behavior patterns. First, you may find further insight about yourself and your workplace behavior in other chapters. But we recommend reading all twelve for another reason as well. Even if you fit only one of the patterns, chances are good that you know, manage, work with, or work for—or will in the future—people who exhibit one or more of the other behavior patterns. Understanding how other people operate and why they do the things that they do can be a tremendous help in getting along with them, managing them, and working with them as peers.

We want to underscore that the case examples we've included to illustrate our points are *real*, culled from the hundreds of people we've consulted with. Understandably, however, the names and other identifying information about them has been changed. As you read through each of the twelve chapters, some of the people we describe as examples of the patterns may seem to be so extreme that you are inclined to dismiss that pattern ("*I've* never wandered around the office swinging a baseball bat! This pattern doesn't apply to *me*"). But we chose to include these examples precisely *because* they're so extreme, so black and white, so clear—each one a quintessential example of the pattern in question, making it easier, we hope, to grasp what the pattern is all about.

So don't judge too quickly—there are many shades of gray exhibited in each of these behavior patterns—and each *can*, under the wrong circumstances, hold you back. The pattern that was fatal (or nearly so) to the person we describe may (merely) be slowing or undermining your advancement. Think carefully about each pattern, and try to identify which one or two patterns best applies to you, even if only under certain circumstances or only to a limited extent. Think about it this way: Even if a virus that was fatal to someone else causes you only to be sick for a while, you're still anxious for a way to become healthy again.

In Part II of the book, we analyze the reasons *why* people fall into these behavior patterns. Each one stems from some combination of four developmental issues, or psychological dynamics, that people have trouble with. We refer to one or another of these four issues in the various behavior patterns in Part I. When you're finished reading Part I, we encourage you to read on in Part II, learning more about these four dynamics and what you can do if one of them is fueling one of the twelve patterns of behavior in your life.

CHAPTER
ONE

NEVER FEELING GOOD ENOUGH

IN A WORLD OVERPOPULATED WITH OUTSIZE EGOS, PAUL seemed to be an anomaly. He had an ego that was too *small* for his considerable abilities and his position. A big international bank in New York had hired him away from a smaller bank in Texas for a high-profile job taking charge of a group of loan officers who, after some heady early successes, had involved the bank in several dangerous arrangements in Latin America. When the Mexican peso collapsed, the bank had taken a financial bath, suffering tens of millions of dollars in losses. Paul's assignment was to rein in the lending group, to ensure that the necessary "due diligence" had been done on major loans before any further commitments were made.

Paul, who was in his early forties at the time, clearly had both the intellect and the experience to handle the job. Although he had never been a manager, he had considerable know-how as a banker, and Latin America was his specialty. Moreover, Paul had succeeded at everything he had ever done. He had been a top student in both college and graduate business school, and he was promoted quickly through the bank he joined in Dallas after getting his MBA at the University of Texas.

But in his new position Paul was suddenly a misfit—or so it appeared, and so he felt. He was self-conscious and awkward, unable to speak with authority, and unable to command the respect that he needed to excel. He felt like a little fish tossed into a very big pond, a small-town kid from fly-over country way out of place among East Coast elites. Sure, he had been at the top of his class in school, but in schools without prestigious names. Now he had to take charge of a herd of headstrong and arrogant deal makers with degrees from Harvard, Columbia, and Wharton.

The coterie of loan officers who had been operating on their own before Paul arrived understandably were not delighted to welcome an outsider charged with keeping them under control. Still, if Paul had presented himself as a confident manager, he might have been able to defuse their resentment quickly enough and establish himself as their skillful leader.

But he never demonstrated that confidence and as a result never took command in the fullest sense. He had a look of intensity and concern that sometimes seemed to approach panic. He worked long hours, much too long—and work that he should have been delegating, he took upon himself. His superior, who had hired him, was afraid that Paul was going to burn out. In the eyes of the lenders Paul supervised, he was respected as a hard worker and a technical specialist, but not really admired and certainly not looked up to as a commander.

Troops want a leader who exudes self-assurance. In a battle at sea, sailors want to look up at the bridge and see "the old man" calmly overseeing the battle—not struggling nervously into his life jacket! But everything about Paul said worry. He had no stature in the lending group; people avoided him.

But at his new job, instead of strolling through offices in comfortable command Paul scurried down the halls with an intense, innerdirected gaze on his face that signaled to everyone that he was in trouble. His body language broadcast concern, discomfort, and isolation. When he stopped to talk to people he was all business, almost curt. There was never any small talk.

Paul was telling people, without knowing or intending to, that he couldn't get away from them fast enough. It was as though if he lingered too long, people would see through him and would recognize that he didn't belong, would know that he was in over his head—and the fact was, he did feel in over his head. Instead of looking upward and contemplating whether he might be CEO someday, or at least head of all of International, he was frightened that he had already risen too high. He wondered whether he didn't really belong a peg or two below where he was.

Those in the department followed his instructions when necessary, but they didn't seek out his advice. Nobody invited him to lunch. Meetings were held without Paul being aware of them. One of his colleagues said of Paul, "He's a hard worker . . . and it shows." Another said, "He's very smart, and everybody respects him—but no one wants to *be* him." When Paul stepped outside himself and took a close look, *he* didn't want to be himself, either! That was the point at which he came to us.

THE DYNAMICS OF THE PATTERN

Paul's actions and feelings fall into a pattern that we've come to think of as a kind of career-related *acrophobia*. Acrophobia is the term for a fear of heights or, more to the point, of *falling* from those heights. Paul's "career acrophobia" was born of his belief that he was incapable of surviving on the heights he had somehow scaled. He felt in his heart of hearts that he didn't deserve to be where he had been placed. It's a feeling a surprising number of people have to a greater or lesser extent.

There is a metaphor involving an elevator that graphically conveys his agony and that of those like him. People like Paul feel as though they are on an elevator with their feet stuck on the fifteenth floor while their heads have been carried to the fortieth floor, with their bodies stretched in between. They feel—in fact, they absolutely *know*—that they're "fifteenth- (or tenth- or first-) floor" people; other people think they're really fortieth-floor people and promote them accordingly. That tension sounds excruciatingly painful, of course, and what these people experience is indeed anguishing—we are not, after all, made of rubber.

In fact, the tension is so difficult to bear that people have only two choices. The first is to somehow unhook their feet from the floor down below and "rise to the occasion" of having been picked to move up to that fortieth floor. This is the happily-ever-after scenario. Less happily, people in this position commonly sabotage their own careers, doing things that get them demoted to the level where they think they belong. One person we worked with had committed a series of gaffes so spectacularly stupid that he actually got himself fired—for no better reason, as we discovered, than because he felt he didn't belong where he was.

Of course, Paul's case is somewhat extreme. But a lot of people, because of lack of self-esteem, feel that way and, subtly or more calamitously, undermine themselves or find ways to hold themselves back so they never "suffer" the fate of rising too far or too fast in an organization in the first place. They simply never rise out of their comfort level. One of our clients, a woman who was a competent scientist in her own right, had spent her career acting as the aide-de-camp to a series of others. Another client worked for many years as an editor of others' work. He wrote his own essays and articles but only occasionally allowed himself to "rise up" and take the risk of submitting them for publication.

This pattern of acrophobia carries some special dangers. If you are "running roughshod" over people (Chapter 5), it's going to be obvious to those around you, and you can see evidence of it by stopping to look at the bodies you leave behind. Not feeling that you deserve to go higher and sabotaging your career advancement, on the other hand, is likely to be invisible to other people, and the fear is so difficult to face that it may be invisible to you as well. It takes an extremely astute and psychologically minded friend or manager to notice what you're doing to yourself and point it out to you. Yet without facing the ways you are hamstringing yourself—perhaps by being late with projects, by procrastinating, by failing to exercise initiative, or by not going the extra mile you know will get the job done right—you may lose out on new assignments, be overlooked for raises or promotions, and potentially even jeopardize your job if the environment changes.

Michael, for example, discovered this pattern of acrophobic behavior in himself when he was interviewing for jobs in his last year of law school. Michael was a generally self-confident individual with an apparently high level of self-esteem. He was unaware that he was communicating a sense of uncertainty about himself in his interviews. It was brought to his attention by an interviewer, who pointed out to him that during the interview, every time she (the interviewer) signaled to him that he was the sort of candidate they were looking for, Michael started backpedaling, expressing concern that maybe he really didn't have the experience they needed, saying that he wanted to make sure they knew what they were getting, and so forth.

It was both insightful and forthcoming of the interviewer to give Michael this feedback. Unfortunately, it was too late to salvage his contact with that firm, and even more unfortunate, he had already done himself in with most of the other recruiters he had signed on with. But by recognizing it in himself, he was able to face his fears and change his pattern of behavior in future interviews. The fact is, even if this pattern isn't the one you'd call "home," even if it's a pattern that few other people would associate with you, it is important to recognize it for what it is and factor it into how you behave wherever you are in your career. Even an occasional occurrence of such a "fear of heights" can, if acted out at the wrong moment, do substantial damage to your career aspirations. Everyone is afraid at times of a particular assignment, a new responsibility, a new environment. The key is to not allow that fear to leak out, in unintentional ways, into your performance or behavior.

Moreover, few of the behavior patterns we describe have consequences only for a person's work life, and this is not one of those exceptions. The individual who doesn't feel good enough in his or her work is very likely to carry that into the arena of personal life. There are many possible manifestations of the pattern, from sabotaging dating relationships with appropriate partners whom we feel are "too good" for us to holding back from striking up a friendship with someone we see as "above us" in some sense to being uncomfortable in settings (dinner parties and so on) in which we feel we "don't belong."

Sometimes the cost of the acrophobic personality is even more subtle. One client of ours described how his mother, a career economist working for a prestigious international organization, carried with her a sense of inferiority throughout most of her career. The organization where she works is very "credential conscious." In an environment where compensation is limited, status is attached not only to social and political connections, but to events more remote in time: where you attended undergraduate and graduate school and whom you studied with when you were there. Our client's mother was highly talented and had a notable career of promotion and recognition, but she never really felt fully accepted. "It's as if she doesn't feel comfortable in her own skin," our client told us. He went on to describe how even though his mother is seen as a strong performer and is regularly sought out for her advice, *she* feels that she is in an unspoken way seen as lacking because her education was not at a big-name university. Part of this dynamic is attributable to a dysfunctional aspect of the organization's culture, but the dynamic has clearly been magnified by her own feelings about her place in the world.

The failures that result from this pattern of behavior are most often not spectacularly catastrophic falls from the top (obviously there is only a limited amount of room at that altitude to climb and fall *from*). Most often we see regular people falling—or about to fall—from much lower pinnacles or holding themselves back from climbing as high as they could.

It may be an obvious point, but we want to make abundantly clear that this kind of self-sabotaging and self-limiting behavior is never conscious. No one wakes up in the morning and says, "You know, I just don't feel comfortable being vice president, so I think I'm going to go in today and screw things up!" Nevertheless, people do act in stranger and more self-destructive ways than that. Often it is only in retrospect that they can see that what they did, they did for some powerful—but unconscious—reason totally outside of their awareness.

There is a personality test, the California Psychological Inventory, that we have found to be a good indicator of whether someone falls into this acrophobic behavior pattern. Among the twenty scales on which it provides information, two are relevant. The first scale gets at whether you look at the top level/"inner circle" (the executive level, managing directors, partners, or management team) in your organization and see yourself as belonging there. This scale assesses people's imaginations of themselves, of how high they think they *deserve* to ascend. The second scale assesses the individual's ambition, drive, and willingness to work for that goal.

If you have high *or* low scores on *both* scales, you are likely to feel satisfied. In other words, if you see yourself as deserving to be the CEO and you have the drive to try to become the CEO, your sense of yourself and your drive and ambition are in alignment. You may or may not make it to that top level, but these two elements of yourself are going in the same direction. At the low end, if you have little drive and at the same time don't believe that you are capable or deserving of achieving much, then you might feel satisfied as well. At the very least, you are unconflicted.

What distresses people is a mismatch between their sense of themselves and their drive and ambition. The middle manager who believes that he deserves to be CEO but does not have the drive to get there may constantly complain about how unfair it is that he hasn't been lifted to the mountaintop, how he's just as smart as the president or his own boss, it's just not fair. We've all encountered such people.

People in the acrophobe pattern suffer from the opposite mismatch. Their drive and talent have carried them to lofty heights, but their self-imagination is low. They don't believe they deserve to be where they are. Even though they are well within their depth, they *think* they are in over their heads. The central developmental issue (of the four we describe in Part II) that people who experience this mismatch haven't negotiated successfully is that of forming a positive self-image and battling elements of negativity. Despite all evidence to the contrary, they still see themselves as the hick from the sticks, or the short fat kid other kids teased, or the little brother or sister whose older sibs were so much more successful. One of our clients, Andy, was a commercial real estate broker who felt fine—and in fact *did* fine—as long as he was talking to clients who were from socioeconomic backgrounds more or less like his own (middle or lower middle class). But when he was introduced to the representative of a client company who was clearly someone from a privileged background, Andy would freeze. He became less articulate, clearly less confident, and visibly uncomfortable to the point of making other people feel uncomfortable. Andy's acrophobia wasn't a factor in his career all the time—only when he hit the occasional slick spot, that combination of patterns and contexts that set him off and sent him into a skid.

Most people who fall into this behavior pattern are also uncomfortable with using power (see Chapter 15 in Part II). They see nothing morally wrong with it, but they simply don't feel as if they know what to do with it or how to use it. Often they don't feel as if it belongs to them, as if they really "own" it. But that is not the *cause* of the person's pattern of feelings and behaviors. Rather, it is a symptom or sign, a result of the acrophobia. That said, however, one element one can use to overcome career acrophobia is to learn to use and feel comfortable with whatever power you do have in your position. *Acting* the part (including using your power) can help you *feel* as if you really belong in the role.

We had a client we'll call Steve, a very talented, good-looking man who had an MBA and a BS in electrical engineering from two top schools. He worked hard and rose rapidly through the management ranks of a company that makes medical devices. Before long the board made him president. But his poor self-image became his undoing.

The gap between Steve's high drive and low self-imagination was enormous. "Sometimes," he told us, "I'd be sitting in meetings of the executive board and I'd think 'Uh-oh, these people are grown-ups!" At other times, he told us, "in meetings I really felt like my suit was too big, like I was a little kid wearing my father's suit."

Steve had never known his father, who had abandoned him and his mother before Steve was born. So Steve grew up without a father to teach him how to be comfortable with success and power. And because he had no father, he grew up feeling that there was something wrong with him and his family. At the same time, he experienced a sense of guilt about supplanting his father (literally, providing support for his mother; metaphorically, wearing his father's clothes). So stressful was the distance between the heights Steve had achieved and the depths where he thought he belonged that he eventually sabotaged himself. He committed a series of political blunders, gaffes so obvious that no one would think someone with his intellect and corporate experience could have made them accidentally. For example, he fired a close friend of a major shareholder without first consulting board members or anyone else in the company.

Eventually Steve himself was fired and fell back to earth, where he felt in his heart of hearts that he belonged. (The good news in this story is that Steve became much more aware of this dynamic and its effects on his behavior. He is now the head of another technology company, which he has led successfully for many years without any self-sabotaging behavior.) Obviously Steve suffered greatly in this course of events. It's worthwhile taking a moment to consider all the costs of this pattern.

THE ACROPHOBE IN AN ORGANIZATION

When a career acrophobe sabotages his or her success, and fails, the cost both to the person and to the company is huge. But it is often a hidden cost, unlike the damage caused by most of the other profiles we describe in this book. Some other types of the Achilles' heels we discuss can cause clear, obvious damage: good people quit because of them, customers are lost, project deadlines slip, quality levels are not met, morale declines (all depending on circumstances and the particular type of Achilles' heel, of course). With the acrophobe pattern of behavior, the organization loses simply because some of the best and brightest—the people you want at the top of whatever pyramid you're considering (whether the CEO or the manager of the customer service unit)—don't *get* to the top. Philip was an extremely competent information systems professional. From the company's standpoint it would have been better if Philip had been one level higher, managing the work of a group of more junior, less talented IS professionals. The company, however, was unable to persuade him to leave the security of his position and step up a level. He just wasn't sure he was up to it. It was his loss, of course (although he certainly wasn't mortally wounded by this pattern), but the company lost, too.

This may not sound like as big a problem as the fallout from those more obvious patterns of behavior we outline in the book, but consider this: Suppose you have an investment company, and working for the company is a young clerk—call him Jeremy—reconciling each day's stock trades. Now let's say that Jeremy has a high school education, is very bright, and is very keen on the investment business. When he has downtime he reads *Institutional Investor* and *Barron's*, and he knows his way around OneSource and First Call on the Internet. He trades his own account (carefully keeping to any SEC guidelines, of course) and makes very good returns.

One day his manager asks Jeremy what he'd most like to do in his work life, and without a moment's hesitation he replies, "Be a trader!" "So go talk to the head trader about your interests and goals, and ask for advice about how you can make that jump to an assistant trader position," his wise manager advises, sensing that Jeremy's true talents—and certainly his interests—would be well expressed on the trading floor. Jeremy screws up his courage, talks to the head trader, and five years later he's in his dream job, trading equities for the firm's account. But he never feels comfortable, never as good as the other traders, despite the excellent profits he makes. So he leaves.

Who loses? Well, first, obviously Jeremy does. But think about your firm. You lose the 28 percent returns Jeremy would have continued to produce if he'd stayed in place—which you feel and notice for a while, but then forget about, erasing that "loss" from your balance sheet. This is the hidden damage to the company that loses an acrophobic top performer, that person's contribution over the course of his or her entire career. Take Jeremy's "lost" gains and then think about what those profits in turn could have produced over the next twenty years. Albert Einstein once said that man's most powerful discovery is compound interest. If you have some time, figure out the lost compound interest on this one! Even without doing the math, we can see that Jeremy's leaving is more costly to your company than to him.

Then consider the cost of the contribution this person would have made to your company after successive promotions—at the next level up and the level after that and the level after that. Then the compound interest really comes into play, and the cost to any organization of losing the talented acrophobe—for no good reason (for example, not having been lured away for more compensation or to join a start-up with equity)—really becomes clear.

THE ORIGINS OF THE ACROPHOBE

Where does this career acrophobia come from? We will describe several primary causes, any or all of which may be driving this feeling and behavior in any given person. The roots of this Achilles' heel almost inevitably go deep into the person's childhood, deep enough to overcome the most basic of all our "drives": the drive to grow and make full use of our potential.

In some cases the causes are cultural. Most of us have heard our parents say something like "Don't get too big for your britches" at one time or another. In fact, this is so universal that it's really a culture message our parents just happen to be charged with delivering. But in most cases they are outweighed by countervailing expressions we hear from our parents, teachers, and other adults around us, such as "You can be anything you want to be." In some societies, however, there are no declarations of encouragement to balance the cautionary note. The Japanese famously live by the phrase "The nail that sticks up gets hammered down," a severe warning not to see yourself as, or aspire to be, the exceptional performer who stands out. It's much safer to be a member of a team of equals.

For example, we had a client who had grown up in England in a working-class family who kept hearing the admonition "Don't be behaving like a big Mick" from his parents. It's easy to understand how that kind of thinking becomes ascendant in a rigid classist society; where there is a hereditary ruling class, it is dangerous to aspire too high. If you're not born into the privileged class, you will never be accepted by it—instead you will be resented, ridiculed, and punished, at least economically. So this fellow's parents were trying to protect him from what they saw as the inevitable punishment that would come if he tried to rise above his station—no matter how talented he was. (In fact, he eventually graduated from the Massachusetts Institute of Technology with honors—but still felt himself held back by these messages.) His parents delivered the message, but the real culprit in the story was the society and its cultural norms and proscriptions.

In Christianity, too—a powerful cultural and religious force for hundreds of millions of people around the world—pride is one of the seven deadly sins and modesty a virtue. There is a certain kind of pride born out of arrogance (which is, in turn, born out of deep insecurity). This kind of pride is haughty and attempts to aggrandize the self by demeaning others. The pride of a four-year-old at going into school with her big sister or brother, on the other hand, or the pride of a six-year-old at learning to ride a two-wheeler—these are examples of healthy pride and self-esteem that enable a person to believe in himself or herself. But these feelings, too, are considered sinful by some—and that kind of message can weigh down a person's aspirations.

The roots of the acrophobic pattern can also be very personal, very idiosyncratic, to the individual. Even though the surrounding society may be based on meritocracy, and schoolteachers and parents are encouraging, a more subtle and deeper message may still tell a particular child to avoid the heights. The relationship between parent and child is crucial in the child's understanding of how he or she grows into a confident, self-governing adult. If, for example, a child's very successful parent is aloof and distant and a workaholic, the son or daughter may grow up feeling very ambivalent about authority. They see that "people at the top" (extrapolating from the one very important data point they can see) are unavailable and emotionally cold and have no time for family or pleasure—all combining to form a high price for having ascended to that level of success. And because of that aloofness, the child never sees at close hand how someone in high authority handles (and, yes, sometimes mishandles) his or her power. Because the child has no real window into the parent's world, he or she is never allowed to develop a real understanding of success, of its rights and responsibilities, of how authority should behave, its prerogatives and its limitations. That was Paul's case. His father worked many hours and traveled extensively, and even when he was home he kept his distance. In some cases, then, the person's ambivalence about attaining the highest level of career success may be born of an abhorrence of what he or she sees that success as entailing.

The fear of ascending to high levels of success can also have its roots in that conflict we all feel and struggle with at one point or another in our lives, the conflict that Sophocles wrote about in the tragedy *Oedipus Rex*. Oedipus, of course, unknowingly killed his father and displaced him in his mother's bed. When he realized the horror of what he had done—patricide compounded by incest—he went mad and plucked out his eyes. The story plays out the guilt we feel about wanting to best our fathers. Do I really want to be more successful than my father? If I am more successful, aren't I in some way "killing" him? How can I resolve these conflicting feelings? Most of us handle those anxieties successfully, and generally we do so with the help of our parents, who *want* us to surpass them—millions of immigrants came to America so their children could prosper as they had not, after all. But not everyone overcomes that primal guilt and anxiety.

Sophocles' play dealt with the most elemental aspect of the Oedipal struggle—the son's wish to kill father and take his place as mother's husband. But the Oedipal conflict is not restricted to a *son* wanting to and not wanting to defeat and displace his *father*. It can engender a son's guilt at overshadowing his mother or a daughter's concern about surpassing her father or mother. One of our clients was the daughter of a school custodian. She rose to a high position in a high-tech company that gave her prestige and wealth unimaginable to her father. But she was terribly conflicted because of her guilt at having achieved so much more than her father had.

Yet another cause of this discomfort with success is the negative self-image (Chapter 16 in Part II) that results from being psychologically abused by parents, teachers, siblings, and/or peers. Being told you're stupid, you'll never amount to anything, you're a loser, and so on time and again as children can have a devastating—and lasting—impact. The person who begins to succeed in spite of that treatment can find those messages being replayed in his or her unconscious like the unwanted signal of an unlicensed 250,000-kilowatt radio station. It's a message that may reassert itself just when you are about to say something in a meeting, or ask for a promotion, or make a presentation, or interview for a new job. ("Who do you think you are?" "You don't belong in here!" "Don't say anything stupid, Stupid!") Tuning out those signals is difficult, and some people find it easier simply to move back down a level or two or three, down to where those messages imply they belong.

PAUL REVISITED

How can someone who habitually feels and acts this way acclimate and learn to love the heights? Let's return to Paul, the banker. Because Paul is very analytical, a "quant" rather than a "touchy-feely" personality, we laid out his alternatives dispassionately, to fit his personal style. "Do you really *want* to be a manager, or would you rather return to your very successful career as a specialist in Latin American debt?" we asked. Paul assured us that he did want to be a manager and that he believed he had the intellect and talent to excel in the job. We were engaged to help him learn how.

We spent many hours with Paul at the office, watching him interact with the loan officers he managed, with his own boss, and with colleagues outside his department. We saw how he conducted meetings and watched him as he questioned the viability of lending relationships the bank had and of proposed loans. As we watched and studied Paul, it became clear that he would have to learn to carry himself in a way that reflected his ability, the capability for command that he had inside. He needed to exude confidence, to walk tall, to walk his own version of what we sometimes call "the matador's walk."

Think about people who are full of confidence. They do things slowly. For example, people who eat slowly are sending a message. They're saying, "I'm not hungry. I'm wealthy enough to be able to eat enough often enough to be able to savor my food—not just gulp down the calories my body craves." Successful executives sometimes fold their hands *behind their backs* and stroll slowly down the hall. They are saying that no matter how much time you take to look, you will discover nothing but quality. It can also be a way of showing that the executive is unafraid of any attack, he or she is invulnerable and doesn't need his hands in front for protection. Such a person is not afraid to linger. Day-to-day crises come and they go. The confident executive can deal with them. He or she is in charge.

We persuaded Paul to adopt that look. We got him to fold his hands behind his back when he walked. That simple gesture seems superficial, but it worked. It forced him to slow down. We also persuaded him to use hand gestures when he stopped to talk to people, to put his hand gently on someone's arm or shoulder in a fatherly gesture that says "Don't worry. I understand the difficult situation you're dealing with, and we'll get through it together." We persuaded him to come in later and leave earlier, to delegate more. In short, we got him to start *acting* the part, even if he didn't yet *feel* it. We were counting on his new actions generating enough feedback from the world around him that it would fuel even more positive, self-confident actions—and that the actions would in turn create a *feeling* of self-confidence from within Paul.

The strategy worked. Not overnight, of course, and with a lot more happening than we've detailed here. But over a period of months, the loan officers and others in the bank began to see Paul as a relaxed and confident leader. Most important, Paul responded to their evolving attitude and growing admiration with even more genuine self-assurance. By (literally and metaphorically) "walking the walk" as well as talking the talk, he began to *feel* the confidence, the assuredness, of the matadors.

And over time something quite remarkable began to take place. Paul began to truly enjoy his job!

IS THIS ME?

What are some of the "signs and symptoms" of this problem? One is a chronic, nagging feeling that everyone else knows what's going on and how to play the game; that they all feel completely at home—it's just me who feels anxious and insecure. ("I'm the one they admitted by mistake," thinks the person. "They really meant to send that admission letter to another applicant with my name.") This feeling may be in the background much of the time and leap into the front of our consciousness only on occasion, but it is a pattern that continually reasserts itself.

Making spectacularly dumb mistakes that result in being cast out from "on high" is another tip-off of this dynamic, as is holding back on making contributions in meetings for fear that they won't be seen as important enough—or will be laughed at. (In some cases the acrophobe loses himself in thought in the meeting, as a means of getting away from that terrible feeling of not belonging—and then is loath to speak for fear that the topic has already been discussed!) Yet in both cases the person in fact has already displayed the talent and drive to have arrived at that place on high to begin with, and to be in that meeting.

Another indication that this dynamic is at play is an up-and-down, fast-and-slow, accelerate-and-brake pattern to the person's career. In fact, the acrophobe/driver seems to be shifting constantly between pressing down hard on the gas pedal (when the drive and ambition we described earlier are in command) and hitting the brake pedal—hard—when the imagination of self element takes over. In fact, this ambivalence (what social psychologists call "approach-avoidance behavior") is really the key when it comes to this pattern.

HOW TO BREAK THE PATTERN

If this sounds like you, how can you help yourself? The first step is, as always, self-observation. You need to become aware of feelings of insecurity and inferiority as you actually experience them. Perhaps as you're walking down a hall to a meeting, you notice that you're feeling anxious and have, in fact, been worrying about the meeting for days. It is a brief meeting, and the agenda is not a major one—so why were you thinking about it when you were trying to go to sleep? Then think about who will be at the meeting. What are their backgrounds and credentials? How do you feel when you're with them? Do you feel that you have their respect? Do you feel that your ideas will be weighed the same as theirs? If not, pay attention to these feelings. Are they familiar? When have you had them before, and in whose presence?

You need to learn to notice these feelings of *not being as good as,* of *not being good enough,* whenever they come up. Becoming more aware of what you feel, and under what circumstances you feel whatever you feel, is the vital first step toward practical insight, insight that you can use to change. Once you are more aware of your feeling states and what triggers them, you'll be in a much better position to see and change specific behaviors.

Career acrophobia has both internal and external elements, and to deal with this issue you have to tackle both. First, to "stop the damage," you need to take a careful and objective look at both the work and the nonwork elements of your life and search for those behaviors that you may be engaging in whose effect is to cause you to fail. Make a list of them. Include "negatives" in this list, such as *not* returning phone calls, *not* completing assignments on time, or *not* making the sales calls you need to. We include the nonwork part of your life because you may be doing things when you are not at work that jeopardize your success (having extramarital affairs, for example, or drinking too much when traveling).

It is of the utmost importance that you be scrupulously honest in this process. The pattern is deep-rooted and unconscious in its origins, so rigorous self-appraisal is both critically important and extraordinarily difficult. You might want to engage the help of one or two most trusted friends (your spouse, perhaps, or a close personal friend—either from your work world or not) to provide you with feedback.

Be as concrete as possible at first ("I'm late for work *on Mondays*" or "I don't speak up in situations involving people with *more education* than I have"). Then look for underlying themes and patterns-within-the-pattern ("I feel generally insecure about my level of education and formal business training"). The reason to look both at the specifics and more generally is twofold. First, the themes can help organize your battle plans—because the struggle itself is going to be at the level of mundane, yard-by-yard gruntwork, nothing fancy and—sad to say—no magic shortcuts.

Like gaining ground in the infantry, changing our behaviors requires two things: motivation and action. So after you make your list, or maybe three theme-focused lists, decide which items you are going to tackle first. (Our suggestion: Choose either the easiest or the ones with the biggest and most immediate payoff). Then, one by one, tackle each behavior, reducing or eliminating—or increasing—the behavior in question. Keep an objective record (how many times, how much— whatever the appropriate metric is) of your progress and your inevitable slippages. If you got feedback from someone else earlier in the process, you may want to ask them to provide a "second opinion" regarding your progress. Once again, it's crucial that you be honest with yourself. Like "cheating" on your diet or exercise regimen when you're trying to lose weight, being less than objective about your efforts here will hurt only you.

The second reason we want you to look for "subpatterns" among your acrophobic behaviors is that they may help you with the other part of your work in combating your career acrophobia: looking for and confronting the root causes of this feeling that you shouldn't be as successful as you are or are becoming. There are countless variations on the themes we described above (in "The Origins of the Acrophobe"), and understanding just what internal assumptions or messages from the past you are grappling with will in the long run help you to win the fight. Pure insight is not enough, but it is a tremendous help, *when combined with committed efforts to change the everyday behaviors that result from those assumptions and messages.* The two together, action and reflection, make for the most potent combination possible for personal change.

FOR MANAGERS

If this pattern of behavior sounds like someone in your organization—specifically, someone you have managerial responsibility for—how can you help them (and, by extension, help yourself and your organization)? The answer to this question lies in another question: What is it about this person (call him Bob), and about what you have been reading, that makes you think Bob may be suffering from this particular Achilles' heel? In answering this second question, be as specific as possible ("Over the past two years Bob has done the following three times: The first was . . ."). If you're going to be able to help someone with this issue, you're first going to have to be able to spell out the actual events and actions that make you associate the person and the issue.

Then you, as Bob's manager, can do either or both of two things. One is to talk to him about what you've noticed, how you see it as forming a pattern, what your concerns are about his career as a result, and what you think he might want to do, or at least think about. Obviously this conversation is unlikely to be helpful if all you can say is that you "have a feeling" Bob might fall into this category. The advantage of having this straightforward discussion is that it opens things up for you and Bob to talk very specifically about what you might be able to do to help him, and it makes clear to him that you value him enough to *want* to help. It also allows for the two of you to use both the action and reflection discussed above.

You might, however, feel uncomfortable having this kind of direct discussion with Bob, either because of the kind of person you are, because of the kind of person you believe he is, or because of the nature of your particular relationship. If so, your options are more limited—but not eliminated. If you were correct in thinking that Bob is suffering from career acrophobia, you know that his basic sense of himself is of not being good enough, of not deserving his level of success. So one thing you can do is to gradually increase the frequency of positive comments you make to him about his work, his contribution, his general level of value in the organization. For example, "I'm sure I don't say this often enough, Bob, and I think we all go home sometimes wondering if we're really making a contribution to the company—I know I do—so I just want you to know how much I personally appreciate you for all you do." You can also take on one or two of the behaviors you notice as undermining Bob's success and "protect him from himself," insulating him from his self-defeating behavior by building in a compensatory safeguard. For example, you might install a final proofreading of important reports Bob writes, knowing that this is one of his self-defeating behaviors. Or you might make it a point to call on him in meetings where you know he has a significant contribution to make but sense that he feels anxious and uncomfortable.

Clearly, taking these steps requires a high level of commitment on your part as the individual's manager—not something you will want to do for just anyone. But if you choose wisely and do this for a person with very high potential, the benefit to your organization can be enormous. Not only is it a *good* (altruistic) thing to do, it is a good thing to *do* (in terms of the return on your investment). This pattern is one of the most difficult Achilles' heels to repair. It is rooted in attitudes about the self and the world that are established early in life and that are often largely unconscious. Changing this pattern is never accomplished once and for all—it takes determination, self-observation, and deliberate action over not a span of months, but years. It will require a continuing resolution on your part. That said, though, finding a way to allow yourself to ascend to each successive level of responsibility, challenge, and reward—whatever elevation that might mean in your particular case—is well worth the effort. As one of our clients put it, "Whatever it takes, it's got to be better than sitting around when I'm a hundred years old saying, 'You know, I *could* have been . . . but I wasn't.'"

CHAPTER

TWO

SEEING THE WORLD IN
BLACK AND WHITE

Sometimes the world behaves in wonderfully rational ways: the team that scores the most points wins the game, the person who spells all the words right or answers all the math problems correctly gets an A, the company promotes the best and most deserving employee. And sometimes, as most of us know, it doesn't. Someone gets a job because of "connections," sons and daughters of alumni in many private schools get preference over other applicants, the company promotes someone who talks a good game and is always careful to rub shoulders with the right people—but is a petty tyrant to those under and around him, and incompetent to boot. Despite the fact that most of us know this, some people never moderate their faith or belief in the perfect rationality of grammar school test questions and answers. They see the world in black and white, with answers that are right or wrong, all weighed on a perfectly fair scale and judged accordingly, on their merits alone. Pam was one example of such a true believer.

Pam was a creative thinker, a talented writer and editor, an innovator who was able to come up with fresh ways of solving problems. She was also a skilled critical thinker, someone who could dig into problems, sift through hundreds of pages of data, pull out the relevant themes, draw the correct inferences, form and test the right hypotheses, recognize the unstated assumptions being made. In short, she was, and always had been, the "sharpest knife in the drawer." She had been a stellar student in high school, a member of the debate team and National Honor Society, had top grades and scored well enough on the SAT to be a National Merit Finalist. She had then gone on to Harvard College, where she was a government major and had taken some very demanding advanced courses as a cross-registrant at MIT and at the Fletcher School of Diplomacy at Tufts University.

Now, ten years later, Pam was a member of the Washington policy community, a group of people who have never been elected to office and generally don't manage many (if any) subordinates. They are "applied scholars" by and large, some with university positions but many without, and they generate many of the new ideas on everything from arms control to health care policy to Social Security reform that ultimately get debated in the halls of Congress.

For a decade Pam had established an enviable reputation as a valuable analyst of the problems of poverty and pollution and as an innovative thinker about their solutions. She was bright, good-looking, and articulate, even eloquent. But Pam had a serious problem. She couldn't hold a job.

Through her career in Washington she had never stayed with an employer for much more than a year. She was forever quitting—or quitting rather than being fired. Always with a good reason (in her view), and always the same reason. The organizations were always pressuring her to do something unethical or were engaging in some sort of unethical behavior themselves. And she didn't want to be a part of it; she was unwilling to accept that kind of "shady" behavior.

Just before Pam came to us for help, she was working as director of communications and publications for a research institute, one of those collections of scholars and analysts in Washington that are commonly known as think tanks. Businesses, labor unions, foundations, wealthy individuals, and others eager to help direct the course of policy provide them with funds. Pam's particular institution was going through a difficult financial period. Some of the foundations that funded it were questioning whether the institute still had an impact in Washington. The sponsors were losing confidence and, with it, interest in continuing to put money into the institute.

Pam came up with a dramatic idea for revitalizing the institute and generating a great deal of attention. The institute would sponsor a week-long conference on rural poverty, a subject that in recent years had been largely ignored and overshadowed by its urban counterpart. Working on her own initiative and after hours, Pam drafted the program in great detail. She designated a keynote speaker and created a dozen panels, naming the panelists and moderators for each. She then presented her plan to the president of the institute.

The president was properly impressed but noted that Pam had left a celebrated and flamboyant advocate for the poor off the list of participants. Pam told the president that the omission had been deliberate. She thought that others presented the same case more intelligently and without the podium banging and other histrionics of the advocate in question. Pam frankly despised his style. The president acknowledged that he tended to be melodramatic. On the other hand, his name on the program would boost attendance. Also, he was a longtime friend of the president, and not inviting him would be considered a direct slap in the face, a humiliating insult. They would needlessly be making an enemy of a friend. We really *have* to invite him, the president told Pam.

Pam refused, calling him a "celebrity hack" masquerading as a policy planner. "I'm not asking you to invite him," the president said, "I'm insisting. *Put him on the program.*" Pam implied that she would not prostitute herself by doing so. Her refusal to accept the politics involved in her PR efforts at the institute had already caused several minor skirmishes. This, as they say, was the last straw. "Pam, I hate to lose you, but this is not going to work out. You'll have to find another job," the president said. "There's just no place for this kind of rigidity here. We're dependent on the goodwill of others. We can't survive with that kind of attitude." So Pam left, having driven herself into a stone wall one more time.

THE DYNAMICS OF THE PATTERN

Pam is what, for the sake of convenience and brevity, we sometimes refer to as a *meritocrat,* one of those people who *insist* that proposals, ideas, products—virtually everything in life—must be considered *strictly rationally,* on their inherent merit, their absolute, true value. They see the world in black and white—without colors or even shades of gray. If the meritocrat ruled the world, all decisions would be put through some sort of merit-weighing machine. Emotions, politics, sentimentality, loyalties, and favoritism would play absolutely no part. That is the way the world should be, according to the person who lives life in this pattern. The auxiliary verb "should" plays a central role in the vocabulary of the meritocrat. He or she consistently talks about the ways things "should" be, about the unfairness of life, railing about how the well connected, the meretricious, and the conniving rise to the top, while the honest and the principled fall by the wayside.

Sometimes it seems as if the meritocrat lives in a remote "parallel universe" where emotions, relationships, and accidents of good and bad fortune have no place. But it is a world that exists only in his or her mind. Most of us recognize early in life that our peers do not rise and fall by their worth alone. The boss's son may or may not be the brightest penny on the table, but in the real world the boss's son often gets the desirable job whether he is the most qualified candidate or not. Most of us shrug in the face of that reality. We either accept it or leave for another job, but we don't deny that this is a factor in how the world works. For most of us, this ideal, perfectly rational meritocracy exists for the most part as just that: an ideal; as such, we look for organizations that are more rather than less meritocratic. But we harbor no illusions about the fact that such perfection seldom actually exists (outside the world of many sports, perhaps, though even there, sports such as gymnastics, diving, figure skating, and boxing, to name a few, are judged relatively subjectively). The meritocrat, however, insists on fighting the "good" fight until she exasperates her supporters to the end of their patience. She is either relegated to the corporate backwaters or she is canned. Certainly she will never be promoted very far. Her victories, such as they are, are Pyrrhic.

While Pam is an example of such behavior in its purest form, many people fall into the trap of the meritocrat more often than they might tend to realize or admit. And in doing so, they leave themselves open to misjudgments and political faux pas that damage their careers. So if you know in your heart of hearts that you even occasionally slip into such rigid black-and-white thinking over a topic, beware. You may be hurting yourself in ways you're unable to see.

One example of such a person is Sam. As long as he didn't feel threatened, he was able to see all the angles and colors of a given situation, appreciating subtleties and nuances that many people missed. But if someone began to push him, to question his sources (he was an academic), he would bristle and his ability to discern the shades of gray would quickly fade. With his back up, he was able to see only in black and white, and there was *only* one way to do things right—his way. Ask him the same questions in a more easygoing, less pointed or aggressive way, and his response would be dramatically different. Was Sam a "meritocrat"? Not by most people's definition. In fact, he rarely displayed such tendencies at all. But when he did, it was a dramatic shift from his more typical demeanor, and his thinking became easily as rigid as Pam's.

One real danger of this pattern is that it can hinder your success even if no one else ever sees any evidence of such behavior. As a result, often there is no one to point out to you your error or mistake in thinking. When you "run roughshod" over others (see Chapter 5), other people notice. Unfortunately, the symptoms of meritocratic or black-and-white thinking may be entirely hidden. One person we know forms judgments instantly on the basis of how people address her or whether someone responds to her e-mail within twenty-four hours, and once that judgment is rendered it is *very* difficult to change. She operates very much out of the black-and-white behavior pattern, but most of the people in the offices around would never know it. Meanwhile she may be alienating people, underutilizing potentially valuable employees, or turning away valuable business contacts for no reason other than the fact that they have failed at some hidden test only she knows about or understands the rules to.

Of course, such thinking isn't limited to work. If you tend to view things in black and white in the office, you're very likely to use that same approach in your personal life, in your family relationships, and in dealing with children as well. People are complicated, with many shades of gray. Our interactions with each other necessarily involve nuances and subtleties that black-and-white thinking blithely ignores. And there can be serious consequences to such thinking. Most people are highly sensitive to being judged. What may be "unacceptable behavior" to you may well be perfectly acceptable to someone else. Communicating about differences and accepting a certain amount of other people's differences is part of what makes strong, healthy relationships possible. If you use a black-and-white measuring system on colleagues, friends and acquaintances, and spouses, it's not unlikely they'll soon become *former* friends and acquaintances, or *ex*-spouses. At the very least, they will certainly be more cautious around you and more distant. Moreover, by passing this black-and-white view of life on to your children, you will be giving them an inheritance that will serve them poorly in their own lives.

It's important to reflect on whether or not your thinking ever crystallizes into rigid black-and-white imagery, and if so, when and why. When you react in a way that surprises you or makes you feel uncomfortable, think about what is causing that discomfort. Could it be a tendency, however mild or occasional, to slip into this kind of rigid behavior? If so, it is important that you recognize it for what it is. Or you may recognize this behavior pattern in someone you work with.

People who fall into this pattern may sound entirely logical and on target. We rightly admire the idealist who tries to protect good ideas from being trammeled. After all, such legitimate rebellion was the basis of the formation of our nation. The underdog who sticks to his guns and fights the good fight for what he believes is right is widely, and understandably, admired. As a result, this pattern has a great deal of cultural support. What others may miss, though, especially in the case of the occasional meritocrat, is that they aren't fighting for the right reasons or to do what is best in the given situation. And in the case of more extreme meritocrats, like Don Quixote, they are forever tilting at windmills. Nor, often, are they even particularly good fighters, for the very reason they've joined in the battle to begin with. Sometimes to win the battle you have to negotiate and compromise—promise something to someone to get him or her to join your side—which goes against the code of rationality (this person should join because it's the right thing to do, period).

As a result, the meritocrat often fights the battle alone. And frequently loses. For example, one of our clients, whom we'll call "Dan," went to work for a family business after college—someone else's family, not his. He knew from the beginning just what the situation was and that he would never get a share of the business. Moreover, he knew that several members of the family his age and younger would have a say in how things were run that, all else being equal, would outweigh his. Dan had bought into this arrangement, but once in it he began to chafe. It wasn't fair that just because they had the right last name they got the goods. He worked as hard or harder, was just as smart or smarter, but still they finished first. What began as chafing rapidly progressed to outright anger and rage against the system. He fixated on the unfairness and on what was denied to him, ignoring both what was available to him and the fact that he had entered into this contract with full awareness. He confronted his boss with the unfairness of the situation. The owner's response was that he could see how Dan felt, but it wasn't going to change and that Dan had to either accept it or leave. In the end, he left. Dan had in this context acted as much like a meritocrat as Pam did. If he'd understood himself and his needs better, he would never have accepted that job in the first place.

The person who thinks this way is acting almost as an anti-Machiavellian, someone who loathes politics and flattery and the compromises of deal making. Most of us, it is true, would rather deal with the meritocrat than his polar opposite, the unprincipled schemer for whom ideals have no value. The schemer is loathsome in his treachery; the meritocrat insufferable only in his self-righteousness. But most of us would much prefer to work with someone who, while not dishonest and manipulative, is aware of how the world works and not constantly denying and fighting it. We would instinctively recognize that such behavior is almost guaranteed to bring about failure.

The fact is, such individuals are tireless defenders of the ideal as long as the ideal is his or her own. But suppose you have a different ideal, and *your* paradigm of excellence is teamwork. Let's say you believe that the way an organization progresses is by moving a large number of people in the same direction and that to do that you sometimes have to settle on a strategy that is less than perfect. The meritocrat would have no patience for *your* ideal. You would have just joined the ranks of the unprincipled, the enemies of the idealistic rationalist.

Later in the book we identify another behavior pattern we call being "emotionally tone-deaf"—exhibited by a person who has so successfully buried his emotions that he doesn't even recognize them in others. Meritocrats, by contrast, recognize the existence of personal loyalties, self-interest, and passions—but they see them as wrong, factors that shouldn't have any bearing on decision making. They want to eliminate them. They tend to value ideas at the expense of the relationships that make all organizations work, whether the organization is a political party, a corporation, a university, or a football team.

Renowned psychologist David McClelland of Harvard wrote about three basic motivators in people's work: need for achievement, need for affiliation, and need for power. Most successful business professionals' scores on these three motivations form something of a checkmark. They tend to be moderately highly motivated by a need for achievement, not much motivated by need for affiliation, and highly motivated by a need for power. The meritocrat, by contrast, is *very* highly oriented toward achievement, moderately highly motivated by need for affiliation, and almost negatively motivated by need for power.

That may be why people who strongly exhibit this behavior pattern tend to worship at the altar of the quantifiable. Keeping score, numbers—those are ways of determining the "achievement value" of an idea or program. The "soft" measures, including things like goodwill and relationship value, or "turf," are nonquantifiable and to many meritocrats are therefore of little or no value.

Interestingly, although such people go through life trying to make the world conform to *their personal* ideal of fairness and justice, and can seem utterly egotistical in their judgmentalism, meritocrats are *not* typically driven by ego. They want to see that whatever they're working on is done right—as they define it—but they don't necessarily seek to have their names emblazoned on it or to get all the credit for it.

Of the four developmental issues we discuss in Part II to better understand how the twelve patterns of behavior discussed in the book develop, the meritocrat will particularly benefit from reading both "Taking Others' Perspectives" and "Using Power." Meritocrats are typically so focused on their personal agendas that they simply forget about other people, whose perspectives may be different. And when this is pointed out to them, they discount it, because those people's personal (nonmeritocratic, selfish, inappropriate) perspectives *shouldn't* exist. They *should* be focused only on the merit of the task at hand. They find using power repellent, feeling that one should not *have* to use power, that people should simply recognize the best ideas on the basis of their *intrinsic* merit and adopt them accordingly. People who fall into this pattern of thinking or behavior disdain power and its users, find the use of power undignified, demeaning, almost repellent.

Meritocrats sometimes fail to negotiate a third developmental task discussed in Part II—coming to terms with authority. Several of the other career Achilles' heels discussed in the book are directly *caused* by difficulty with authority (the rebel, for example, described in Chapter 6 comes immediately to mind). In the case of the meritocrat, difficulty with authority is more a by-product. The person has no need to butt heads with those in authority—if only they would see the light, stop playing politics, and jump on the meritocrat's bandwagon. The problem, of course, is that people in positions of authority would never have come to hold these positions if they had consistently exhibited this behavior pattern. As a result, meritocrats are likely to run into trouble with those above them, although by chance rather than (like the rebel) by choice.

People who are extreme meritocrats are relatively rare in business, and are rarely very successful, perhaps because business almost *always* involves a compromise with perfection. One place where we have seen people who exhibit this pattern (albeit with moderately severe cases) succeed is in the investment management industry. Given that ethics and adherence to Securities and Exchange Commission regulations are a key part of the business, this pattern, if not too extreme in its manifestation, can be neutral or even something of a positive. Far more often, though, compromise in business is the rule. For example, sometimes a business deal is so imperfect that it loses money for one party. But the company knowingly enters into it because in the long term, the deal will preserve a client relationship—and that is where its profitability lies. But even when an issue at hand is spelled out as clearly as that, the meritocrat often has trouble swallowing it. "But why do we need to lose money just to preserve our relationship with the customer! If two years from now we come to them with a great deal, they should jump at it, regardless of whether we do this one." And their consternation is multiplied if the decision is *personal:* We're doing this just to please the customer's vice president of sales. Typically, the meritocrat is outraged.

The meritocrat may be successful in a research and development department—the closer to basic research and more removed from the demands of the market, the better. And such behavior is more tolerated in the arts—music, literature, the movies—and in the halls of academia than elsewhere. But even people who bring the idea out of R&D have to be willing to compromise. Yes, it's a perfect laboratory product, but to be marketable it has to be manufactured below a hurdle cost *and* work outside a climate-controlled laboratory environment *and* be easy to operate *and* be sufficiently superior to whatever consumers are currently buying to lure them away. High-definition television is truly spectacular, but few people will buy sets at $10,000. The early pre-Windows PCs required some working knowledge of DOS—a consumer-unfriendly system that constituted a significant barrier.

No matter how wonderful the creator may think a product is, it doesn't have any value unless the marketplace agrees with that assessment, and even the backroom R&D scientists at the Du Ponts, Lucents, GEs, and Hewlett-Packards of the world have to recognize that fact. So even there the meritocrat has to learn to adapt or else be so brilliant that his or her shortcomings are tolerated.

But companies' tolerance for the "brilliant but impossible to get along with" individual is waning. Most managers today factor the "maintenance cost" of this kind of person into the equation of his or her worth and would prefer a slightly less brilliant but much lower-maintenance employee.

Meritocrats sometimes fare a bit better early on in their careers (if they are doing work sufficiently valuable for their managers to be willing to cut them some slack). Many managers are willing to chalk up the meritocrat's firebrand idealism to the excesses of youth—up to a point and up to a point in time. The overbearing meritocrat, no matter his or her age, is likely to be in career trouble. And the excuse of youth fades rather quickly as one moves through his or her twenties and enters midlife. The wunderkind gambit usually works only while you are a *kinder,* a child, if at all.

THE MERITOCRAT IN AN ORGANIZATION

When meritocrats are in charge of a company, the company tends to produce solutions that are looking for a problem, products that are beautiful in design and technological elegance but that no one wants, at least not yet.

In his thesis of "disruptive technologies," Harvard's Clay Christensen describes a cycle in which a company, with great intensity of purpose and effort, develops an idea into a breakthrough product. This is a good thing, a very good thing. But with meritocrats leading the charge, the company continues to invest vast amounts of money in R&D, creating follow-on products that are truly meritorious but are more sophisticated, complex, and expensive than what the market wants. To a degree, Xerox got caught in that cycle by producing more and more intricate copiers with more and more functions. Meanwhile the companies that profit from the technology are those who turn it into a commodity and figure out *just* what the customer wants and provide that and no more—and *cheaply!*

One company that fell victim to its meritocrats is Digital Equipment Corporation, the Boston manufacturer that came out with a string of sensationally successful computer and peripheral products, such as their VAX computer system. But as the market moved toward PCs, their engineers didn't. They continued to develop great new ideas, and no one could figure out what the market for those exotic products might be. The engineering people would build machines and chips and devices and tell the marketing people to find a market for them. "There *is* no market," the marketing people would say. "Well then, find one, make one. This thing is really fast, really good." The fact that nobody wanted such a machine was beyond the meritocrat creators' understanding.

Meritocrats can also be destructive to the morale and general atmosphere of a company by virtue of their judgmentalism. Most meritocrats are not people who simply note what they think is right and move on. Even if something is good, they want to make it, or do it, perfectly. "Well, you know, if we were *really* true to our mission we would. . . ." More to the point, if an employee or colleague is found wanting, the meritocrat often feels compelled to point that out. On both counts, the meritocrat succeeds in making people feel bad—and, sooner or later, angry. Others just can't be perfect enough for the meritocrat, which makes for a negative climate. Of course, this is worse when the meritocrat in question is the manager of the group, but the meritocrat is a source of organizational damage even if he or she is not the leader, but one of the team.

That said, one individual we worked with, call him Jason, was an exceedingly nice, optimistic fellow who also happened to be a highly talented strategic analyst. He was not the least bit judgmental, negative, or egotistical, yet because he saw the world in black and white he assumed that in the marketplace of ideas the best would win out. So he would come to internal business meetings with his analyses and conclusions, ready to put them forward for healthy debate. What Jason didn't understand until we examined the organizational culture he worked in was that these meetings were being held for the purpose of *publicly ratifying an idea that had already been agreed on.* All the agreements had been made, all the deals cut, before the meeting. So his fellow executives were nonplussed when Jason presented another proposal—and a good one at that—in these meetings. And Jason was baffled when he would be shot down without consideration of the idea's merit, when he would find the "idea marketplace" closed.

Again, the severity of this pattern of behavior ranges from the extreme (such as Pam) to the more moderate. Jason is a good example of someone whose career was impaired by this behavior pattern—but not fatally so. He was simply less effective than he might otherwise have been had he not relied on people to set aside their personal or parochial interests and consider ideas and proposals on their merits. He was still able to influence the course of events in his company, but less so than he would otherwise have been able to do. (Once we pointed out his behavior pattern and how it clashed with the culture of the organization, he shifted his approach and became a great deal more effective.)

Meritocrats are often attracted to public service, although their successes in politics are generally limited, undone by the very commitment to meritocracy that drew them into that arena to begin with. Michael Dukakis, unsuccessful Democratic candidate for the presidency in 1988, was essentially a meritocrat. He defeated himself, in many people's view, because of that disability, because he eschewed passion. He seemed incapable of emotion, responding to any and all questions on the campaign trail with a listing of the merits of whatever issue was at hand. One big, although dubious, issue in that presidential campaign was the William Horton case. Horton, a convicted murderer imprisoned in Massachusetts, was allowed a forty-eight-hour furlough from prison, as were other felons who were considered good risks, not only in Massachusetts, but in other states. Horton fled the state, later attacking a man and raping his fiancée in Maryland. Dukakis was governor of Massachusetts at the time, and the Bush campaign's television advertising campaign made it sound as though Dukakis had personally opened the cell door for Horton and driven him south.

Dukakis *could* have undermined the Bush campaign by expressing his own outrage over what Horton had done. He could have said, "Of course I'm outraged, and saddened, and a part of me wants revenge. But in a civilized society, although we can *want* revenge we can't exact it. We try to rehabilitate people so that when they go back into the world they'll be able to live by the rules. Any system makes mistakes. In Horton's case the system made a terrible, tragic mistake. And if Mr. Bush had ever been in charge of such a system himself, mistakes like this would have occurred on his watch as well."

But Dukakis didn't do that. He dryly replied to the Bush attack with a meritocratic defense, a defense of the *merits* of the furlough system, stating that in its weekend release program the Massachusetts penal system was adopting the most up-to-date thinking on rehabilitation. He carved that cold meritocratic image of himself into the voters' minds forever during a national television debate. A journalist asked Dukakis what he would do if someone raped his wife. The correct answer would have been an immediate outburst of rage followed by a rational disclaimer "but of course, we can't do that. . . ." But he didn't respond immediately. He pondered the question as though he were trying to come up with the proper meritocratic response. Dukakis paused, fatally—and then *did* give a level, even-handed, cool, meritocratic answer.

President Jimmy Carter was a meritocrat as well, although his symptoms were not the same as those of Dukakis. Carter's great shortcoming, at least one of them, was that he refused to play politics. By measures of integrity and intellect and a number of other virtues, no one deserved to be president more than Carter. Few presidents have had a higher IQ. But the meritocrat in him insisted on being an outsider and refusing to play the Beltway games of backslapping, flattering, cajoling, and the rest. The reality of Washington is that unless a president strokes congressional egos and at least pretends to respect them, he will not accomplish much. At times, Carter's White House didn't even return the calls of congressional leaders. He relied on the merit of his ideas to carry the day, and today most people consider his presidency to have been a failure.

THE ORIGINS OF THE MERITOCRAT

Unlike some of the other Achilles' heels discussed in *Maximum Success*, the meritocrat does not seem to be shaped in early childhood by an unsuccessful struggle to come to terms with authority. Rather, meritocrats have a naive reliance upon a certain kind of authority, the authority of objective, measurable facts.

The meritocrats we have worked with or researched all did very well in school. They excelled at formal tests, especially those tests with quantifiable answers. The SAT test they took to get into college is a meritocrat's paradigm of how life *should* be. It doesn't make any difference whether you are tall or short, ugly or beautiful, male or female, black or white, from the East or the West, smile at the teacher or scowl. If you know all of the answers on the math and verbal sections, you score 1600. If you don't, your total score is something less. Your father's position as chairman of the school board won't add a point to your score (except that the more well-to-do often get private coaching).

If you get all the spelling questions right, or did the problem set correctly in your college engineering class, you don't have to lobby the teacher. You don't have to work to make sure that the principal funds that class for the rest of the term. Your score is what it is. And since the meritocrat's score is usually pretty good, she concludes that this is a pretty good system! We all like systems that are fair, but we like them even more if we can excel under that system. So the meritocrat decides that if this is the way life is in class, it's the way life should be *after* school. The difference between the meritocrat and other people is that the meritocrat simply never gives up on this idea.

So the meritocrat believes in his or her heart of hearts that all of life should be scored as fairly and objectively as the SATs. But in real life, of course, even the SATs don't function as a perfect objective determinant in channeling people into college. The SAT score counts. Merit counts. But a whole lot of other factors count as well. Is that *right?* Should a college pass over a very bright girl from New York City in favor of a young man from Wyoming with a lower score simply because there are already too many people like her in the entering class and too few like him? Maybe not. But that's the way the admissions process works—and that's the way the world works. To rail against it as unfair, to insist that only merit should count, is an exercise in futility.

Compared with many other countries, the United States indeed does value meritocracy. If you invest in the stock market and your stocks go up, it doesn't matter who your parents are (or are not). If you develop and secure the patent for a new kind of microchip, it doesn't matter what college (if any) you went to. America is a country that eliminated the aristocracy and that prizes personal ambition, talent, and work ethic. Horatio Alger's stories of young men like Ragged Dick who, by dint of their virtue and hard work, become successful and respected are part of the fabric of American culture.

But America is hardly a pure meritocracy. American institutions, public and private, commonly boast that they are meritocracies in which the best people rise to the top. "Meritocracy" is a virtual buzzword in American business. But it also matters who your mentor is and where your alliances are in the organization. In the real world you need patience, the ability to compromise, and the willingness to accept an occasional defeat.

HOW TO BREAK THE PATTERN

If you realize that you fall into the trap of black-and-white thinking, even if only occasionally, what can you do? The first step is recognizing that this is something you do. Next, you have to ask yourself a very tough question: "Do I really want to change?" Many meritocrats *really, truly don't want to change*—it's easier for them to hold on to the fundamentalist view that the world is *all* black or *all* white. And if that's you, and you really don't want to change your viewpoint, why kid yourself about trying to change? You'll only frustrate yourself. You simply need to know this is how you tend to act, and you should try to find a job or position where such thinking is most likely to be tolerated.

If you really *do* want to change, though, you need to acknowledge that changing how you think and behave is not going to be easy. You're going to have to struggle (repeatedly) with whether you are giving up too much principle in a given situation in the interest of advancing your agenda. And sometimes you'll find yourself grieving over the compromises of your agenda. This is an easy thing to write or say, but a very difficult thing to live. Once you give up the notion that the end and the means must be wholly pure, then you'll find yourself wrestling with the dilemma of when the means are not justified by the ends you are seeking to accomplish.

You'll need to work at being aware of your thinking, feelings, and actions when you find yourself raging against the injustice of the organization's politics. One of our clients noticed that he used to clench his teeth and jut his jaw forward when his sensibilities were affronted. Another realized he sat or stood rigidly straight, like a military officer at attention. Still another found himself shaking his head slowly, saying (to himself), "Typical, that's just so typical."

You need to learn to listen in a nonjudgmental way and think about how your boss, your co-workers, and the customers of your organization experience the world. Doing so will not only make you politically more effective, it will lead to greater knowledge and insights about the challenges and problems your team and company face.

When we work with people who suffer from black-and-white thinking, we often suggest that the person take his or her ideas to a manager and present them *as if* they were not yet fully formed ("just something I've been kicking around, it's not really fully thought out yet, but I wanted to get your ideas and input"). In reality the meritocrat may have spent countless hours analyzing it from every conceivable angle. But by presenting the sketch, he allows his manager to have a sense of ownership. It's the "managing your boss" equivalent of cake mix makers' learning that if they allowed the buyers to add the egg to the mix (rather than supplying dried egg in the box), they felt as if it were *their* cake that *they* had baked. In the case of the rural poverty conference, we would have encouraged Pam not to present a complete and final conference program to the president but, instead, to go to him and say, "This is preliminary. This is what I'd like to do, but I want your thoughts as well." If you validate the ideas of other people, they find it much easier to validate yours.

We also teach these clients specific phrases to use in disagreements to avoid communicating a judgmental stance that is sure to have the listener go on the defensive: "I wouldn't dream of questioning your technical data, which are impressive, but I wonder if there isn't another way to look at this situation." By using words and phrases that suggest they see the shades of gray in a situation, clients are more likely to avert battles. In addition, they usually genuinely *are* then more able to appreciate those points of view that they would previously have been blind to.

When you find yourself wanting to "take a stand" on something, step outside yourself and the situation and apply a variation of the "reasonable person principle." Ask yourself, "Would a 'reasonable person' think I am being too rigid?" (A "reasonable person" would have told Pam just to put the guy on the program and get on with it.) Ask yourself, "How would a sage, wise mentor, advise me on this matter?" One meritocrat we know, a private client services professional with an investment bank, was so rigid in his approach that he refused to allow the husband of one of his clients to be in the office when he talked with her about her investment account—it was the letter of the law, his law. He could recognize other people's rigidities, but he was blind to his own. So try hard to step out of yourself. If you have, or have ever had, a mentor, ask yourself, "What would s/he think?" (This assumes, of course, that your mentor was not a meritocrat him- or herself.)

Next, move into action. What (or who) are the barriers to the program or idea being adopted, what are the others' concerns, what are the idea's selling points, whom do you need to get buy-in from, what points can you yield on, are there things you can build in to your agenda that you can give up later to compromise? What are the "hot buttons" of the people you need to enlist to make this happen, when and how should you start garnering the support you're going to need? Read "Taking Others' Perspectives" (in Part II of *Maximum Success*)—especially the subhead entitled "What Do People *Really* Want?" Ask yourself that question with regard to the people whose cooperation and support you need to achieve your goal. Then try to supply each person with some of what he or she really wants or needs as part of this alliance.

Certain fencers are noted for their unwillingness to "give ground" during a match—as if the outcome were measured by real estate gained, not wounds inflicted. Once they advance on the strip, they will never retreat in the face of a counterattack. They are easily disposed of by more skillful fencers. As a meritocrat you probably have an analogous tendency. Be aware of it (it can leave you, metaphorically, mortally wounded), and know when to give ground and live to fight another day. Remember, life is a long campaign, and if you risk death in every battle, your chances of fighting on and winning the war are pretty slim.

Guy Kawaski, best-selling author and former Apple Macintosh VP and evangelist, espouses the doctrine "Don't worry, be crappy." His point is that if your product or idea is at least ten times better than what came before (comparing even the very *worst*, most primitive toilet paper to leaves, for example), it is good enough to take to the market. Try to adopt a bit (if only a bit) of his attitude and just *get things done*.

The person who sees things in black-and-white, all-or-nothing, perfectionistic terms is not going to have a long and fruitful career in the world of Internet business and software development. Success in this world is about grabbing market share, getting things out to the consumer. The winners worry about getting out all of the bugs and polishing all the features in the next release or the release after that. A company that bases its business strategy on building the very *best* mousetrap and trusting in the marketplace to see its merit and cast aside competing products will fail. Sony's Betamax tape and Apple's Macintosh operating systems are prime examples. If compromise and full-color thinking are what are fueling the world's hottest industries, it may be a signal that you should think long and hard about using a black-and-white screen for your own career and life.

We are not trying to turn idealists into cynics or to say that merit doesn't or shouldn't matter or that you must be ready to sacrifice any principle to achieve your goals. But meritocrats often have very good ideas, and they fail to see them adopted just because they are not good at advancing them. Our point of view is more that, just as force equals mass times velocity, progress equals the merit of an idea times the skill of its implementation. And a successful career is much more a function of how much progress you are responsible for than of how many meritorious ideas you conceive.

MANAGING THE MERITOCRAT

Meritocrats are not easy to work with—as colleagues or managers. Often when we first begin working with a meritocrat, they spend a lot of time talking to us about their ideas, wanting us to "certify" that they were indeed right, that their plans for the reorganization of a division, or the launch of a new product, or a change in their job description, was the best approach and that their co-workers and manager lack insight and are blind to the truth. One of our clients spent three-quarters of his time trying to convince us that his co-managers were crippling the company with their antiquated methods.

Our approach with meritocrats (and one that managers we have worked with have used successfully with such employees who report to them) is to immediately jump onto their side, to ally with them in their anger that the "MQ" (meritocracy quotient) of their companies is not higher. We listen and agree with them that their ideas are excellent and sympathize with them over their inability to get others to see their value. We commiserate with them.

Next we draw an obvious but critically important distinction that often eludes the black-and-white thinker. That distinction is between being right and being effective. We often use Presidents Carter and Reagan as examples. "Let's assume for the sake of argument," we say, "that President Carter was right as rain in his policies, and that Reagan was the devil in disguise, whatever your actual politics or political affiliation. Even the most diehard proponents of that view agree that Reagan was enormously effective in advancing his political agenda, and that Carter was largely ineffective in advancing his. Clearly, being 'right' has absolutely nothing to do with being 'effective.' Right now you are so focused on being right that you are incredibly ineffective. Is that what you want?"

We put to them a question, just as obvious as the distinction between rightness and effectiveness, that they stubbornly ignore: "What's more important to you, being right or getting your plans enacted?" The usual response is, "Both." And our counterresponse is, "You can't have both. Perhaps you can get 90 percent of 'your way'—but only 90 percent. Or you can insist on 100 percent purity and get none."

With Pam, the client we discussed at the beginning of the chapter, we asked, "Is it more important that you keep the celebrity hack off the program or that you mount and get credit for an important conference on rural poverty and revitalize your group in the process?" Pam agreed, painfully, that the overall conference was more important. Yes, her meritocratically purist peers in other Washington organizations would likely snicker to see his name on the program. But just as certainly they, too, had made similar compromises.

To successfully manage someone who sees things in black and white, you have to first sympathize. Yes, it really is unfair. Then you need to try to move them beyond the judgmental mode into one of action, soliciting their help in getting them to confront the reality of whatever the situation is. What (or who) are the barriers, what are the concerns, what are the selling points, whom do we need to get buy-in from, what points can we yield on (a painful subject for someone who thinks like a meritocrat, of course—but necessary), are there things we can build in that we can then give up, what are the "hot buttons" of the people we need to enlist to make this happen, when and how should we start garnering the support we're going to need?

It's a little like trying to jump-start a car. If you ask the meritocrat to think about all the questions you just posed and come back in a day, it won't work. But if you galvanize the person into immediate action, throw your energy into it, he or she can be carried along and get into it. Present it like the landings at Normandy beach: "We're going to plan this operation and carry it off, and they won't even know what hit them!"

Once you establish the dual importance of correctness *and* effectiveness, you may be able to engage the meritocrat's interest in solving the problem by presenting the issue as a puzzle, almost a game, to be figured out. "We want to get your idea adopted. Let's put together a plan to ensure that happens!" And one thing about success is that it feels good and is a tremendous reinforcement. The very act of being successful is a powerful inducement in encouraging your career meritocrat to be a little more flexible the next time and to think about "effectiveness," as well as what is "right," in the future.

When black-and-white thinkers self-destruct, it is an enormous loss to the organizations for which they were working. Typically they are bright and hardworking, with hearts in the right place. In fact, they're just a little *too* bright and hardworking, and their hearts are just a little *too* much in the right place. If you can just help them come to see that being smart is not enough, that being right is not enough; to see that having the right product or idea is necessary but not sufficient; to see that selling that product or idea is the essential second half of the battle; and to see that, bright as they are, they may not be right all of the time—then you will have salvaged someone who is likely to stay with you for a long time and provide a great benefit to your organization. It is an effort well worth undertaking.

CHAPTER
THREE

DOING TOO MUCH, PUSHING TOO HARD

As far back as she could remember, Stephanie made extraordinary demands on herself. It wasn't enough that she was an A student from the moment schools started to grade her performance. She insisted on extra-credit homework as well, studying late into the night, every night, from the time she entered adolescence. She was president of her class at her high school in rural Oregon, a member of the debating team, a gymnast, and the head of the drama club. Stephanie wasn't just an aspiring actress; she was an aspiring everything.

At first Stephanie's obsession with taking on more and more responsibility, to work harder than anyone else, was a source of amusement to her friends. In college the smiles began to fade. She persuaded the faculty supervisor of the drama club to mount a production of *King Lear*, perhaps Shakespeare's most difficult tragedy, with Stephanie as both director and Cordelia. The other members of the company thought she would have been better cast as Goneril or Regan. As director she drove them mercilessly, keeping them at rehearsals late into the night again and again. Never satisfied, she had them repeat scenes dozens of times. Three days before the opening four members of the cast, including Lear, walked out. The play never went on. Stephanie had developed what we refer to as a "hero" behavior pattern.

THE DYNAMICS OF THE PATTERN

We use the term *hero* not as an accolade, but as shorthand for a behavior pattern in which people constantly try to do too much and push too hard—both themselves and other people. The person who falls into this pattern takes on the impossible, or near impossible, time and again and, even when she or he masters it, never feels that is enough. The hero does not believe that a grade of 99 percent is acceptable or that a production—any production—is good enough and must go on. In the workplace such a person's rallying cries are, "More, better, faster," "No guts, no glory," and "Twenty-four/seven" (working twenty-four hours a day, seven days a week).

Setting ambitious goals and working hard to achieve them is not a bad thing. It is the compulsive nature of the pattern the hero lives out that is the problem. The individual who sets his or her sights on a goal, works toward it consistently and achieves it is to be admired. But the person who drives him- or herself, and others, relentlessly for more and more, who works obsessively and usually joylessly, is neither fun to be around nor at all fun to work for. This is one of several reasons that heroes, while frequently prospering early on in their careers, have limited success later on. The fact is that any business comprises the people within it, and if those people are unhappy and "burned out," they will begin to leave, setting off a disastrous cascade of even greater stress and burnout, further departures, and so on.

In times of high unemployment, and in an industry in which machines, not people, play the key role and at lower levels—given all of these conditions, this scenario *might* be tolerable. Absent any one, though, the results are totally unacceptable. Certainly in any company in which the people are *the* key to success (as in the form of "intellectual capital"), a hero can unwittingly exert a deadly influence over time, and once this pattern is recognized by upper management, the hero is going to be forced out.

In working with one top management consulting firm, the following situation was described to us: "The project manager we want you to work with, Dick, is one of the brightest people we have, but we can't get anyone to work with him. Clients love him, the other partners love him, his peers tolerate him, but we can't staff his projects with consultants, other than at gunpoint. He drives people too hard, even for us, he has no sense of humor, no warmth, he's totally task focused. He's not, so to say, 'developing a following within the firm,' and we won't be able to promote him to vice president (our equivalent of partnership) unless he can change." Dick's response was telling: "Look, our clients pay us a lot of money to analyze their strategies, and we pay our consultants a lot of money to work here [this is a firm that pays its young MBA consultants upward of $200,000 a year to start]. They deserve total commitment and value for their dollar, and we deserve it from our consultants. I'm not going to waste anybody's money asking people on my teams how their vacations were, how their kids are doing, or how they may have liked a movie they saw. We're here to work, not to chat." And in fact, Dick wasn't there much longer, either to work or to chat. He wanted to do it all, and for the first four or five years he was with the firm that worked in his favor. Then it swiftly led to his ouster.

Heroes tend to bite off more than they can chew and in the midst of one project are already looking around for something else to tackle. It isn't greed that drives them. Money, including easy money, doesn't interest them at all. What attracts them is the unattainable. They whip themselves and others at top speed, constantly ignoring the fact that machines, animals, and other humans that run endlessly at top speed without time for recovery will eventually falter and fail.

Rafael Lopez-Padrazo, a celebrated Venezuelan psychoanalyst, wrote about what he calls "titanism." In Greek mythology, even before the gods appeared and occupied Mount Olympus, the Titans had emerged from the chaos as raw and savage forces with insatiable appetites. They devoured everything around them with abandon. Heroes are like Titans; they feel impelled to do more and do it better and then to do more, better, again and again. Lopez-Padrazo once described a patient, a businessman in Caracas, with "titanic" appetites who would regularly schedule simultaneous lunch meetings with as many as three different clients. He would begin the first with an apology that he was going to have to leave early; begin the second with apologies for being late and for having to leave early; and meet his third appointment with profuse apologies for his lateness. His appetite, by the way, was not for the food, but for the work, for getting more done—as if he could split himself into a team of three and accomplish three times as much!

A hero is not merely a perfectionist. A perfectionist might hold on to a project forever, constantly correcting and refining, determined to get it "right." The hero not only insists on perfection, but keeps expanding the project to include more and more work. The "too much too hard" pattern is one that tends to persist tenaciously throughout a career. What is worse for those around him or her, the hero likes to lead a team, charging like Teddy Roosevelt and the Rough Riders up San Juan Hill (or, less successfully, leading the famous "charge of the light brigade" to their death against overwhelming Russian opposition at Balaklava during the Crimean War).

The people who fit this pattern are often inspiring, sometimes charismatic leaders. They have grand visions, and when they are able to communicate those visions and goals to others, they can inspire them to broaden their goals and ambitions and activate their own "inner heroes." When the leader says, "We can do it!" the unspoken statement behind these words is, "*You* can do it, *you* are able to do anything, you are capable of greatness, I believe in you," a message that is hard to resist. We all *want* to believe that we are capable of great things, and to hear such a call to arms can inspire renewed efforts.

This tendency to try to "do it all" is a common theme in the private lives of these individuals as well. Most of us know at least one or two people socially whom we watch in amazement (and sometimes in sympathetic exhaustion) as they juggle demanding careers, travel, coaching their kids' soccer teams, helping with homework, decorating, entertaining, supervising an array of home help, doing the shopping, handling the family finances, and planning vacations (activity filled, naturally). Like the heroes of work, they are not only personally more active by a factor of ten than most people, they often push others to a high level. These individuals' own activity level often extends to their children, who are overscheduled in the extreme, with numerous sports (games, practices, and private lessons), music and other arts, play dates, religious instruction, and so on—all on top of the regular schoolday and homework. Little downtime is built in, to the detriment of the children themselves. One child psychologist we interviewed put it this way: "Kids need a lot of time just doing nothing—time when they can wonder about things, come up with ideas, and be creative. They need time to be kids. They're not little adults!" The "hero" is often oblivious of the ways his or her thinking may negatively impact children and friends.

People who fall into this pattern of thinking and behavior tend to do best in "heroic" businesses where burnout is expected and accepted—such as a business in turnaround or a start-up that is planning to go public. When seventy-hour workweeks are the norm, the stakes are high, and the goals are indeed extreme, the hero may fit right in. This is the case on Wall Street, for example, or in high-powered corporate law firms, where the monetary rewards are so great that people are willing, for a time, to sacrifice their lives and relationships in order to "make it." The hero may also find a comfortable fit as management consultant, salesman, or some other type of independent contributor. By contrast, in slow-growth, more bureaucratic companies where teamwork is prized above individual contribution, such a person, even if initially praised for his or her productivity, will eventually drive everyone else away.

After college Stephanie joined an energy company in Houston. Because she was smart and worked very hard, by her late twenties she had advanced to a high-level marketing position. She was a demanding manager, but no harder on the people reporting to her than she was on herself (as both she and her subordinates would agree—she burned at least as much midnight oil as they did). Some heroes are screamers who bark commands and insult their underlings. Stephanie, however, never raised her voice. Her way of showing dissatisfaction was to sigh and shake her head in acceptance of the fact that not everyone was as bright or as dedicated as she was.

Because she didn't lose her temper, Stephanie didn't think of herself as a tough boss. But, in fact, she was unbearable to work for. She used all of the tools of high technology against her teams—and against herself. She called them constantly on their cell phones wherever they were and whenever she felt the need, including evenings and weekends, and made it clear that they could (read *should*) do the same—so even if she wasn't calling them, they felt that she was expecting a call *from* them! Their home fax machines hummed through the night with her latest thoughts about a new marketing campaign. They were expected to check their e-mails at least a couple of times a day over the weekend *and respond to her messages*. There was never any downtime for them, and they always felt as if "Big Brother" (or "Big Sister") were watching them. In a previous era, when presentations had to be written on typewriters and slides had to be prepared manually, there was a limit to the number of revisions people could make within the allowed time. And even if there were more time, at a certain point someone would say, "Well, it would be better if we changed such and such to _____, but is it really worth retyping the whole document?" Today, with Microsoft Word, PowerPoint, and other programs, it's possible to edit and polish documents into oblivion. Previously, practicality reined in the hero's desire to produce a document that the teacher would grade A+; now it requires self-discipline to say, "It's good enough," and turn off the machine. Stephanie didn't have that self-discipline, and she didn't allow others to use it, either.

THE HERO IN AN ORGANIZATION

It is said of some champions that they don't know the meaning of defeat. Heroes don't know the meaning of victory. They don't recognize that they have won, that it is time to enjoy their accomplishment, rest on their laurels for a while, and give their bodies, minds, and spirits a chance to recover. Nor are they able to allow the people who work under and around them the chance to ease up a bit from time to time. In fact, it never even occurs to them that other people might need a rest, because they quickly get so focused on the next task that they scarcely see the drawn faces and the rolling eyes when they announce the next great goal.

This is not to say that such individuals are cruel taskmasters or Scrooges who squeeze the most from their people and then discard them. Some, of course, do beat up on their people (or, as a result of their own stress levels, are abrupt and curt, "all business all the time")—but even then, they do so usually not out of meanness, but in their blind obsession of achieving the goal. Others may be likable, friendly, essentially good-hearted people capable of managing with finesse, praise, and generous rewards. Nonetheless, they overtax their employees just as they do themselves with their constant time urgency, intolerance of imperfection, and insistence on taking on the next big thing.

Organizations tend to love "heroism" on the part of their employees, at least for a time, for the obvious reason that they get so much done. What could be better than an employee who, when you say, "Jump," asks not only "How high?" but "Where?" and "How many times?" and "On one leg or two?" and "Is there anything you'd like me to be doing while I'm jumping?" There are two problems, though, that lead to our qualifying the organization's love with "for a time." The first is that most people who fit this pattern, tireless as they may appear and feel, are not in fact tireless. Ultimately they do fatigue and burn out. They may last longer than other people, who either tire more quickly or simply don't want to drive themselves at that pace, but few last forever. One characteristic of the *way* they burn out is noteworthy. Some objects or materials, when stressed, "fail" gradually. For example, a long piece of two-by-four lumber supported at each end and stressed with a heavy weight at its center point will begin to crack and splinter and then, relatively slowly, will break in the middle. Other materials fail suddenly and with little advance warning. The hero type is much more likely to follow the latter pattern. Everything will look—and in some sense *be*—great, and then it's gone. This is unfortunate for the individual's manager, who will not be able to easily see the signs of strain that signal him or her to pull off some of the load, to "pace" the person a bit.

The second reason the love affair with the organization is unlikely to last forever is that people who work for the "hero" begin to leave, either after they are simply spent or when they recognize that they are going to be driven into the ground unless they get out. As a result, talented people leave the company. Word spreads that the person is a slave driver, and he or she has trouble getting people to join his or her work group. (In a conversation with a group of executives, it was noteworthy that all agreed that one of the worst things you can do is to go to work for someone who is recently divorced. "All they have is their work, and they expect you to keep them company.") Overall, morale suffers as people begin to say things like "Do you have to give your entire life to the company in order to be promoted here? This just isn't the place for me." The company gradually begins to see the hidden cost of all those astonishing accomplishments.

Those costs, however, are often overlooked or simply do not show up for a considerable period of time. In the meantime, the person who pushes relentlessly can both achieve a great deal and do a great deal of damage. If you are a manager, then, it behooves you to look closely at people in your organization who fit this pattern and carefully watch for those hidden costs.

Another characteristic of the hero is poor listening skills. He is so internally driven that he doesn't hear those under him saying that they are spent and can't wait for the weekend or really need some vacation time. The hero refuses to acknowledge that there is a rhythm to stress and recovery and that without those peaceful valleys after ascending a stormy mountaintop, the army will collapse. Even Genghis Khan recognized that he had to stop and let the horses graze and grow fat in summer so that he and his troops could ride hard and fight the following winter.

Sometimes the person with a "doing too much" behavior pattern is faulted for being reluctant to share information with people in other groups. These other people imagine (occasionally correctly) that the "hero" is interested in building an empire at their expense. The real reason for being less of a team member—unless he or she is leading it— and acting solo, though, is that a heroic achievement ceases to be heroic if too many people are involved. James Watson and Francis Crick, discoverers of the double-helix structure of DNA, became heroes (and Nobel Prize winners). But had they been merely two members of a team of twenty researchers working together, both the glory and the sense of accomplishment would be so diluted as to remove the sense of heroism. At some level the hero is a loner, even if he or she leads a team to the greatest heights. The net effect in a larger organization in which teamwork is essential, however, can be the bottlenecking of information that is useful or perhaps even essential to others.

Heroes often justify their solo actions and behavior by saying, "But my team doesn't need any help! Why should I bring other people in on things that we can do better ourselves? They'll just be in the way." Heroes suffer from a chronic tendency to overestimate not only their own personal abilities, but also their resources. They think their groups can do more than anyone else's can. So at those times when they really should be attacking a hill with a battalion, they decline the help and go for it alone, sometimes with disastrous results. Remember, no guts, no glory.

Human nature being what it is, people who attempt to do too much and push too hard can engender both envy on the part of others in the organization and anger at what other people may consider a kind of "rate busting." If you think of such a person as someone who works either as a renegade commando or the head of a small platoon of commandos, working against impossible odds behind enemy lines, risking everything, only to return successfully to glory and commendations, you can see how the rank-and-file employee could be a bit jealous. Especially when the employee's boss says, "Joe and his team worked around the clock for two months straight to get that product out the door, and can do two hundred push-ups besides! Why can't you?" It's easy to see how more than a little enmity could be created as well.

But even in those cases heroes don't wear out their welcome; they tend to *burn* it out. A client we'll call Kim worked for a medical devices company in Minnesota. Many of those who supervised her and worked alongside her describe Kim as the most brilliant colleague they ever worked with.

Kim's description of her childhood was unremarkable. Her parents were not implacably demanding. Their expectations of her were rather ordinary and moderate, hoping primarily that she would get a good education and a good job. Kim's "heroism" seems to have been self-generated. She graduated with honors from the University of Chicago and earned a master's degree in biology with distinction from UC Berkeley. The brilliance of her intellectual light was not accompanied by much warmth. She was in her mid-thirties by the time we met her, and she had never had a serious intimate relationship. She would date a man for a few months before the relationship would fizzle.

One reason for that was that all her passion went into her work, which often occupied her for thirteen or fourteen hours a day, seven days a week, and for weeks at a time. Simultaneously she added on to her workload the incredible burden of preparing a doctoral dissertation, even while her superiors were counting on her to bring to market a new device for diabetics, an instrument that would help the company sustain its spectacular growth.

Kim's brains and energy level were perfect for the task; but her heroism undermined her. She wanted all of the credit for the development of the new device to go to her and her team, so she instructed her thirty subordinates to bring to her personal attention all glitches and stumbling blocks that they couldn't work through. They were not to go to anyone else for help and were to communicate as little as possible with other members of the organization outside their group.

Kim was authorized to hire an additional twenty team members. But she wouldn't delegate the job of hiring to her subordinates. She insisted on screening people herself, and because almost no one else came up to her standards, which is to say nobody was as smart and as obsessively devoted to the job as she was, few candidates made the final cut. Kim wanted only the best, when she should have been hiring people to take over some of the relatively lower-level work to free up time for her star performers. As she delayed hiring, the growing workload fell on those members of her team who were already in place, crushing them with its weight. Several quit, and two went to work for a competitor. As a result, of course, the burden multiplied for those who remained. At that point the CEO told Kim that she would have to change her management style, and the company sent her to us for help.

Few companies can tolerate heroes indefinitely. Once a failing company is turned around and set on course, or a start-up has successfully started up, everyone from the stockholders to the stockboys want the company to steady itself and stay the course. The hero, however, is never satisfied. He or she wants to keep repairing and redesigning the boat even when it is under full sail—businesses don't have the luxury of dry docks! But mere mortals cannot operate in crisis mode forever, so they begin to jump ship. And because the most talented have the most options, they are often the first to leave. Companies that have been "reengineered" run lean these days, and one of the consequences of a trim structure is that each worker who remains fills an important slot. There is little redundancy or margin for error. Companies can't afford to lose good people, especially to the competition, and in this age of "knowledge work" a company's most valuable capital investment is its "intellectual capital"—the people who work for it—that (unlike factories, machinery, or real estate) can get up and walk away.

Companies with dominant positions in their industries see even less value in heroes. Another of our clients, Alan, was an ambitious MBA who had gone to work for a large and successful publisher of trade magazines. In addition to handling his normal work responsibilities, Alan began to work on his own, nights and weekends, almost in secret, on some new ideas. After several weeks he came up with a plan for revamping and repositioning one of the firm's most successful "flagship" magazines and took his ideas to the publisher.

Fascinated, the publisher listened as Alan presented his compelling ideas. At one point, though, he put up his hand and signaled Alan to stop. "You know, Alan, this is really *very good*," he said. "It's clear we made the right decision in hiring you, because you're obviously very smart and these are great ideas. But the fact is we don't want to change this magazine. It absolutely dominates the market and is doing just fine. Think of it as an ocean liner. If we do change its course, we will do so very slowly, one degree at a time. I really want to thank you for the time and effort you've put in, but more than anything else we just want to keep doing what we're doing and not screw things up! I'm sure you can understand that." Alan did understand, but he quit soon after, not waiting around long enough to find out whether there was another magazine in the company that *did* need heroic intervention.

Similarly, the company Stephanie worked for could not long endure the turmoil her relentless ambition created. The marketing department she supervised was not composed of world beaters. It was composed of smart enough people with modest career goals (relative to Stephanie's) who believed it was important to spend nights and weekends with their families. Those knowledgeable and experienced employees, moreover, were the temperaments top management wanted in the marketing department. They didn't see the need for a department made up of world beaters like Stephanie.

Things came to a head when in a routine upward feedback perfor-mance evaluation, eleven of the twelve people who had worked for Stephanie on a recently completed project admitted that it was an un-pleasant experience; eight said they would strongly consider looking for jobs elsewhere if they were required to work for her on another project. When another project she was concurrently managing wrapped up a few weeks later, eight of the ten members of that team said they would consider alternative employment; two others had quit the company be-fore the project had ended. Her executive vice president ordered Stephanie to come to us.

Like so many heroes who tend to be blind to their subordinates' re-actions, Stephanie was both surprised and deeply wounded by her fail-ing grades as a manager. Heroes get straight As; they certainly don't fail.

THE ORIGINS OF THE HERO

With some people we've worked with, the roots of the hero syndrome seem fairly clear. Their parents had extraordinarily high expectations of achievement and were never completely pleased. The highest praise the hero received was, "You can do better." That's flattering in a way; the intended message is, "You're so talented you can set a new standard." The problem for the child is that he or she never knows what the limits are, where it's okay to pause and rest and say, "I *did* it."

In other cases the parents may be emotionally and often physically distant; they are absentees who do little to make the household function. The inchoate hero takes on a parental role, even as a child, and grows up believing that everything depends on him or her alone, that unless he or she keeps performing everything will fall apart. This is the formation of the "hero" type of behavior, as the individual insists on doing absolutely everything him- or herself, controlling every project.

But adults are not always to blame. Stephanie's parents, for exam-ple, were not absentees, and early on they became concerned with her obsessive work habits. They urged her to slow down and take it easy when it became obvious that Stephanie was not just an overachiever, but an over-the-top achiever. Stephanie's compulsion perhaps came from somewhere else, dynamics in her emotional development that we were never able to identify, but that were extremely powerful whatever their genesis.

Children feel acutely vulnerable in an environment they are unable to control, so they tend to identify with and take on the roles of heroes, from Hercules to Superman, who *are* powerful and able to dominate the forces that threaten. But heroes are never allowed to rest. There is always one more Herculean labor, one more master criminal for Superman to subdue. And children, whose identification is for some reason unusually strong and enduring (at an unconscious level, of course), may be at risk for slipping into this pattern of thinking and behavior. This is especially true if the child's efforts at accomplishing great objectives meet with early success. He or she comes to see that by being willing to work hard and long enough, he or she can effect changes at school or in life. Should that knowledge push the person into a compulsive behavior pattern and life stance, the result can be detrimental to the individual's psychological health as well as to his or her career.

This kind of compulsive achievement may be a mechanism for countering chronic feelings of emptiness or even depression. The thinking (again, at an unconscious level) is, "If I keep working, I won't have time to be depressed." The fact is, if you're driving 130 miles an hour down the highway, that does tend to take all your attention, not leaving much time or energy to think about or feel anything else. But consider the person who has lost a parent or a spouse or a child whose response is to begin working eighty hours a week. It is an effective way to avoid feeling grief, but is it healthy? What are the psychological costs over time? Similarly, there are effective therapies for depression that could allow the person to continue to work and accomplish his or her goals, but in a healthier and happier manner.

Success, especially heroic success, can have an almost addictive quality. Participants in so-called extreme sports talk about the "high" that comes with the activities; they, too, often describe their relationship to the sport in terms of addiction. So, too, do people we've worked with who have just come off projects in which they made almost superhuman efforts to ensure the engagement's success. This kind of career adrenaline burst can serve to produce—and maintain—a hero behavior pattern. Most of us have periods in our work life when we experience the "high" of pushing hard to get an important project done. This type of experience is an important element of any career. The hero, however, *knows no other way of working.*

HOW TO BREAK THE PATTERN

What can you do if you recognize yourself in the portraits of such people as Stephanie, Kim, and Alan? The first step is to become aware of what you are doing. Do you push too hard as a normal way of working? Do you tend to push those around you in the same way? Ed Sullivan used to have performers who would spin dinner plates atop wooden dowels mounted in a table; in a frenzy the person would run madly around the table, spinning plate after plate, returning to those that were slowing to keep them going, until at last all were going around. Does that describe your life? One of our clients described his life as "juggling hand grenades with the pins out while riding a unicycle downhill." Do people describe you as constantly stressed out? Do your subordinates describe themselves in that way? Do you lose a lot of people from your group? These are key signs and symptoms of the hero behavior pattern.

We need to draw a distinction between acting heroically and living the pattern of the hero. Applied judiciously, heroics as such can produce substantial benefits and be very useful over the short term. If you act heroically on occasion, when the situation calls for it, no cure is necessary. The problem arises if you have adopted this as a way of life—as a normal function of your career. We put Stephanie, for example, through an extensive self-examination in which she confronted the issue of whether she was cut out to be a manager. She concluded in the end that she was not. As a result, she eventually left the company and became an independent marketing consultant. Because she works incessantly, she makes each of her half-dozen clients feel like her only client, and they love her for it. Is she missing out on much of life by choosing to spend almost all of her time focused on work? Perhaps, but that's her decision.

The only victim of Stephanie's heroism these days—if there is one—is Stephanie.

Even those heroes who genuinely want to advance, and are willing to change, have a tough job doing so, largely because it's hard to modify a pattern that has brought so much success. Unlike Stephanie, Kim decided that she wanted to remain a manager. We persuaded her that she would have to change her style radically and that she probably could not do it on her own. At our suggestion, the first of the twenty additional team members she eventually hired was an assistant whose most important assignment would be to stand up to Kim and tell her when she was demanding too much of those under her. She was also charged with handling Kim's calendar to avoid double and triple scheduling of meetings and with screening the sometimes hundreds of e-mails she receives in a single day.

The first assistant Kim chose for the job was a woman who suffered from a heroism syndrome almost as severe as her own and as a result was no help at all. When we pointed that out to Kim, she acknowledged (with a bit of a smile) that she had been just a little ambivalent about the change. Finally she gave the assignment to someone with a metabolism close to normal and who, taking Kim at her word, doesn't hesitate to tell her when she is pushing too hard. The screen saver on Kim's computer now reads "-(U)≠(U)," a kind of scientific notation for our reminder: "People who are *not* you are not necessarily *like* you."

We've also given Kim standing orders to "think like a general," meaning to consider the value and status of the entire army, not just her immediate staff. She was able gradually to let go of her death grip on the hiring process and found that her reports actually made pretty good hiring decisions on their own. She's gradually learning to delegate—something any effective manager has to master—and her group's productivity is increasing as a result, a pleasant surprise for Kim. And we have worked with Kim to change her natural inclination not to share information with others in the company. Frankly, that has been the single most difficult change for her to make, not, as it turns out, because Kim is afraid that other people will steal her ideas, but because she just doesn't want people to meddle in her group's work!

We train people who fit this pattern in some other "dos and don'ts" as well. One of the dos is to take the temperature of their teams, to do it often, and to use someone else as the thermometer to make sure they get an accurate reading (most people are reluctant to tell the hero him- or herself that they're tired). We train them to be better observers of other people's facial expressions and nonverbal communications. There are almost always areas of the work that the hero refuses to delegate (like Kim's hiring). We try hard to get the person to try it, just for a little while, with one or two people or projects. Our hope is to get the door open a little bit, so the client sees that it really is okay, they don't have to do it all.

Our ultimate goal is to help the hero build some boundaries around his or her own work schedule, reducing that 24/7 to, say, 20/6—or even a bit less! But we forcefully insist on immediate limits around pushing work into subordinates' night and weekend time. If the environment is "interrupt-driven," as a telecommunications network might be, beepers are normally worn. But in other work settings we "forbid" our heroes from night or weekend calling/faxing/or e-mailing people they work with (unless in the e-mail mode they explicitly state that the person doesn't have to attend to this matter until the next day or week).

Finally, with this Achilles' heel, as with many of the patterns that can hamstring one's career, it is enormously helpful to have someone else act as an observer/feedback provider in the work setting. For the hero it is virtually essential. This is a behavior pattern that is richly rewarded and therefore strongly reinforcing. It is a behavior for which the "volume" must be turned down but not turned off. It is like changing one's eating behavior (from eating too much and too rich to eating less and eating more nutritiously) compared to smoking tobacco, which people breaking the habit try to eliminate entirely. As a result, it is critical to have someone with a more normal range of hearing to help you adjust the volume.

Again, the pattern that results in hero behavior is hugely valuable in the short term and in certain jobs and almost—*but not quite*—invulnerable as well. Of all the Achilles' heels discussed in this book, the hero, perhaps, has the greatest potential for enormous career success, *if* he or she can address the dysfunctional aspects of his or her work behavior and personality. The world needs heroes, but those heroes—if they are to achieve all that they are capable of—need in turn to find a fuller and more balanced way of operating in the world. We need heroes, but those heroes need to be compassionate and understanding of others. Otherwise they may find themselves wounded like the original hero Achilles himself, undone by their very heroism.

CHAPTER

FOUR

AVOIDING CONFLICT AT ANY COST

Brian was fuming, his stomach on fire. His tormentor and nemesis, Donald, had humiliated him again, not just in front of their boss this time, but before the entire management committee. Brian had left the meeting mute, returned to his office, and shut the door behind him. He banged his fist on his desk and then just sat, furious and bitter, for an hour or so, daydreaming about revenge. But that's all he would do, daydream about it. The fact was that Brian would never confront Donald verbally, much less physically, for Brian was what we sometimes refer to as a *peacekeeper,* someone who steadfastly avoids conflict at any cost—and that pattern was destroying him.

THE DYNAMICS OF THE PATTERN

A peacekeeper is someone who is determined to avoid conflict at any cost. Although most of us have some healthy degree of aversion to angry confrontation, we accept that it is inevitable from time to time. We also recognize that conflict, although painful, serves a useful purpose. The clash of opposing ideas and strategies is a dynamic, creative process

that reveals the strengths and weaknesses of each and leads to reconcil-
iation at a higher level. To put it more simply, you can't cook without
heat.

The peacekeeper is phobic about the possibility of confrontation.
He or she goes out of the way to avoid conflict, because of uncertainty
about how it will end up. The fear with such people is that in the heat of
confrontation, the conflict will spiral out of control. Things might be
said that should have been left unspoken, arguments might get personal,
people might get hurt, quit, or get fired. People who think this way associate anger with virtual annihilation and fear that their own power (as
well as that of others) would rage out of control like some sort of nuclear meltdown.

The peacekeeper believes that this aversion to battle is a form of
self-protection and preserves the orderly functioning of the organization he or she is in. But that perception is wildly off base. In fact, it is a
subtle and insidious behavior that ultimately can undermine relationships and groups and become destructive to the organization. How?
Peacekeeping is a barricade that blocks the healthy interplay of conflict,
resolution, and progress. It *literally* keeps the peace, but at an enormous
cost to the organization and the people in it. Peacekeepers see themselves as individuals who "put feelings first," when the fact is he or she
puts the *suppression* of feelings first.

Brian, a warm, bright, and outgoing person, had been raised in Utah
by a family in which no one was allowed to express anger. Family members, in his recollection, never broke the rule. Brian vividly recalled a
camping and hunting trip he and his father took one summer into the
desert. Brian was fourteen and old enough to handle a gun responsibly.
While his father was loading the car for their return home, Brian
pointed his father's powerful hunting rifle at the windshield. Sure that
there was no cartridge in the chamber, he pulled the trigger—and a shell
shattered the windshield.

Fortunately, Brian's father was out of the line of fire. Less fortunately, Brian's father said nothing. He gave Brian a stern look that
showed he was disappointed, but that was it. There was no outburst, no
yelling, no dressing-down. Brian's father must have been furious, as
well as frightened. Brian would have welcomed some sign of anger,

something! But his father said nothing—all his feelings were held rigidly in check. Tense with anxiety, Brian wanted the release that would have come with a strong reaction from his father.

Brian told his father that he was sorry, hoping his father would at least offer a stern warning. But his father simply nodded. They drove back home across the blazing desert with a huge hole in the windshield and, consequently, no air-conditioning—almost three hours in total silence, in stifling heat that was a constant reminder of Brian's foolhardiness. When they got home Brian's older sister asked what had happened to the windshield. His father simply said there had been an accident but did not elaborate. The windshield was fixed, and the incident was never mentioned again.

But something remained broken or, more accurately, something remained unbuilt. Brian didn't experience the natural unfolding of anger and its aftermath. He didn't learn about encountering strong conflict, working it through, and coming out the other side intact—and with everyone else alive, too. There *should* have been shouting and apologies and more shouting and tears and finally resolution. The net result would have been a closer bonding. Father and son should have talked it out. The incident should have become part of family history, something that in the future father and son would share a couple of beers over, shake their heads, and laugh about. That would have built both a closer relationship between Brian and his father and—much more important—a level of confidence and comfort in Brian when dealing with anger and conflict. Instead he was left with fear and avoidance. It was an opportunity squandered. Brian never felt that the incident had closure to it— many years later it was still an open wound. This incident, of course, was just one in a lifetime of interactions between father and son, but it shows how Brian's father worked to avoid conflict at any cost—and the costly effect that squelching difficult emotions had on Brian. It shows how anger was handled—or rather, not handled—while he was growing up.

Anger and its resolution are an essential part of the human experience. Peacekeepers can't accept that reality and thereby learn and master the process. As a result, they are seriously handicapped. We want to make an important distinction with regard to the term *peacekeeper*. We are not talking about people who recognize when a conflict has gone far enough and try to find ways to bring it to a successful resolution— peacemakers. Peacemakers act by rational choice. Peace*keepers*, on the other hand, do whatever they can to keep the heat of conflict from rising to begin with. They act out of fear and compulsion. And they act by suppressing natural reactions and emotions and thereby increasing the tension in a group or relationship as unvoiced feelings or reactions are swept under the carpet.

Many people are not as extreme in their peacekeeping role as Brian. Although they may shun confrontation personally and find it their natural default reaction, when conflict arises they don't actively enforce it on others. Nevertheless, their peacekeeping reaction can affect their thinking and behavior much more than they know, causing them to go way out of their way—and encourage those under or around them to do the same—to avoid conflict. In the process they suppress creative ideas and initiatives that might improve the organization and further their own careers—but that would elicit some "push-back" or resistance from some parties who might feel threatened or oppose the ideas for other reasons. Such people, without their being aware of it, handcuff themselves as they worry about whether other people will react negatively to plans or actions they have taken or are thinking about taking. They become conservative in their thinking in order to minimize the risk of conflict.

Alternately, they may avoid a certain aspect of their job because it involves dealing with someone about an issue that may precipitate an argument. One manager we worked with would never, *ever* push for an idea, for his department, for his people. This ultimately came to be seen as a near fatal flaw in his management ability when his key employees began to jump ship, moving to opportunities with leaders who had more "backbone." Ultimately he was moved into an individual contributor role where there would be less demand for him to "stand up" for things and fight.

One employee who worked for one of our client companies, a large biotechnology firm, was in general not at all afraid of conflict. A bright, intense individual, Victor had earned a black belt in karate and spent his weekends whitewater kayaking and rock climbing. But there was one woman in the company with whom he avoided any and all conflict. She was someone who would come on *very* strong in virtually any argument, seemingly adopting a strategy of "the best defense is a good offense." "If Nancy said, 'I told you about that yesterday,' when in fact she really hadn't," Victor told us, "the forcefulness and aggressiveness of her presentation could make you go away wondering why you hadn't remembered her telling you what she hadn't told you!" As a result, rather than risking conflict, Victor would just agree with her or avoid her as much as possible. By thinking about how Nancy was able to elicit this response in him, Victor clarified his feelings about her and how they led to that behavior. "I could deal with the conflict as it was—over who said what when, or whatever. But Nancy looked in those moments like she could absolutely lose control and go ballistic. I don't know if it was a conscious tactic or not, but it sure worked. I was afraid she'd lose it and start pummeling me. I know that's crazy, but that was what I thought." (Once he identified his fear, he was able to call Nancy's bluff by pointing out her behavior to her and break the hold she had.)

Larry was another "occasional" peacekeeper. He avoided dealing with a certain subordinate because he felt the person was quite fragile, someone who would be devastated by even mild criticism. Instead of confronting him with the fact that his work was not of sufficient quality, Larry did the work himself.

The fact is, when you slip into the peacekeeper role, even if only in specific situations, you don't act in the way that you otherwise would— and should. Some people avoid conflict with others in every area of their lives. But even those of us (which is to say, most of us) who fall into this behavior pattern only in specific situations will benefit from facing up to those specific conflicts that we avoid or gloss over and taking positive steps to resolve them.

As you might imagine, this fear of conflict can spill over into every aspect of life: marriages, parent-child relationships, sibling relationships, and friendships all inherently involve conflict. One of the hallmarks of a successful marriage is the ability of both partners to face up to the conflicts they have with each other and resolve them. The same is true with any other kind of intimate relationship, whether with siblings, parents, children, or close friends. If you recognize that you instinctively avoid conflict in your relationships, think about the effect it has on you and on those close to you. Do you genuinely stay closer together because of your ability to avoid conflict? Or does it, as we suspect, in the long term prove to be a wedge that drives you apart? And is handing down a fear of conflict to your children a legacy you really want to bequeath them?

PEACEKEEPER IN AN ORGANIZATION

A peacekeeper fears conflict with peers because it might be construed as an act that violates friendship, resulting in the termination of the relationship—or at least a distinctive cooling of it. He fears conflict with subordinates because it might be seen as an abuse of authority and result in the end of the positive relationship. He's not sure how to handle things in the aftermath—he's not confident of *his* ability to survive such conflict and worries about his future relationship with them. He fears conflict with a superior because it might be interpreted as an attempt to usurp power and result in deterioration or termination of the relationship. People who exhibit this behavior pattern avoid conflict because they dread what they feel, deep down, is its inevitable price: the loss of the relationship. So a sort of catch-22 comes into play. Because a peacekeeper has no experience in going through and resolving conflict, he fears the loss he is sure it brings, suppresses his anger, and avoids conflict; as a result, he is never able to successfully gain the experience he needs and so continues to fear the loss, suppress his feelings, and avoid conflict.

On a personal level, of course, what this means is that such an individual's relationships are doomed to be lukewarm and rather distant. Closeness and intimacy inevitably result in the friction of conflict that the peacekeeper is so fearful of. Professionally, such a person never develops a level of comfort in bringing creative ideas into the crucible of conflict, where good products are reshaped into better products before being introduced to the market and where just okay strategies are torn apart and reconstituted as winning strategies. While conflict avoiders fear that if things get too hot, the pot might crack, they are oblivious of the fact that a far greater danger is of things not getting hot enough to properly harden the clay.

Moreover, the peacekeeper pattern poses a serious obstacle to leadership roles. Getting to the top of any organization requires a willingness to take risks and battle rivals. Once on top, a leader sometimes has to require people to do things they don't necessarily want to do. Because people who avoid conflict suppress their real thoughts or feelings, those who are not afraid of doing so are never sure how peacekeepers really feel or what they really think. Peacekeepers often have high needs for affiliation and a high need simply to be liked. Needless to say, if their managerial role calls for them to call someone on the carpet or terminate them, they're going to do everything they can to avoid those responsibilities. And although they want everyone to think well of them, ironically enough they are often seen as weak and untrustworthy by those who manage or lead them, as well as by their peers and subordinates. They "like" everyone, so no one trusts that they *truly* value them as individuals. And no one would think of depending on them to fight for more budget or compensation for them.

An organization can unwittingly develop and nurture a peacekeeping culture—with disastrous consequences. Here is but one good historical example. Prior to the ill-conceived and ultimately disastrous invasion of the Bay of Pigs in Cuba, several members of President Kennedy's national security circle had grave doubts about the plan and in fact privately predicted the calamity that resulted. But in the cabinet meetings leading up to the invasion, they kept their mouths shut. They didn't want to oppose the consensus and precipitate conflict. No one knew that there were others around the table thinking and feeling the same way, and no one was willing to "take the heat" and stand up in opposition. The blow to the Kennedy administration—and to the United States' relationship with Cuba—was enormous.

Similarly, managers at the Morton-Thiokol company knew that certain O-rings used on the space shuttle warped out of shape when exposed to temperatures below a certain level—but in the interest of keeping the peace, no one would come forward and precipitate the conflict that would have resulted. Instead the *Challenger* shuttle exploded, and its crew was lost.

Less catastrophic, but significantly painful to their sponsors nonetheless, are the bad ideas that are brought to the commercial market every year because those who knew they were bad ideas feared the consequences of speaking up, whether because the people in question were peacekeepers themselves or because their companies' cultures discouraged open expression of conflict and disagreement. (Typically, after the disaster, there is a rush to point fingers. As Fran Lebowitz put it, "It's not whether you win or lose, it's how you lay the blame!")

This conflict-suppressing culture was once found frequently among organizations that enjoyed a preeminent position in their fields—perhaps because they felt they had a lot to lose and little to gain by change and the conflict it often engenders. The enormous acceleration in the pace of change and level of competition in the last ten years has altered the culture of such organizations for the better. One of our former client companies did fit this description; one of its most senior executives, whom we'll call Ron, appeared to spend the great majority of his time making certain that no one spoken above a metaphorical whisper. Ron was well suited to this role, being personally uncomfortable with conflict of any sort, and he raised hushing things up to an art form. During his entire tenure there was virtually no internal conflict or messiness to be seen (although plenty was swept under a large number of expensive rugs). Ron kept things rigidly under control—passive control, to be sure, but control nonetheless. Everything was fine (it wasn't), everyone was incredibly nice and terrific (they weren't), everything was going along smoothly (it wasn't), and everybody got along fine (they didn't). And nothing changed. Not for the worse, not for the better, not at all. And that was just what the company wanted from Ron—and from itself. The result over the long term was predictable—the company lost ground and market share in the competitive race of business.

THE ORIGINS OF THE PEACEKEEPER

There is a predisposition in our society to think that women are more likely than men to fall into this pattern. But this is not so. It has been argued that girls are more likely to have been brought up to think in terms of relationships and of the family and communal good first and their concerns second, and that boys are more likely to be raised to distinguish themselves from the crowd, to see the peak of accomplishment as that of the quarterback rather than a stalwart teammate on the offensive line of the football team. If so, the difference in rearing doesn't seem to be a determining factor in whether or not one is a conflict avoider. Over the years we have seen about an equal number of men and women who fit this picture.

The etiology of this pattern of conflict seems to arise out of four often overlapping causes. The first is a generally weak sense of self, including the fear of not being able to put one's ideas across in the face of opposition. This is not the same as having low self-esteem. For example, a quiet introvert who is the sixth of nine boisterous children could grow up feeling that he or she can't get—and hold—the floor around the dinner table and will inevitably be drowned out. This might be a quite accurate assessment in that family context, but by generalizing that feeling to the rest of life, the person in a sense gives up on ever fighting to be heard.

The second cause is the result of growing as something of a loner on the fringes of the family. The person might be the only member of the family who isn't interested in football or religion, or the child who is ten years younger than the others and is essentially "left behind" by his or her siblings and parents in their much more advanced pursuits. This person craves acceptance, and that unmet need may be exacerbated when in a social or work setting where people of his or her race or socioeconomic group are not well established and comfortable.

One client of ours, an African American, was the third son of a father who worked in a highway tollbooth. He became the director of computer services at a prestigious university hospital. This peacekeeper was so grateful to have an important job in a world that once seemed out of reach that everything was always "okay, fine" with him. He let his subordinates, none of whom were black, walk over him. They would show up late or not show up at all, and he would pretend not to notice, for if he did, he would have to reprimand them. Instead he would cover for them, stay late when they left early, correct their errors, and fill in the gaps they left. The peacekeeper himself, of course, was only one victim of his subordinates' dereliction; another victim was the hospital, which was cheated of services it was paying for. The employees, too, were cheated, in that they were never called on the carpet and forced to confront their slack behavior and genuinely become better employees.

The third force that can create a peacekeeper is family dysfunctionality. Brian's family, for example, suppressed all expressions of anger. Such families superficially conform to a 1950s American TV series picture of the family: *Ozzie and Harriet* or *Father Knows Best*. Everything was okay even if it wasn't. The tension underneath the surface in such families is usually enormous. Another type of dysfunctional family is one in which anger boils *all* the time and no one is able to turn down the temperature. There are few compromises or apologies, no real resolution, no kissing and making up. The household's default position is rage. It's hardly surprising that one outcome of this kind of family is a person who will do almost anything to avoid a conflict, because to him or her once you stumble into a well of anger there is no way out. One of our clients told us that in her family people woke up yelling, left for school or work yelling, came home and started yelling again, and stopped only when they went to bed. As an adult she herself alternated between feeling comfortable with conflict (after all, that was what she grew up with) and feeling overwhelmed by it and shying away from it.

Children, being ultimately powerless in the face of the adults surrounding them, want power, want to be adults, want to displace Dad or Mom and take over control of their own lives. They often fantasize about their own importance, attributing to themselves powers they simply don't have. After a fight with Dad, or after seeing an argument between the parents, they wish to themselves that their parents would just get a divorce. Later, if that actually occurs, they feel responsible for Dad's leaving. They may wish, in a moment of anger, that Mom was dead. If their mother does, in fact, fall ill or die, they come to believe that it was because they got mad and momentarily wished her dead. If Dad loses his job, the child is convinced it was because he or she got mad after Dad missed an important event in the child's life and wished Dad didn't have that job. The child imagines that his anger is an omnipotent and uncontrollable force that can destroy people and therefore has to remain locked up inside. As an adult, such an individual recognizes intellectually that this isn't true, but at a deep emotional level he or she continues to believe it and thus behave as though it were. This kind of root emotional feeling frequently produces conflict-avoidance behavior in specific situations. The person may not behave this way most of the time. Rather, he or she feels this way only in the context of relationships with people who have power and authority over them.

The cost of the peacekeeper's emotional suppression does not generally show up early in his or her career. When you begin your career you're expected to be quiet, to watch, and to learn. To challenge authority before you know what you are talking about is a disability at the other end of the spectrum, the rebel's affliction, described in Chapter 6. But later on in one's career its effects can be devastating. Brian's avoidance of conflict didn't become a serious handicap until he was fifteen years into his career as an architect with an Atlanta architectural firm that designed suburban office centers. Brian was talented and well regarded, although his inability to handle conflict ensured that he had not become a partner in his firm. Nevertheless, Brian was content enough with his job and his standing—until Don came along.

Don was brought into the firm to help Brian with his workload. In character and style he was Brian's polar opposite. Brian was honest, almost to a fault. Not only did he refuse to exaggerate his own importance to a project, he bent over backward to give colleagues more credit than they deserved. He insisted on pointing out to clients possible cost overruns, even when the chances of such overruns were remote.

Don, on the other hand, was less scrupulous—and was clearly trying to grab Brian's job. He habitually lied to Brian, assuring him, for example, that he would support Brian's solution to a design problem and then undermining him by going to the boss and saying Brian's plan wouldn't work. When Brian found out he was outraged, but he did nothing and said nothing. Don lied to clients as well. He slandered competitors and gave clients absurdly low estimates to win contracts, padding their bills later.

The subterfuge went on for months. Brian burned inside but remained silent. Finally Don inveigled himself into a position in which he was no longer Brian's subordinate but his peer. That was a turning point for Brian. Although he was an inveterate peacekeeper, he wasn't stupid; he could see that in a few months Don would be in an even stronger position, while Brian would be on the street with a ruined stomach lining. His fear of isolation and rejection surpassed even his fear of anger, and he came to us for help.

We listened to Brian's description of Don's activities, and then he asked us if we thought he was overreacting in being so upset. "Well," we said, "they hire a guy to work for you who starts acting like he owns you. He castigates you, lies to customers and colleagues. He acts in a manner that humiliates other people, takes credit for your—and other people's—work, and tries to undermine you in the eyes of your boss. If I told you that I was upset about somebody like that whom *I* worked with, would you think I was overreacting?" What we had done was to put a little psychological distance between Brian and a Don "type," a Don who was ruining *our* life, which allowed Brian to see that his experience of Don was not out of line.

"Okay, this guy is making your life miserable? Is he good for the company?" After a little equivocating Brian had to admit that Don's presence constituted a significant negative to the organization and that it had been a mistake to hire him. It was clear that a head-to-head confrontation with Don wouldn't work. Brian wouldn't have been a contender in that kind of fight. He didn't feel comfortable going to his boss to tell him the truth about Don, and even if he had, it was too late—Don would simply have lied one more time and slipped out of it.

"So," we said "why not devise a plan to let this guy reveal who and what he is to management, so they can act on this situation—or not, as the case may be?" Together we designed a strategy that would allow the partnership to get a better view of those aspects of his character that Don had so skillfully kept hidden. Don loved e-mail, and he made it a practice to send Brian "flamers," insulting messages. Brian was the target of the flamers, but Don frequently copied other members of the firm. Brian began forwarding all of these e-mails to the head of the division. That revealed something about Don's style to the boss, but by themselves the e-mails, were not enough to unseat Don.

The real change came when Brian stopped protecting Don. In the past when they had worked together, Don had drafted project cost estimates that were ridiculously under what any professional knew the real costs would be. Brian would then go over the figures and correct them before presenting them to the client. It happened that the firm was competing to design a major office center, and an important part of the project had been delegated to Brian and Don. This time, instead of covering up Don's duplicity by correcting the figures before anyone else saw them, Brian decided to call in the partner in charge of the project and ask him to review the projections Don had come up with.

Before he knew what was happening, Don found himself in the partner's office going through his numbers with the partner and Brian. The partner was baffled by Don's calculations at first and then infuriated by them. Don's proposal, obviously aimed at suckering the client with a low bid, would fall apart under the client's scrutiny, he said. Don quickly countered with some maneuvers he had in mind to keep the client from figuring that out. The boss looked at Don in amazement. Not only was the plan unethical, it jeopardized the entire project, not just the part of it Don and Brian were working on.

Within weeks Don was forced out of the firm. Brian now understands how dangerous peacekeeping can be—both to himself and to the organization. He still isn't comfortable with the blunt confrontation that leadership sometimes requires—and probably never will be. But then, not everyone is cut out to be a CEO. At least, though, he can now recognize when the situation has gone from self-limiting to potentially terminal and has some weapons to fight with. Moreover, he will find it a little easier to fight back if a similar situation arises in the future.

HOW TO BREAK THE PATTERN

If the pattern we've described causes a shock of recognition in you, or if you recognize the pattern in someone who reports to you, you'll realize it's not subtle. Most peacekeepers act out this set of behaviors in a consistent way. The "diagnosis" is easy; the treatment is not. First, we encourage you to read Chapter 15 in Part II of the book, which discusses how to acquire and use power (and why so many people have trouble doing so).

When we coach a peacekeeper we have two goals: to desensitize them to conflict, and to build their skills at handling conflict. The people in this pattern are phobic of conflict in the same way that some other people are phobic of spiders. In both cases logic holds little sway over the person's feelings of anxiety, so it does little good to reason. The person already "knows" that expressing anger or having a heated discussion isn't going to make the other person die or kill you or the other person—or cause you to lose your job.

One thing we do say to our clients is that they don't have to become karate experts to become skillful enough at dealing with conflict. The fact is they don't *want* to metamorphose into hyperaggressive corporate street fighters, even if they could. We also assure them that they can't, so they don't have to worry about going overboard, from conflict avoiders to conflict seekers, which is a fear some people have.

Sometimes we use the analogy of zebras and lions in discussing this fear of conflict with our clients. They're both fine animals, both with a place in God's choir, but if you're a natural-born zebra, you have to do one of two things. The first is to surround yourself exclusively with other herbivores who aren't going to attack and eat you. The second is to learn to act like a lion when necessary. You're never going to *be* a lion, and that's all right, as long as you can act like one when you need to. But right now, as a zebra among a group of lions, when the lions see you they start to think about lunch—and you're not a guest, you're on the menu. To avoid that, we want to design a lion suit for you to put on when necessary, so the other lions will think you're one of them, someone to be respected and not messed around with.

One task we assign our client is to become more of a naturalist at work—a careful observer of the carnivores in their organizations. How do such people dress, walk, talk, sit, look at people, and so forth? If there is one person in the group whom they admire for his or her fearlessness in dealing with conflict, we ask the client to pay special attention to him or her. This exercise serves two purposes: to gain real and useful information, and to begin the process of desensitization. This is no longer some mysterious and scary thing, it is now *merely* a *phenomenon* to be examined, turned this way and that, studied and learned from. By doing so, they're able to put some emotional distance between themselves and this thing called conflict, while at the same time becoming more comfortable with it—in effect, being able to get closer to conflict.

As we discussed earlier, a major reason for peacekeepers' avoidance of conflict is their fear that it will result in irreparable damage to the relationship with the other part. Put simply, they don't know how to "normalize" relationships after conflict has occurred. There are two methods we teach in this regard. The first is to just stop in to see the other person a few hours later (postconflict) and chat briefly either about a work-related topic ("Hey, Joan, the contracts we were waiting for just came through, I'm having copies made right now and should have one to you within about a half hour") or about something unrelated to business ("Joan, I forgot to ask how your son's recital went" or "You won't believe what I just saw when I was out for lunch! There was this . . ."). Either one serves to reestablish the relationship as a positive one, regardless of the conflict that may have occurred.

The second method is to address the fact of the conflict directly. Here the person might say something like "Joan, we were both pretty heated in the meeting this morning, and I just wanted to tell you that I really do see your point of view and why you hold it. It's just that I see things differently. But I don't want you to feel like I was in any way attacking you personally." Or perhaps something like "Joan, things got a little heated in our meeting this morning, at least too much for my comfort level. I just want to make sure that *we're* okay, or if we're not, to do whatever we need to do to get okay." Some people prefer the indirect approach, some the direct. In some instances, though (if the conflict had been particularly heated), the indirect could be seen as just glossing over what is now a real problem, so being skillful at using both is important.

In working with clients, we often think in terms of helping them develop strength in a particular muscle. Depending on which muscle it is, and how strong or weak it is, you might start with a twenty-pound weight, or ten pounds, or two—how much is not important. What counts is that you begin a weight program based on where the person is at that point and work up gradually. The worst thing you could do would be to give the person too much weight to attempt, causing them to fail and lose hope. By analogy, we ask our clients to make an exhaustive list of all the situations and people they avoid conflict with—including people at work, family, neighbors, merchants, anyone at all—and then to rank order them in terms of difficulty. This tells us who "weighs" fifty pounds, who is twenty, ten, five . . . 1. Then we start at the bottom.

For each person or situation, we work with the client in two ways: as "screenwriters" and as acting coaches. First, we help script out what he or she wants to say when going to the dry cleaners to complain that they keep putting starch in his shirts or her blouses when asked for no starch (remember, we start with the lowest weights). We work and rework the script until it is just right—both in the client's opinion and in ours. If this seems silly, we point out that when we have important phone calls to make, we often do the same thing: write out what we want to say, then follow that script as closely as possible. This works wonderfully well for voice mail messages, obviously, with no possibility of interruptions on the other end, but it serves as a guide and beginning even in live conversations.

The advantage of the telephone, of course, is that the other party doesn't see that you have a script in front of you. For face-to-face contact, you need to have your lines memorized. What this really means is that (just as with the phone) you need to practice what you're going to say. Here we move into our role as acting coaches with our clients. First we play the role of the client and have him or her play the role of whoever the other party is. We then go through the scene a few times, allowing the other person to make things as difficult as possible—and usually rewriting the script along the way. Then, when we feel as if the situation is under control, we switch roles, the client plays him- or herself and we play the other protagonist. We practice and practice and practice some more until we both feel that the "script" works and that the "actor" can play the part. Then the client goes out on the stage, in front of a real audience (the other party), and acts out his or her role.

Again, we choose the easiest person and situation to deal with first.

After the client plays out the script in real life, he or she comes back for a debriefing. We then use the insights gained from the first trial case when we draft the script for the second. We practice, revise, practice more, then go on stage, play, come back, and debrief, then repeat again. Over time the client gets stronger and stronger at this, until he or she can take on the toughest situations on the list.

This, by the way, is very much in keeping with what is termed "systematic desensitization," a treatment used by psychologists to treat people with specific phobias. The therapist might start by showing the person the written word ("spider," for example), then have the patient hold the paper with the word on it, then show a picture, move it closer, have the patient hold it, then show a rubber spider or a videotape of a spider, then a live spider, and so on. At each step the patient is a bit stronger, a bit more confident, a bit less frightened.

At some point we craft and practice some "normalization" scripts similar to those we described earlier as well, so clients have the tools at their disposal when the need to heal a wound arises. We encourage them, always, to think carefully about what they want to say, how they want to say it, and to practice beforehand if at all possible.

We teach them a few other tricks as well, such as to allow the other party in a conflict to exhaust his or her energies, take lots of time to talk, get it all out, be as emotional as he or she may feel—all the while nodding attentively and perhaps jotting down a note or two. And only *then* responding, thoughtfully and to the point. Or letting someone come at them with an argument that they (our clients) have anticipated and are already prepared to yield on, and before the person has even begun to make the argument, break in (politely) and say, "You know, I think you are absolutely right on this one. I agree with you, and I think we ought to move on."

Perhaps scarred by the tragedy of World War I, Neville Chamberlain, England's prime minister before Winston Churchill, was desperate to avoid conflict with Nazi Germany and advocated a policy of appeasement toward that end. He returned from a meeting with Hitler in Munich in 1938 proclaiming that he had attained "peace with honor . . . peace for our time." By insisting on peace at any price, Chamberlain succeeded only in delaying the coming conflict and, in the opinion of many, raising the price England and other countries would eventually pay in World War II. In contrast with Chamberlain, the peacekeeper would be better served by recalling the lines from the American poet James Russell Lowell in *The Bigelow Papers:* "Ef you want peace, the thing you've got to du / Is jes' to show you're up to fightin', tu."

CHAPTER

FIVE

RUNNING ROUGHSHOD OVER THE OPPOSITION

Mᴏsᴛ ᴏꜰ ᴜs ʟᴇᴀʀɴ ᴇᴀʀʟʏ ᴏɴ ᴛᴏ "ᴘʟᴀʏ ɴɪᴄᴇʟʏ ᴡɪᴛʜ ᴛʜᴇ other children," as our mothers tell us. Some of us don't. One such example—albeit an extreme one—is a former client of ours named Jim. Jim used to stroll—or perhaps a better word would be prowl—the corridors gripping a baseball bat, which he would occasionally slap into his fist. If he had been a prison guard, this threatening behavior might have been a little excessive but not completely out of place. But Jim was a partner in a prestigious New York law firm, where his menacing demeanor was utterly incongruous.

Picture the setting: a handsome suite of offices decorated in rosewood, Persian rugs, and Impressionist paintings high up in a building on Wall Street, in New York City's financial district. Efficient secretaries quietly tap away at their computer keyboards, and young associate attorneys in starched shirts and gray flannel slacks intently sort through thick legal folders, reading briefs and other documents. Through this dignified bustle walks Jim. He is dressed appropriately in an expensive suit—but he is carrying a baseball bat, looking like a Neanderthal in a Paul Stuart disguise.

THE DYNAMICS OF THE PATTERN

Jim is an extreme example of a behavior pattern that we sometimes refer to as the *bulldozer*, talking and acting tough, bullying people, taking no prisoners, and leveling anyone and anything that gets in the way. Like the offensive lineman in professional football, the bulldozer's role—and goal—is to flatten people, to run as roughshod over them as necessary. The person who displays this behavior pattern is hyperaggressive and so narrowly focused on how to solve a problem—crush it—that he often ultimately undermines his career. Although he may think of himself as the irresistible force, ultimately he runs into the real immovable object, something he cannot roll over or plow through, and because he has never learned the skill of moving *around* resistance rather than over or through it, he is stopped and defeated.

Of the twelve behavior patterns we analyze in this book, eleven of them are as likely to be women as men. This is the exception. Although a few women do fit this pattern—women such as Margaret Thatcher, former prime minister of England, and Leona Helmsley, sometime queen of the New York hotel industry, come to mind—it is a condition seen much more frequently in men than in women.

The person who exhibits this pattern, however, is not necessarily a man born in a bare-knuckles neighborhood, one in which he had to learn to fight just for the right to some space on the sidewalk. Rich kids in prep schools can grow up to be bulldozers. Nor is the pattern found only in occupations that require and reward raw physical strength and aggression. The chairman of the college English Department can fall into this pattern, as can the head of a corporate research laboratory or those in authority in any calling, from moviemaking to the priesthood.

The "default option" in this pattern is to view all transactions from a win-lose perspective. Generally this is also an all-or-nothing view, but even if the person can see the situation as one in which one party will achieve only a partial victory, it is still win-lose rather than win-win. People who think and act in this way view any and all situations as zero-sum games and adversarial in nature and focus on how to get the biggest piece of the pie (if not all of it). This is true, by the way, whether the interaction is with a customer, a vendor, a colleague, or a manager. Bulldozers give "office politics" a bad name.

In addition to the adversarial, win-lose perspective bulldozers apply to life, they have a notably difficult time seeing things from the position of what is good for the group. If what's good for the group happens to coincide with what's good for the person who shows this behavior pattern, that's great—but it is coincidental rather than thought out or intended. But if it comes down to the group sharing credit for a piece of work, or sharing a commission, for example, or the bulldozer getting it all, there's no question of the bulldozer's attitude.

People who fall into this behavior pattern are almost fatally impaired in the "taking perspective" function that we describe in Part II of the book and frequently have difficulty dealing with authority as well. They are often oblivious of the fact that they are making enemies, as well as to the fact that by making enemies, they are hurting their long-term performance and ultimately endangering their careers. Leaving something on the table for the other player is a concept that does not readily occur to the bulldozer. In fact, bulldozers often espouse a sort of social Darwinism: the winners of the game are the ones who deserve to be at the top, the losers sink to the bottom and deserve no tears, sympathy, or regrets. It's the law of the jungle, the food chain brought to the world of business. (Not surprisingly, such people are less keen on this perspective when *they* suffer reversals of fortune.)

People who fall into this behavior pattern don't listen well to what other people are saying, and as a result, they don't absorb information around them that would enable them to lead complex organizations. General George S. Patton was a bulldozer. The tanks of his Third Army crushed the Nazi legions. But Patton was so ferocious, so single-minded, so unyielding, that he never could have risen to the next level of command. He could not have led a complex alliance as General Eisenhower did. The two steps forward/three steps to the side/one step backward maneuvering often required of top leadership is beyond the capacity of the bulldozer. In addition, bulldozers lack empathy— that is, the ability to put themselves in the place of other people and imagine what others are thinking and feeling. Empathy is a very important skill, but not necessarily a morally positive one. Morally, it is neutral. You can have empathy for another person and act compassionately toward him. But you can also use empathy to manipulate someone else for your welfare and against his own. Hitler, it would seem, had empathy. He understood the fears and frustrations of the German people and manipulated them to his advantage. Stalin, on the other hand, probably did not have empathy. The century's archetypal bulldozer (who took the name Stalin, which means "man of steel") ruled by brute force.

As with all of the habits we describe, there are many shades of gray in terms of how strongly and how frequently a person exhibits this pattern of behavior. One client we worked with named Alexis had a very pleasant demeanor, but when she really needed something from a colleague or from someone in another department she would pay a visit to them (without calling or e-mailing first), tell them what she needed and why, mention that her boss had assigned a high priority to this project, and ask when they thought they could get it done. No baseball bat here, no ivory-handled pistols, but people still felt as if they had been bulldozed. Or, more accurately, they felt as if their agenda for the day had been blown up and that now they had to do what Alexis wanted before anything else. They resented it, and as they complained (through their manager) to Alexis's manager, it became an issue that held Alexis back in the organization. Alexis was running roughshod over people, not with cleats but with deerskin slippers, stepping lightly, yet in her determined way flattening them nonetheless as she took no one into account but herself.

People are often inclined to say, "Well, I don't act like *that*—that's not me." The fact that someone doesn't physically run roughshod over others in their office doesn't mean that they don't slip into acting in this manner at times, especially under pressure. Most of us are hoping we *don't* see ourselves in any of the twelve patterns that can hinder success. Never underestimate the power of denial as an impediment to coming to a better and clearer understanding of yourself.

Refusing to see the truth presents a grave danger. Many of the people we're called in to work with deny that there is a real problem, even as their managers are telling us that if they don't change—fast—their jobs will be in jeopardy. By the time someone tells you that you run roughshod over the staff and are not just a "tough negotiator" or "someone with high standards" (as you might think of yourself), it may be too late. Neither Jim (from earlier in the chapter) nor Alexis saw themselves as their colleagues did.

It's useful to think about the severity and frequency of bulldozing displays separately. Jim was over the top in his behavior (severity), and he was over the top most, if not all, of the time (frequency). Alexis, whom we just described, was much less extreme (she didn't create the hurricane force that Jim did), but that was her "climate," day after day. In other words, it's possible to act out this pattern in much less dramatic ways and at a much lower decibel level than Jim—and still find it holding back your career. You can also be at risk as a result of an *occasional* stormy episode. Perhaps running roughshod is something you do not do every day, but only once in a while, under certain circumstances. Yet that can be enough to damage your career—even badly. This is because the wounds left by the bulldozer are so slow to heal. Others remember such blowups long afterward, and it colors their perceptions of you. You can also make a long-term enemy—someone who can lead to your being passed over for advancement. As one of our colleagues put it, "I'm really not the kind of person that anybody who knows me would call a bulldozer. But given the right set of circumstances, the right level of stress, I know I can be—and have done it."

Harvey ran roughshod over people by controlling airtime in meetings (and thereby exerting *de facto* control over the agendas) and by instantly squashing any opposition. We once sat in on a meeting—in which Harvey was one of the participants, not one of the leaders or experts. Yet by our estimate, at least 75 percent of the meeting consisted of either Harvey talking or someone else responding to something he had said. Another element of Harvey's behavior pattern was his almost reflexive defense against any questioning of or disagreement with his position or opinion on anything. He was highly intelligent and well versed in most subject matters and instantly brought those tools to bear against what he felt was opposition ("Well, have you read . . . ?" "Did you look at . . . ?"). The result was that people gave up trying to offer even the slightest suggestion. Of course, people who know much less about a particular topic can offer wonderful suggestions and ask important questions, precisely *because* they stand further away from the issue. Harvey lost this input, and his career was further hampered because people grew tired of attending to what were billed as meetings but turned out to be lectures.

It is critically important that you recognize whether or not this is a behavior pattern you fall into. Ask yourself whether you are ever seen running roughshod over others, even without cleats and a baseball bat. If the answer is "Yes," then ask yourself when and how you're most prone to acting this way. It's important to be aware of even the occasional "spikes" in behavior and of the possibility that you're a more constant but lower-level pusher—a 5 on a scale of 1–10.

This pattern of behavior shares some common elements with the pattern described in "Rebel Looking for a Cause." Both are aggressive and essentially egotistical. But the rebel is more aggravating to his colleagues than threatening. His slogan is "I'm me, and don't try to change me." The bulldozer's inner motto is, "I'm me, and we're going to do things *my* way."

Consider as well whether you show any inappropriate bulldozer behaviors in your life away from work. Pushing too hard to get your own way, even when done nicely, can alienate friends and acquaintances—not to mention causing marital discord and alienating your children (while teaching them to grow up either to be bulldozers or the exact opposite). Don't be misled if the other people go along as if they don't mind, by the way. The fact that they're acceding to your wishes (read "demands") doesn't mean they're happy about it.

THE ORIGINS OF THE BULLDOZER

Bulldozer behavior usually originates in childhood, when one or more adults, by word or example, teach children that the world outside is an extremely hostile place. "It's a tough, dog-eat-dog world, son, every man for himself, and the sooner you learn to fight for what you want, the better." Such parents at heart view life as war, and childhood (if it's done right) as boot camp.

The person who displays this behavior pattern learns that everyone is out to take advantage of everyone else. The only way one can succeed is to beat the other guy into the ground before he gets a chance to do the same to you. "Do unto others before they do unto you—plus 10 percent" is one such lesson, or interpretation of the world. It is based on a mistrustful, paranoid view of the world and other people. Such people are taught that there will not be enough to go around and that they'd better be ready to elbow their way in to get some of the food—or go hungry. This may account for part of why people in this pattern are often absolutely terrific to work with much of the time but are occasionally able to flatten you by their stubbornness and aggressiveness. Jose, for example, was seen as charming, funny, and agreeable—as long as his position was secure. But if his position were threatened, if he were "hungry" or could even foresee being hungry, out of his way!

Now this is sometimes true, in some circumstances. But people who exhibit this pattern of behavior are usually *not* taught to see the countervailing point of view, that people will often treat you fairly and reasonably. It is as if such people, growing up, hear every day of their lives that the weather is stormy and *never* hear that the weather is clear and sunny. Of course, if the information being imparted were actual weather reports, they could look out the window, see the sky themselves, and know better. The bulldozer's parents, however, are presenting a report on what is in other people's hearts ("watch out, people want to take advantage of you; if you're slow, you'll lose out"; and so on)—and sadly, there is no window to look in on other people to give the lie to these messages.

Consciously or not, people who grow up with this world perception become disciples of a variation on what Douglas McGregor wrote about as the "Theory X" view of people. This point of view holds that people will work only if they are forced to. At heart, bulldozers believe (call it "Theory XX") that people do only what is best for them and that only brute force, threats, and coercion—not what is the right thing or even the subtle art of persuasion—will change that.

In psychological terms, members of this group engage in "projection," imagining that other people feel, think, and act just as they themselves do. They "project" *their own* attitudes onto others and then react as if those people were bulldozers themselves. And of course, if they act according to the pattern for long enough, at least some other people *will* adopt the same tactics, once they see that bulldozers aren't going to play nicely in the sandbox. Jerry was one such "occasional" bulldozer, neither outrageous nor constant in running roughshod. But his behavior occurred often enough and pointedly enough (for example, he would literally edge people out of conversations by gradually shifting his position to stand in front of them) that people came to mistrust his intentions. Some days he was perfectly reasonable and pleasant; he'd listen and be respectful. But at other times he'd insist on his own way on something and refuse even to hear anything anyone else had to say. Jerry, by the way, was completely unaware of his behavior, and when it was pointed out to him (as it was on more than one occasion) he dismissed it as the other person's problem. As a result, he was genuinely surprised when people stopped wanting to work with him.

Let's look again at Jim, perhaps the most extreme example—the lawyer with the baseball bat. Jim was born to a well-to-do family in Ohio, attended a fine boarding school in New England, and from there went to Bowdoin College and University of Virginia law school. So it wasn't that Jim didn't know that it was inappropriate to walk through the office swinging a Louisville Slugger—even if it *had* been given to him as a souvenir by a former client company. And it wasn't just a nervous twitch, a substitute for cigarettes or worry beads. Jim knew that the bat had shock value. It was a message, loud and clear, that nobody was tough enough to get the best of him. He *wanted* to send a message, that he would metaphorically beat others into submission if he had to.

Physically, Jim was probably strong enough to do just that. He wasn't tall, a couple of inches below six feet. But he was powerfully built, with broad shoulders and an expansive chest. In prep school he started playing lacrosse, one of the toughest contact sports, and continued to play well into his thirties. Jim never struck anyone in the office—or anyone else, as far as we know—but he used his physical presence to intimidate people, frequently backing a subordinate—man or woman—up against a wall or desk during a reprimand (or just a demand).

Fresh out of law school, Jim was attracted to a branch of the profession well suited to his temperament, bankruptcy law, and went to work for a firm where bankruptcy was the sole practice. Unlike other legal specialties where even the most ruthless aggression is covered with a patina of civility, in general bankruptcy law makes little pretense about following gentlemanly rules of conduct.

The battles are no-holds-barred. Jim's firm represented suppliers to large retailers. When a department store chain, for example, declared bankruptcy, Jim's goal was to get as much money as he could for his clients, the chain's creditors. His enemy in this endeavor was both the foundering chain and every other creditor circling it, trying to get the maximum share for itself. Jim was one of the best bankruptcy lawyers in the business, a bulldozer who never backed off, who never gave up a dollar he didn't have to. If the image suggests hyenas or wild dogs fighting for a piece of the fallen wildebeest, that isn't far from the truth.

But several years ago Jim's world changed around him and he suddenly found himself working on unfamiliar terrain. What turned Jim's world upside down was the merger of his firm with a large general practice firm. Like many other small firms, Jim's found that more and more clients wanted a full-service law firm, one that could take care of all their legal needs, including taxes, labor, copyrights, and trade as well as bankruptcy. So against his expressed desire, Jim and his fourteen partners joined—were absorbed by, really—a large and well-known law firm with no bankruptcy practice.

The culture of the new firm was as far removed from Jim's old firm as imaginable. Partners didn't shout at one another; they didn't even shout at subordinates. They didn't behave as though every transaction were a zero-sum game in which someone had to lose. Not all of its business was adversarial. The firm helped create webs of alliances that were mutually beneficial for its clients and even for nonclients. Protecting the clients' interests no longer demanded annihilating everyone else. The workplace Jim found himself in was no longer belligerent; it was genteel.

Most of the partners from Jim's firm made the transition successfully. They were still gladiators in bankruptcy court, but they minded their manners in the office. Several other partners could not make the transition and retired. Jim was alone in refusing either to change or to quit. In so doing, the bulldozer ran into a wall he could not breach.

THE BULLDOZER IN AN ORGANIZATION

The world has evolved in a number of ways to make people who exhibit this pattern increasingly obsolete. The economy has shifted from one based on manufacturing to one based on services. Behavior that *might* be acceptable on a factory floor does not play well in an office setting. Bulldozers *might* do satisfactory work successfully in a factory, if the assignment is clear and straightforward. They do not do so well in face-to-face relationships with customers, where they have to read what the customer is thinking and shape their tactics accordingly. They discover that it is much easier to bend steel than people.

In addition, the increasing diversity of the workforce has complicated their lives. Their rough manners often include crude jokes and even more objectionable forms of sexual harassment, which often gets them fired and their employers sued. Moreover, in an economy with low unemployment and a shortage of skilled workers, employees won't put up with being abused or undervalued.

Most of the people who use bulldozer tactics seem to do better early on in their careers, for several reasons. Their inappropriate behaviors are less visible by senior management when they are farther down the totem pole. And their behavior, in the short term, may be very effective at getting things done. Some will excuse their "bull in a china shop" behavior as a function of youth and immaturity, something they'll grow out of. Some managers view such hard-changing behavior as a sign of drive and ambition that, when tempered with age and seasoned with experience, will transform their bludgeon into a well-honed rapier. (What they don't realize is that the bulldozer without help and the proper motivation will never give up that club.)

Over the years, as people with this pattern log more and more (metaphorical) fistfights with peers and competitors, two things happen. First, no one wants to work with them anymore. They have simply used up the supply of available "playmates," and increasingly others refuse to deal with them. Just as harmful, over time bulldozers develop a "critical mass" of people they have cheated, bruised, abused, and humiliated; when the opportunity presents itself for those people to band together and overwhelm the playground bully, they lose no time in doing so. Charlie was an equities analyst who was, as his manager put it, "brilliant all the time, a great guy almost all the time, and an absolute disaster that remaining 1 or 2 percent, when something makes him 'morph' into a pit bull who locks on to something and won't let go. If I tell him no, he'll go to my boss; and if she tells him no, he goes to the head of the entire firm. And the crazy thing is, *he* thinks this is absolutely okay."

The truth is that bulldozers at any career stage have problems in most organizational cultures, but they do especially poorly in cultures that have strong traditions, that emphasize professionalism and have a strong market position and brand name that they are not willing to risk because of untoward behavior. And that was Jim's undoing. The new firm's senior partners—and even clients—had watched and heard him berate associate attorneys; a few had even seen him patrolling the corridors with the baseball bat. Those partners were not only concerned that the clients were uncomfortable; they were equally troubled that his behavior was demoralizing to the staff. Law firms compete for clients, and they compete just as hard for the brightest law school graduates. They couldn't afford to let Jim chase away talented associates and valuable support staff to rival firms. Jim's new partners saw him as, among other things, someone who was going to flatten their incomes.

A little over a year after the merger, the managing partner called Jim in and informed him that it would be best if he left the firm. He was being fired. Jim was shaken. The only setbacks he had received in life were on the lacrosse field, defeats he invariably blamed on unmotivated teammates who lacked the guts to do what it took to win. He tried a similar explanation on the managing partner. He was one hell of a bankruptcy lawyer, he said, a rainmaker for the firm. If the partners didn't appreciate him, it was because they were too soft and squishy for battle. The failure was with them, not him.

The managing partner didn't buy it. He turned very cold and very hard and stopped Jim in his tracks. He acknowledged that Jim was a producer, an effective attorney in his specialty, but said that on balance he wasn't worth the cost to the firm and its reputation. "Do you know what your reputation is, Jim?" he asked. "People don't see you as one tough son of a bitch, they see you as a bully and a cheat, just this side of the line in terms of formal ethics and way over the line in terms of acceptable behavior. They cross the street when they see you coming, and it's not because you're such a great lawyer, it's because they don't respect you and because they don't trust you—in fact, a lot of people actively despise you!"

Jim was stunned. Ashen faced, he was speechless for perhaps the first time in his life. Then he apologized and begged for another chance. Miraculously, he got a three-month stay of execution.

Jim was tough but not stupid, and he recognized that he could not easily survive as a lone practitioner. He also recognized that there was a lot on the line, and on the advice of his brother (an investment banker whose firm had used both our services and those of Jim's law firm) he came to us for help. He came through the door like the bulldozer he was. He was imperious, full of bravado, sucking up all the air in the room. Jim began by deprecating our profession and kept reminding us that he was paying the fee and was therefore the boss. He staked out his position: We were being hired to convince the managing partner that he had made a terrible mistake. That position, of course, was untenable, but we allowed him to hold on to that fantasy for the moment.

Then we began the difficult job of convincing Jim that he had to change his behavior. Extreme bulldozers, by and large, are deaf to what others are saying. So Jim had not picked up—or had discounted as the grumblings of the malcontented losers—the voluminous signals around him that the attitude toward him ranged from distaste and resentment to fear and hatred, as the managing partner assured us.

We try to speak the language our client understands. In Jim's case the vernacular we used was blunt, simple, and unequivocal. "If a comedian thinks he's funny and other people don't, he's wrong and they're right. The same thing is true here—it doesn't matter whether you think you're right, Jim," we told him. "Your partners think you're wrong, and if you want to keep your job, you're going to have to change your behavior."

We decided on a strategy that would make two points. First, it had to convince Jim that the firm was unanimous in denouncing his behavior. Second, it had to persuade Jim's partners that he was willing to face his affliction and reform. The managing partner reserved a private dining room in a quiet restaurant in midtown Manhattan, and we (Jim and his brother, about a dozen members of the partnership, and the two of us) gathered for an after-hours meeting. Over dinner everyone was allowed a glass of wine, no more, to loosen inhibitions just a bit. The conversation was general, polite, and strained. Over dessert we explained what we were trying to accomplish and invited Jim's partners to tell him what they saw as his problems. (Variations of this technique, sometimes called an "intervention," are routinely used to confront alcoholics and drug addicts with their behaviors.)

The partners unloaded mercilessly. They told him that they regarded Jim as crude and obnoxious. He treated his partners like opponents and everybody beneath him like dirt. The partners acknowledged that he was skillful in his field but said that the business and income he brought to the firm didn't come close to compensating for the damage and risks incurred. He was useless in any project that required cooperation rather than combat. His manner was fit for a bear pit, not for a law firm; and on and on. Occasionally Jim tried to defend himself, but he was unsuccessful. The partners had the baseball bats and the lacrosse sticks now, and they kept pummeling him. In the end, Jim could only say the one thing he had never said before—and the one and only thing the other partners wanted to hear: "I'm sorry."

When the last of the partners trailed out the door at about midnight, Jim was left with us and his brother. His brother, red eyed, turned to him and said, "Jim, you know I love you, but I agree with them. They're right." Jim walked into the bathroom (to vomit, we later learned). When he returned he didn't make any excuses. He recalled a couple of lacrosse matches in which he had been beaten up so badly that he couldn't move without pain for weeks and said he'd rather feel that pain than the shame he felt now. He'd had no idea how people thought about him. He'd believed his behavior was more or less normal, that everybody saw life as dog-eat-dog and that although he might have been more demonstrative than others about expressing that worldview, he wasn't much different from anyone else. He figured that other people were intimidated by him, feared him, were sometimes angry at him, sometimes envious. But he'd had no idea that they held him in contempt, that they found his behavior despicable; the night had opened his eyes and ears.

To Jim's great credit, we have never had a client who took to coaching better and more seriously than he did. He took the same relentless, straight-ahead drive that had nearly been his undoing and turned it on himself for a job of reconstruction. He enlisted the help of one of his partners, asking him to correct him whenever he got out of line. He forced himself to go through the entire roster of the firm, down to the secretaries and mailroom crew, and made apologies to those he had treated badly.

Jim will never be a natural charmer, but he is working to transform himself from a bulldozer into, say, a backhoe—and to know when to turn it on and off! And in a firm that values hard work and a professional approach to a problem, his determination has been enough to save his job. And one day, soon after what Jim came to refer to as "the last supper," the baseball bat quietly disappeared from his office.

HOW TO BREAK THE PATTERN

If reading about Jim is distressingly like listening to a brief history, however exaggerated, of your own career, you need to turn off your engine. You *can* do it. Adults often train children to be polite by asking, "What's the magic word?" with the answers being "Please" and "Thank you." We, too, have a third magic word (or phrase): "I'm sorry." And the first thing you need to do if you realize you use bulldozing techniques is to get comfortable saying it. Because contrary to the hackneyed dictum of the movie *Love Story,* in which Ali MacGraw's character admonishes Ryan O'Neal, "Love means never having to say you're sorry," love—and life in general—means frequently having to say you're sorry. And if you're a bulldozer, even an occasional one, you no doubt have a roster of people you need to apologize to. But, being a bulldozer, those words may not come easy to you—especially with people you work with.

So start small and work your way up. First, it is essential that you recognize exactly when you fall into using bulldozing tactics. Make a list. Next, find reasons to say those magic words, out loud, to store clerks, taxi drivers, other drivers, customers, passengers in the subway—anybody at all. The important thing is literally to get used to saying "I'm sorry." That's all. (And if you think this is silly, try it with anything else you don't say or do easily. Frequency creates comfort, whether it's in saying "I'm sorry" or in diving off a ten-meter platform into a pool.) Then, move into the arena of your workplace and practice apologizing for current misdeeds and bulldozing behaviors. "Joe, I'm sorry I lost it in that meeting. I really do think you've done great work on this project, it's just that we have so much more to do—I'm just feeling stressed out." Be prepared for your co-workers to look at you askance, waiting for the blow to come. Remember, they're accustomed to being bulldozed by you, not apologized to.

Then, as you get more comfortable, move into expressing your regrets for past bulldozer behaviors. This is harder, because it is an explicit admission that you have done things in the past that were wrong, and *wrong enough* to warrant bringing them back to light in the present to recount and apologize for. Do an audit of everyone you work with—present and past—and for those on your "enemies list" (those who consider *you* an enemy, regardless of how you feel about them), make notes about what you have done that has damaged those relationships. Then craft a plan for each individual to begin the repair of the relationship. You might begin with just reaching out and making contact of the "How was your weekend?" variety or "I heard that one of your kids had been sick at school—how is he or she?" Next, make an effort to express your appreciation for the person's work in a meeting that includes your manager. Finally, look for a time when you can go back to a past injury and apologize for what you said or did. You might say, "Hey, Jo Anne, I was thinking on my way in to work today about the meeting we had with X and Y last summer, and about what

I said about your work. I was out of line, and I want to apologize for what I said. Your work really was fine. Moreover, I had no business saying what I did. I was wrong and I'm sorry." We are big believers in scripting and role-playing difficult conversations, and for apologies that goes double. Writing out and editing and reediting the words, and then practicing saying them (and then editing them yet again), can make them come out just the way you want and make you feel a lot more comfortable.

Be prepared for two things: an amazed expression on the part of the person you're clearing the air with, and a feeling of immense relief on your part. If you know you've hurt somebody in the past, it's a weight you've been carrying around a long time; apologizing will allow you to put it down. And, as we advised earlier, customize your approaches to the people you need to work things out with. With one person you may need to go through the long ramp-up we just described, with someone else you might go directly to the final step. With another person you may need several meetings before the anger they've been carrying can be diffused. It is critical, when you're apologizing and making amends, that you don't get defensive if the other person takes the opportunity to express his or her anger: If you say, "I'm sorry I bulldozed you, Janice," be prepared for her to reply, "And well you should be, you were such a jerk!" Don't get defensive, complaining to her that you *said* you were sorry. You can't contaminate your *mea culpa* with a *j'accuse* or it won't have the salutary effect you intended.

So far we've been focusing on taking care of past sins. Now let's talk about the present. If the motto of the bulldozer is "Do unto others before they do unto you—plus 10 percent," the motto of the *recovering* bulldozer is "Do unto others as you would have them do unto you." Period. The Golden Rule. Yes, as corny as it sounds, this is the sound bite you need to put on your screen saver and imprint on the front of your mind. Because what this message does is to force you to think about how other people feel about what you're doing, and saying to yourself, "How would I feel if Jack did this to me?" Now, if your conclusion is, "Hey, I'm tough, if Jack did that, I could live with it," then think to yourself, "Do unto others as *they* would have you do unto them." Because the fatal flaw of the bulldozer is a lack of perspective, a lack of empathy, a lack of understanding of how other people feel. And no matter how you might feel, you need to understand how *they* feel. And as a bulldozer you need to practice *acting accordingly.* You need to practice understanding and caring—like lifting weights to build up a formerly atrophied muscle or stretching one that is tight. Simply learning to say you're sorry, and understanding when you *should* be sorry (so you can anticipate when you're about to bulldoze someone and stop in advance), will go a long way toward fixing the problem.

Another tool for use in turning down the volume on your bulldozing habits is to learn to be more aware of when you're just about to lose your cool. Do you start to clench your jaw? Get (literally) hot under the collar? Does your voice start to shake? Once you've identified the early warning signs, try to put some solutions into place (counting to ten before you speak, asking yourself *why* the person you're getting annoyed at might be acting or speaking as he or she is, (taking perspective), pretending your beeper has just signaled you so you can take a minute or two outside the meeting to regain your composure).

It's always a good idea to have an outside ally who can give you feedback ("You were great in that meeting, you followed through on your plan to let at least three people speak before you did" or "You did it again—Jack was trying to make a point and you interrupted him four times"). If you tend to overheat in meetings that include your "buddy," you might even ask this person to act as a circuit breaker for you if you start to lose control, with some prearranged signals or code words, or with his or her having the license to step in and say, "Wait a minute, Bull, I think Jack has a point, and you're not letting him make it."

These are very simple things, but they *are* the solution. Simple, yes, but as we all know, simple and easy are not the same thing. Diving off the cliffs at Acapulco is simple, but not easy. Nevertheless, if you do just these few things, you will be more successful in your career by many orders of magnitude. And you can still—*when appropriate*—push your agenda aggressively. But now it'll be *your* decision about how to drive it, and when, and *your* choice whether to knock down a wall or drive around it. You'll be a whole lot more effective in the long run.

MANAGING THE BULLDOZING BEHAVIORS
OF OTHERS

Suppose you've just read the material concerning this pattern and real-ize, "Well, this isn't me, but it sure sounds a lot like Jack who works for me; he's been wreaking havoc ever since he was transferred into my di-vision." Well, the bad news is that there are a lot of people like Jim run-ning around the landscape of business. Unlike science or medicine, business by its nature seems to attract such types. As a business manager or leader, you need to know how to deal with them.

Assuming that you have someone like this on your staff whom you don't want to turn loose as a wrecking ball on your people or your com-petitors, what do you do? First, put down on paper a brief list of the per-son's most egregious offenses. Next, set up a meeting, preferably off site, at the end of the workday; plan for a couple of hours. When you sit down with the staff member, you should first express your appreciation for his hard work, energy, determination, dedication, and so forth. "But . . ."

Next, come right to the point. The fact is, a lot of Jack's (or Jane's) energy is being wasted, a lot of enemies are being created, a lot of ill will is being generated. Here, go through your list of exploits. Don't allow him to argue. Tell him that he is, bottom line, very expensive and begin-ning to run into red ink. You spend too much time cleaning up the after-math of his behavior, soothing the feathers he's ruffled. It's just not working. Most bulldozers need to hear straight out that they have to change *or else*—or they'll discount your message. They tend to think, "S/he just needs to be able to tell people that he chewed me out, but s/he's really on my side." Tell him that it's up to him to decide: change or be fired. But he should understand that this behavior is going to be a problem no matter where he goes, and you want him to stay and work it out here (he needs to understand that although he's being taken to the woodshed, he's still valued).

Provide him with the advice in the section above entitled "How to Break the Pattern." Offer to be his eyes and ears, helping him to see when and where he rolls over others. Role-play apologies for past bull-dozer transgressions with him. When you see him make even small changes—giving airtime to someone else in a meeting, for example—

make certain to bring it to his attention and reinforce it. (Remember, big programs are written one byte at a time.)

If all this sounds like a lot of work, it is. But if you can help a bulldozer to reform, you have someone with a powerful engine and lots of traction on your team. When you save him, you're holding on to a major asset for your organization. So before you write someone like this off, consider not only the cost of helping the person, but the benefit that accrues from a successful outcome.

CHAPTER

SIX

REBEL LOOKING FOR A CAUSE

Andrew seemed determined to defy authority—and everything associated with authority, including societal tradition, company custom, and good taste. He was endlessly confrontational and abrasive in the office—and with clients—always "in your face." He felt it was important to break the rules in the name of honesty, expose the hypocrites, and enlighten the ignorant. *Someone* has to stand up and speak the truth, Andrew would insist. Andrew, in fact, accomplished none of those objectives. Sadly, what he did achieve was the derailment of his own career.

At the peak of his career Andrew was a senior project leader for a large management consulting firm in Boston. His job was to direct teams of between four and ten subordinates who would engage corporations in the difficult, sensitive, and critically important work of defining elements of the corporation's best strategies for success in a risky, unpredictable world.

To understand Andrew's self-destructive behavior, you have to understand the culture in which he worked. Andrew's firm was not rigid and hidebound. You don't achieve the kind of success that firm has achieved in the world by following a dictum that the solution to yesterday's problem is the answer to tomorrow's problem. For the most part Andrew's superiors, peers, and subordinates were very smart and open-minded about new approaches to new challenges, very adaptable.

That said, the firm still had a strong sense of decorum. Everyone in the firm who might be seen by a client during the workday—even a chance meeting with someone else's client—wore a suit, or for women employees a suit or other conservative mode of dress. The firm's dining room was always well stocked with fruit, breads, and cheese that employees could take back to their offices when they had no time for lunch; it was assumed that no one would fill a tote bag of those offerings to take home. Rarely did anyone raise his or her voice in public—and no one ever said anything before an audience that would embarrass a colleague.

Andrew broke all of the rules. He was large and heavy and likely to attract attention anyhow, but he really made himself stand out with his dress. He wore ties, but of the Nicole Miller opera tickets print variety, not the conservative stripes and patterns that were de rigueur. He regularly went a little too long between haircuts. He sported long sideburns long after they went out of fashion. He made a ceremony of stuffing fruits and cheeses into his bag to take home. Most of all, he loved a good fight. His favorite way of drawing attention to himself during a meeting was to explode, "The answer is so obvious. How come I'm the only one in the room who gets it, and I'm not even a partner?" We sometimes refer to people with Andrew's behavior pattern as *rebels*.

THE DYNAMICS OF THE PATTERN

There is a vital, indispensable place for the rebel in American society and in business. Indisputably, if it were not for the revolutionaries George Washington, Thomas Jefferson, and the other Founding Fathers, there would be no United States of America. Throughout our history the country has jumped forward because of the actions of fearless rebels, whether they are artists, military leaders, statesmen, athletes, civil rights activists, entrepreneurs, or inventors.

But what all such revolutionaries have in common is that they were fighting over a long period of time for a cause that was larger than themselves. Rebellion was not their fundamental stance vis-á-vis the world; they were often very reasoned and moderate in their thinking and actions. The Revolutionary War was a course of action pursued because it was the only course of action open. That is what distinguishes them from "rebels" such as Andrew who adopt an oppositional frame of mind as their primary stance in most social settings.

The rebel stance is often dysfunctional in an organizational setting. Rebels are not typically seen as good team players, because they refuse to recognize the value of synergy, to acknowledge that the capabilities of several people working together as a team are usually greater than the sum of their parts. They stake out positions and hold fast to them, because compromise is seen as a humiliating defeat. They fantasize about owning their own businesses so that they won't have to be faced with the compromises that come with working in a team. They are often angry, which can easily alienate them from would-be allies.

For the person with this pattern of thinking and behavior, honesty—and by that rebels almost always mean brutal honesty—is an imperative. Saying what's on our minds, as most of us recognize, is a limited virtue. In extreme form it's what three-year-olds do when they're on the elevator and ask, "Mommy, why is that lady so fat?" Even when we're asked to be candid, most of us know that it's wise to be somewhat guarded. If the CEO says, "Give me feedback. Tell me how I'm doing, and especially what I'm doing wrong," the wise subordinate with appropriate survival skills perhaps gives the CEO some well-modulated opinion about how instructions from the corner office are sometimes a bit confusing. Even the critic would couch his observation carefully in overall praise for the boss's performance. The rebel, however, might send the boss an abrasive, eight-page letter telling him exactly what he thinks.

Although they may define themselves as change agents, rebels usually change very little about their organizations. For the rebel is interested not in spreading the truth, but in gathering the attention. If the rebel's actions go unnoticed, he or she is likely to escalate them until they *are* noticed, until he or she receives the attention so richly craved. Being quietly, subtly different is not what rebels are about. They seek a reaction to their actions. Nor is the rebel interested in destroying the opposition and gaining power. In fact, if you agree with a position a rebel stakes out ("We should be doing . . .") and offer resources to help him or her make the necessary changes, the rebel will likely shrink away and look for ways to abdicate such responsibilities. The true rebel does not fight for noble causes or for the power to carry them forward.

Of course, relatively few of us live so completely in this mode. As is the case with all of the other behavior patterns, there are many shades of gray to the rebel. These shades are seen both in how the rebellion is carried out (its severity) and in the amount of time it goes on (its frequency). Some rebels are extreme, even explosive; others are more subtle in their methods, employing more "passive-aggressive" behaviors (being late for meetings, being late in meeting deadlines, and forgetting to give people messages). In fact, passive aggression appears to be the rebellious weapon of choice among people who want to voice their rebellion but fear reprisals if they do so openly. One manager we worked with "lost" requests for information (in fact, she swore that those e-mails never got to her) with alarming frequency. She would never come straight out and say "No," never take a stand that could put her in the line of fire.

This is not, by the way, the same phenomenon as procrastination. People procrastinate when they delay taking action out of fear that the result they produce won't be good enough. This is a function of low self-esteem, not rebelliousness (see "Looking in the Mirror" in Part II). Passive-aggressive lateness is unconsciously designed to inconvenience other people. If you're dependent on me to get a piece of work done so you can then start another piece, I can passively—yet aggressively— hurt you by making you wait until just before your deadline to get my work to you. Although the "3 Ps" (passive-aggression, procrastination, and perfectionism) may all have the same behavioral outcome, the last two come from the same root, one that is very different from the passive-aggression of the rebel.

Some people are almost constantly driven by rebelliousness; others are more occasional. But if it is a mode of behavior you find yourself falling into—even at a more moderate level, ask yourself why. What triggers that reaction in you? Does the situation you're in or the person you are talking to remind you of something from your past? What do *you* get out of the act of rebelling?

The rebel pattern of behavior is one that is prone to being activated—in any of us—almost without our being aware of it. If you think back for a moment, the odds are that you can come up with a memory of a meeting in which someone started acting in a way that pressed your "hot button" and caused an immediate negative reaction, whether what the other person said made sense or not. Your rebellion button, for whatever reason, has been pushed. The problem is that if you give in to such behavior too often, or at the wrong time, you can seriously taint the way your superiors and colleagues view you.

One of our clients worked for a major bank and was in both word and deed a "corporate man." There were one or two people he worked with, however, whom he perceived as smugly looking down on him, putting down his opinions on any number of topics. Whether his perceptions were accurate or not, they triggered him to respond in a flip, almost adolescent way, metaphorically thumbing his nose at them. Suddenly he felt as if *they* were the representatives of the bank and he was the rebellious crusader. Then, as soon as they were gone, he calmed down and reverted to his normal mode of behavior (feeling somewhat sheepish over having acted in a somewhat embarrassing manner).

Another client we had absolutely refused to adhere to the company's unwritten dress code. He wore sport coats instead of suits, a sweater and tie instead of either a sport coat *or* suit. When one of his colleagues would comment, "My, aren't we casual today!" he acted as if he heard it as a compliment. But in virtually all other ways he was the perfect corporate citizen. He was someone who was constantly—but mildly—rebellious; not so much that his job was in jeopardy, but enough so that people noticed, and it likely held his career back.

A *lot* of psychological energy is tied up in the rebel pattern, and unlike some of the other behavior traps, it's there in all of us. This is why it can be so readily set off by circumstances we don't fully understand. It's important that you try to identify the circumstances in which you've found yourself acting the part of the rebel. Make an attempt to understand when your rebellious instincts are triggered.

Does the behavior pattern manifest itself in your personal life as well as at work? Does the behavior of certain friends or relatives cause you to think or behave rebelliously? Are there certain situations or topics that set you off? Remember, the twelve habits that cause people to falter in their careers don't "go to work" only when you walk into your office and then turn themselves off when you leave. Think about the role this pattern plays in the rest of your life as well.

THE ORIGINS OF THE REBEL

Why does someone grow up to be a rebel? The roots of this behavior pattern arise out of a failure to negotiate a critical element of childhood development, the process of separation and individuation from the parents. As infants, we are effectively (in our own experience) merged with our parents (especially with our mothers), and a large element of what our psychological and essential lives are about until we reach adulthood is separating ourselves from our parents and forming our own individual identities. Most of us are able to do that successfully—albeit not without some substantial Sturm und Drang as children and later as adolescents. We come out of it satisfied that we really are individuals, entirely distinct from our parents. (Only later do we realize how much of our parents, good and bad, we carry through life.) But some of us don't successfully achieve a sense of separateness, and a rebellious behavior pattern is one outcome of not having done so.

Adult rebels act and appear as if they are stuck in adolescence. As a teenager, one of your primary tasks is to continue to separate from your parents in order to feel confident that you are someone who is different from them, that you are the author of your own life. Much of what is typical adolescent behavior—defying authority, breaking the rules, wearing rings through the eyebrows, blasting heavy metal music, experimenting with drugs—arises out of that struggle. The rebel, however, never feels that his or her core being has separated from his or her parents and has become an individual. The rebel is eternally struggling against his or her parents or authority in order to feel free from that authority.

As an adult, the rebel re-creates that struggle, transferring the fight to someone else or somewhere else. Ultimately rebels carry on the fight in the organizations where they work and, more specifically, with those in management above them. The situation is paradoxical; in rebelling, they see themselves as unique, a one-of-a-kind creative talent. But in reality they are conformists, adhering to an out-of-date, adolescent mode of behavior. They think of themselves as free and independent. In reality they are still the captives of a process that most people have worked through, and been free of, for years.

Successful individuals—as distinct from the rebels still mired in separating themselves from their parents—are self-confident enough to join a team without losing their sense of self, without fearing that they will drown and vanish into the group. Rebels, on the other hand, have to continue fighting to make themselves seen, to prove to themselves that they're different from the people around them so that they don't become swallowed up or made invisible.

Usually at some level rebels understand their failure, realize that they are fighting more than they should and tend to "act out" more than is necessary, and feel gravely dissatisfied with themselves. So the process of "reaction formation" (the psychological defense through which unacceptable impulses are denied by going to the opposite extreme) takes over to protect them from what they feel inside. On some level rebels know that they don't fit in, sense that the emotions pulling at them make them different from those around them, and they feel ashamed. Rather than seek help to find their way through the passage, they do the only thing they know how to do: they react (this is the reaction formation) by trying to make a virtue of the fact that they are still struggling for an acceptable sense of self. At heart, the extreme rebels don't like themselves, so they are excessive in their insistence on the virtue of their cause.

Andrew, for example, grew up in a medium-size city in western Pennsylvania, the younger of two brothers born to an immigrant day laborer and his submissive wife. Andrew's father—and Andrew talked about him proudly—tolerated no disobedience from anyone—not his wife, certainly not his children. His father decided—ordered, in fact—that Andrew's older brother was going to be a lawyer. All of the family's financial resources were devoted to that goal and most of its emotional reserves as well. The older brother would hoist the family up the ladder of success. There was little support left over for Andrew.

But Andrew, to his credit, scouted college scholarships on his own and found himself a spot at a good school in Ohio. (And here we see the positive element of his rebelliousness: Andrew rebelled against the unspoken dictum of his father that he shouldn't bother trying to amount to much.) He later earned an MBA at a university in the Southwest. In essence, Andrew launched himself into the adult world. But he wasn't an adult inside; he was still, at heart, an adolescent rebel. Nonetheless, he had raw intelligence and he worked hard, and within a few years a prestigious consulting firm in Boston hired him. The fact that he was not an Ivy League graduate may have helped him get the job. The firm was interested in diversity, a nontraditional point of view, and Andrew seemed to fill that need. What the firm had not counted on was his need to rebel.

THE REBEL IN AN ORGANIZATION

Rebels have a longer career life than one might expect of people who can be mercurial and difficult to be around. First, for reasons of our history—a nation born out of revolution, as well as our penchant for rugged individualism—American culture seems to be far more tolerant of rebels than most societies. Even our outlaws—Billy the Kid, Jesse James, Bonnie and Clyde—fascinate us.

Rebels tend to do best early in their careers, when their rebelliousness can be written off as youthful exuberance, and in industries where rebelliousness is common and, to a certain extent, valued (specifically in entertainment circles or cutting-edge, high-tech environments). One popular title in Silicon Valley is *Rules for Revolutionaries,* giving an indication of how accepted such behavior is in that arena. The rebel may well be able to find a home there—*as long as he or she has enough to offer to make the rebelliousness worth its cost.* But people who fall into this pattern are "high maintenance" employees. *If* they are brilliant in some way, *and* working in companies where this kind of discordant behavior is tolerable (in some organizations rebelliousness is not going to be tolerated regardless of how brilliant the individual is), the cost-benefit balance may tilt in the direction of the rebel. But the "brilliance" has to be perceived in the eyes of the company, not in the eyes of the rebel him- or herself. And the person has to really *shine*, not just be above average or good. Kawasaki says that he looks for programmers "whose bodies have so many piercings, they set off the metal detectors in airports—but they have to be great!" These people are rebels in some sense, but the fact that they're happy to work together with a group of similarly pierced-and-dyed Web designers (instead of spending their time cyberattacking major Web sites) marks them as rebels with self-control. In such a context they're the norm, not the rebellious exception. Rebelling against certain social conventions doesn't necessarily predict the sorts of career troubles and limitations that characterize this behavior pattern.

Rebels themselves tend to justify their behavior by placing themselves in the tradition of those who have fought conventional wisdom and won. In business that includes people such as Sam Walton of Wal-Mart, Fred Smith of Federal Express, Richard Branson of Virgin Airways, and Steve Jobs of Apple. The rebel looks at them and says, "That could be me." But breaking away from convention is not the same thing as defying authority for its own sake. And even breaking away from convention is a high-risk venture. The four names just mentioned are all impressive, but they constitute small islands of success. (Magazines like *Fortune, Inc.,* and *Fast Company* don't write stories about the countless rebels who didn't become highly successful.) The rebel's theme song tends to be Frank Sinatra's "I Did It My Way," and rebels forget that for every Sinatra who really did do it his way, there are thousands of would-have-beens who didn't.)

A favorable economic climate can significantly extend a rebel's career. One client of ours was a middle manager in an insurance company. He was always sending the CEO querulous notes complaining about management's incompetence (although wisely excluding the CEO himself from blame). It wasn't as though his observations were going to change the business. For the most part they were complaints about things like the e-mail system the company used and the need to update reporting systems—perhaps good ideas, but not something the

CEO was going to act on. As long as the company was doing well, the CEO was mildly amused by him.

Then the company ran into trouble, and the CEO's attention turned to the serious business of trying to save it and, not incidentally, his job. The rebel, so focused on his need to do battle with authority, failed to sense the sea change. He kept sending the same notes about the slowness of the elevators and such. To such a CEO, the rebel had lost even his amusement value as an eccentric. He was just annoying. He wasn't fired, but he was passed over for promotions and eventually quit.

Andrew survived at the consulting firm for a while, partly because the partner who had hired him and with whom he worked most closely was something of a nonconformist himself, although of a much lesser magnitude than Andrew. What Andrew failed to notice, or deliberately ignored, was that his mentor was being squeezed out of the firm. The mentor was adept technically, but he wasn't bringing in new business, and when times became tough his partners thought he deserved a lesser share of the profits. Andrew's mentor departed.

Andrew could have stayed on and enjoyed a successful career at the firm. He was smart and skilled in his specialty, which involved understanding the complexities of health and pension plans and the various alternatives for the firm's clients. But when he had to work face-to-face with clients, or when he had to lead a team of the firm's junior associates, he was a disaster. He never insulted a client directly, but he didn't hesitate to embarrass his young colleagues. "I have to be honest with you," he told several of them. "You don't belong here." It was far beyond Andrew's authority to make those kinds of decisions for the firm. He was, in effect, willfully destroying the firm's seed corn, the potential partners of the future. Moreover, Andrew was not so skilled in his specialty that he was irreplaceable.

Andrew ignored a cardinal rule: If you insist on behaving like a rock star, make sure you're a rock star. He persisted in behavior that was pushing him to the margins of the company. He could not see that with his protector gone he was likely to go over the edge as well. At a company retreat he complained to the managing partner that the firm's profits were unfairly distributed. Too large a share was set aside for senior partners, Andrew argued. He didn't actually use the adjective *greedy* during the confrontation—which took place in the company of half a dozen colleagues—but he might as well have.

Within weeks Andrew was fired. He left bitterly, of course, complaining to everyone who would listen inside and outside the firm that he was fired by jerks who couldn't tolerate anyone with an independent mind. He's working now for a health insurance company, helping to design benefit plans. He works by himself. It's an acceptable job, but not a great one. The pay will never be better than mediocre. There is no opportunity to become a partner. What he does now is far too narrow to ever qualify him to move into upper management, or indeed much beyond what he is doing today.

HOW TO BREAK THE PATTERN

One key to successfully curbing a rebel, whether your own "inner rebel" or someone you manage, is to act before it's too late. There comes a time in the career of the rebel when he "crosses the Rubicon" and fatally injures himself in the eyes of his superiors. Unlike some of the other profiles that we have discussed, where the damage is a slow accretion, rebels tend at some point to do or say something almost literally to blow themselves up. So if you are reading this and recognize yourself or someone you want to help, the first counsel we have is to act soon.

As coaches we try to break through the reaction formative "shield" we described earlier, so we use strong and pointed language, allying ourselves with the person's rebelliousness. "We could 'baby you' and pretend that this isn't a big problem, but we're going to be really honest with you. You're acting as though you don't really want to stay with your company. Is that true?" If the answer is "Yes," the coaching is over almost as soon as it began. Usually, though, the response is a rather shocked, "No, of course not! Why do you say that?"

We then talk about the person's confrontational style. Rebels are usually inclined to excuse their behavior with phrases like "I was just kidding the guy." Our response to that defense is: "No, you weren't— and even if you were, it doesn't matter. You're not going to use that smoke screen here. You say things that really offend and hurt people, and that behavior is ruining your career. If it weren't, you wouldn't be here."

Then we give a homework (or, more properly, a "fieldwork") assignment. "Pretend you're an anthropologist. For the next couple of weeks you are going to study the culture of your company as though it were a remote tribe that no one in the civilized world has encountered before. Imagine that this culture is entirely unfamiliar to you and to the people back home. Take careful notes on how the people of your company tribe behave, dress, and interact with one another.

"What kinds of words do they use when talking to one another? What about their tone of voice? Does the second person who speaks acknowledge what the first person has said and show respect before disagreeing? How? What sorts of signals do people observe in knowing that the other person has finished and that it's time to speak up? What's the body language? How do people walk and sit?

"How do people dress? What rules do people observe when deferring to one another? What codes are there about the use of company property, including practices about taking company property home? Who's in charge, and how do you know they're in charge? In other words, how do they assert their authority? What else do you notice about those who are in charge? What distinguishes them in manner, dress, and other outward behavior from everyone else in the firm?

"Keep careful notes, and every week we'll go over those notes."

"But I don't *want* to dress and act and talk like everyone else!" is the likely response. "Why not?" we say. "What do you care? Is it so important to you that you dress and act and talk *differently* from everybody else that you're willing to sacrifice your career for it?"

"Well, no, but . . ." "And do you have any sense of just how much your behavior is controlled by your knee-jerk reaction against the norms you're discovering? You know, if I want my three-year-old to do something, all I have to do is tell her to do the opposite. You're just as hard-wired as she is! Do you really want to allow your automatic reactions to whatever the organizational norms happen to be to control your life? Because that's what's happening."

The notion of being controlled, whether directly by other people or indirectly by our reactions to them, is repellent to the rebel. Framing the dynamic this way presents a double bind to him. He *has* to acknowledge the foolishness of his behavior.

After you've turned the rebel into an anthropologist and eliminated the first layer of resistance to change, two pieces of work remain. The first is helping him to learn to act like other people who are generally more effective than he is. Here you're going to meet the second—and stronger—layer of resistance, and we again use a little judo to get past it. The resistance comes this time because now we're asking the rebel not just to contemplate change, but to enact it. So again the cry is going to go up, "But you're asking me to change who I am, my core, my essence—*I gotta be me!*" And our response is, "Not at all. You are who you are, and that's just fine. But let us ask you a question: If you want to get something done while you're visiting Spain, should you a) speak English, b) speak German, or c) attempt to speak Spanish? Spanish, right?

"Now, what if we told you we'd pay you an extra $50,000 a year if you would be willing to learn Spanish and speak it while you're at work. And that you'll be fired if you don't. What would you say? You'd say yes, of course. Now if you learn Spanish, would you not be you anymore, or would you be you, Version 2.0? New and improved?

"We're not asking you to change how you think or feel, just what language you use. Look, people in your organization speak, say, Mandarin, and you've been speaking Portuguese. They're both fine languages, but if you want to be effective where you work, you've got to learn to speak Mandarin—it's as simple as that. You remain you, but you learn another language in addition to the one you speak now. The only change in you is that you stop railing against the fact that everyone here speaks Mandarin and learn to speak it yourself. You'll be surprised at how much better you'll get along and how much more effective you'll be!"

Now we go to the heart of the matter, asking our client to help us understand why he feels so trapped in a state of rebellion. We ask him to talk to us about the other important authorities he's come into contact with—and fought with—in his life and what those relationships were like. These are frequently personal relationships (parents, grandparents) but sometimes involve groups or types of people (for example, the "cool kids" at school, the police, the CO when the person was in the military). We want to get beyond the current manager, to go deeper. Because if someone really is a "rebel looking for a cause," the cause is not the person's current boss; there *is* a cause, but it's usually buried at least ten years (if not twenty or thirty years) deep in the person's past.

IF YOU ARE THE MANAGER OF A REBEL

If you're the rebel's manager, rather than his or her coach or the rebel him- or herself, you may not feel comfortable going into this material. You may feel it is too personal and that you would be taking on too much of the role of a "psychologist." What you *could* do, though, is to say to your employee something like "You know, Kim, we all wrestle with parts of ourselves that get in the way of our being as successful as we could. Rebelling against authority seems to be your 'opponent in the ring.' It's not my place to get into it with you, but you might want to ask yourself: 'Who am I really fighting?' Because it's really, really important that you stop. I want to help you in any way I can. And although I make incredibly stupid mistakes at times, I don't think I initiated your rebellion." In that way you can at least encourage some introspection on the part of the person you're working with.

IF YOU ARE A REBEL YOURSELF

If you are a rebel trying to get control of your actions and behavior, ask *yourself* these questions. Only you can answer them. If you find yourself unable to get at the root causes of your rebelliousness, seek professional help. A large part of the reason coaches, counselors, and psychotherapists exist is that people have blind spots and can't be objective about themselves. Getting help may help you to get ahead more quickly and achieve the potential you know you have. In more dire cases, it may save your job—or your marriage.

We highly recommend that you read the chapter "Coming to Terms with Authority" in Part II. The chapters on using power and learning to understand the perspective of other people will also be helpful to you. Ask other people who can be more objective to help you; enlisting the aid of someone who knows you well, such as an old friend, spouse, or other family member, can be invaluable. They can help you to recognize your rebellious ways by being honest with you when they see you being self-destructive. Chances are that, like most of us, you operate on "automatic pilot" a lot of the time, unaware of both what you're doing right and what you're doing wrong. Designating a "buddy" (the way you were assigned a buddy while swimming as a kid) whose sole function is to sound an alarm when you're sliding back into your rebel model can be a huge help in stopping.

As a rebel you may have offended key people whom you would do well to apologize to. Do a careful audit of people you work with to identify anyone who should be on this apology list. Then plan what you want to say. Scripting and role-playing can be a great help. Having written out and edited and reedited the words, then saying them aloud in practice (and then editing them yet again) can make them come out just the way you want and make you feel a lot more comfortable. You want to have a conversation in which you say something like the following: "Hey, Mark, I've been thinking lately about the stand I took on the X issue last season, and about how dug in to my position I got. I was really talking more out of stubbornness, and I want to apologize for that. At this point it's clear that you were right and I was wrong, and I'm sorry I got so pigheaded about it." Be ready for an expression of astonishment and disbelief. If you've been the organizational rebel for a long time, you may not be believed at first, but it's important to do it anyway.

As we point out in Chapter 5 regarding the bulldozer, it's important, when you're apologizing and making amends, that you don't get defensive if the other person takes the opportunity to express his or her anger. Don't follow up your peace accord with a new attack!

Learning to be more aware of where, when, and with whom you tend to go into rebel mode is crucial. One way to do that is to learn the signals your body gives you when you feel the need to rebel. Do you begin rolling your eyes, or sighing, or jiggling one of your legs? Be on guard against the rebel pattern in situations where it is most likely to emerge, and take action immediately when it begins. Usually this means finding some way to break off the contact. Your cell phone could suddenly fail. Perhaps you may discover you've left an important paper back at your desk. Or there is another call coming in. These white lies may help you to regain control of your behavior.

We want to make one final point on this pattern of behavior. It's not rebelliousness itself that's the problem, it's the *pattern* that's the problem. There are always going to be times when the right thing to do is to stand up against the authority in power. Constant rebellion, though, like constant loud music or a steady diet of one kind of food, loses its "punch" and effectiveness. If you need to be a rebel occasionally, be a good one, an effective one—and a *live* one. The best rebels know what battles are worth fighting and other ways of getting things done when rebellion is not the answer.

CHAPTER
SEVEN

ALWAYS SWINGING FOR THE FENCE*

THE BATTER STEPS UP TO THE PLATE WITH ONE OUT. THE runner representing the winning run—one of the fastest base runners in the league—is on third. The manager knows he's taking a chance sending a rookie to the plate in his first game in the majors. But all the kid needs to do is loft a nice fly ball to right field, allowing the runner to tag up and run home. Instead, however, the rookie swings with all his might—once, twice, three times—going for the two-run homer instead of trying to bring his teammate home, and he strikes out. It happens in baseball, and it happens in every other arena as well.

It was his mother who brought our client Warren to us, practically dragging him through the door. As far as Warren was concerned, he didn't need help. Sure, he had struck out a couple of times (those were the words he actually used), but he could turn his career around in an instant with a single swing of the bat, so to speak. Warren was twenty-seven years old, and he had never brought home a paycheck. Straight out of school—an excellent Ivy League MBA program—Warren had decided to start his own company. He pursued this avenue against all the

*"Swinging for the fence" is a term used in baseball meaning swinging as hard as possible in order to hit the ball over the outfield fence for a home run.

advice of his colleagues, friends, and teachers, despite the fact that he had no prior business experience. In fact, no one in his family had any business experience.

Warren's first company was a "high end" errand service catering to wealthy residents living on New York's Upper West Side. The enterprise failed in less than a year. Next, he and a friend from business school created an Internet company to help wealthy travelers find exotic vacation spots that had connections to first-rate medical facilities. That one went under in about eight months. When Warren's mother finally persuaded him to come to us, he was about to take a third fling at entrepreneurship, negotiating to buy a vineyard in Washington State.

Stop him, Warren's mother more or less pleaded, before he ruins not only his career, but the lives of his wife and two-year-old baby as well. Tell him to take a regular job. The suggestion that he take an ordinary job made Warren turn away from his mother in disgust.

THE DYNAMICS OF THE PATTERN

Warren is an example of what we sometimes call a "home run hitter," someone always swinging for the proverbial fence, who expects—demands—extraordinary and immediate success. Small accomplishments will not do. The home run hitter wants it all, and he wants it now. In some way it is unthinkable, embarrassing, for such people to work their way up from the bottom.

In the business world, such people refuse to take a position with anything other than the top company or firm in the industry; they want to start, if not at the top, at least in a job where there is a strong chance of standing out immediately. Or the home run hitter determines to go it alone, setting out to create the next Amazon.com or Microsoft. To this individual, the notion of spending time learning more about the industry he or she is going into and learning more about managing, marketing, fulfillment, leading, hiring the right people—all the elements of "business savvy" that one can acquire only with time and experience—is like joining the military as a private when you could be starting your own army!

Such people tend to be overconfident and overeager. They want instant gratification. The home run hitter often hears the applause in his or her mind before undertaking any action. Because home run hitters "go for broke," they sometimes do just that: go broke. They act this way with their finances as well, betting everything on one or two companies in terms of their investments. They may buy houses, furniture, cars, clothes, and vacations as if they'd already hit the home run, when in fact their success is highly questionable. And by overextending themselves financially, they put even more pressure on themselves to make that "big score." One managing director of an investment bank shook his head in amazement at the spending habits of his young associates in their first year out of business school (and thus usually already in some serious debt). "It's just amazing," he said. "They spend as if there's no tomorrow. It's got to be the Lexus, and it's got to be today. Some of them drive more expensive cars than I do!"

We do not want to give the impression that the behaviors in this pattern are reserved for the young and overeager. There are plenty of people who are older and none the wiser—and just as overeager. One client described her father as someone "always chasing dreams, always after the big deal, the 'next big thing.' " And he never stopped. Marissa talked at length about how he was always looking for "sure things" that would be "big things" and about how her mother was the one who had to have both feet on the ground.

"Not having their feet on the ground" is a characteristic of people whose behaviors fit this pattern, and in some way it echoes the big plans that children have. "*I'm* going to be president when I grow up," they say, or "*I'm* going to become the richest person in the world." It is a fantasy we expect in children; we worry when a child doesn't have an active imagination and fantasy life. But unlike most children, the home run hitters never stop such unrealistic dreaming. They continue looking for the grand slam, the deal that will justify their actions to date.

Perhaps we sometimes think of these home run hitters as being young because they *act* young, no matter how old they are. In Aesop's fable of the ant and the grasshopper, the ant diligently works gathering food for the winter, while the grasshopper, living for the moment, plays his life away. People with this behavior pattern are not so much like the grasshopper as they are the opposite of the ant, uninterested in working hard and "scoring singles."

People of any age or stage in life can be seen acting out this youthful fantasy. One client, well into his fifties, "played" the stock market at a level far beyond his ability to sustain the losses he might incur. He looked with disdain at friends who invested in mutual funds or—even worse—index funds that were tied directly to the value of the market. He was going for the big score, the killer investment that would have a return in the hundreds of percentage points and make him a wealthy man. No amount of losses discouraged him from his strategy, betting heavily in hopes of hitting the big one. Another former client who worked as an independent stockbroker spent far too much time and energy trying to win the accounts of individuals with exceedingly high net worth, the heavy hitters. He would have been far more successful spending 90 percent of his time going after the small and medium-size clients he could more confidently land.

Some people play out this dynamic in a completely different arena, that of finding a mate. In looking for a marriage (or other) partner, they hold out for the perfect mate. All of us know someone who is whiling away his or her time waiting for that "perfect pitch," someone who'll score at least a nine in every category, "Mr. or Ms. Right."

This pattern doesn't have to be played out in its most extreme form to impede your career—or other parts of your life. Perhaps you don't set your sights on the million-dollar sales, ignoring all other possibilities. Maybe you look around occasionally and notice one of the smaller but easier to pick, low-hanging fruit. But you still overlook a dozen bushels that you could have picked just as easily.

One can overreach when only three feet off the ground just as easily as when three *thousand* feet up, scaling a sheer rock face. Consider the new college graduate who insists on applying only for jobs for which the probability of his or her being hired is in the hundredths of a percentage point. This is someone right on the ground, starting a career as a home run hitter with a succession of strikeouts. Consider all the people who apply only to colleges where admission is *most* highly competitive (with no "safety schools" in the mix); or the real estate broker who insists on beating his or her head against the wall to get to represent only *the* most highly valued properties. Both are swinging for the fence, with a high probability of failure.

In his excellent book on investment strategies, *Winning the Loser's Game,* Charles Ellis asserts that the most common mistake people make—whether in playing tennis or in picking stocks—is in trying to hit the "killer shot" on the court or make the "killer investment" in the market. In fact, he says, the way to win most tennis matches (excepting at the top professional level) is to simply stay in the match and, point by point, allow your opponent to try to hit the killer shot—and miss. He goes on to prove his point with regard to investing in equities. Home run hitters would do well to heed his advice before they quit their jobs to become day traders.

The truth is that most organizations don't rely year to year on the spectacular—the home run—to get by. They rely on the simply excellent and reliable—on predictable, sustained growth. The movie and book industries count on blockbusters to a certain extent to carry them and therefore tolerate a fair number of failures, but they are unusual. Most industries don't operate that way. An automobile company bringing new models to market, or an investment bank bringing new companies to market, is not likely to survive if two out of three introductions are failures.

THE HOME RUN HITTER IN AN ORGANIZATION

If the home run hitter joins a large company, he or she tends to volunteer to run projects that are far beyond his or her ability. Sometimes the company will be forgiving of young employees who fail in an assignment because they tend to go for it all rather than laying the foundation for future growth. They chalk up the failure to youthful exuberance and a sense of ambition that—in part—they want. But the home run hitter can't stop swinging away, doesn't back off and learn from his or her mistakes, trying something a bit more manageable next time. In fact, the person may now feel even more pressure to do something grand in order to compensate for a previous failure. The pattern almost guarantees that they will fail again.

Ultimately the company encourages the home run hitter to move on somewhere else, giving him or her great references and acknowledging his or her ambition, energy, and ingenuity. Sadly, the home run hitter only repeats the same pattern at the next job, with predictable results. Over the years the home run hitter accumulates a lot of frequent-failure miles.

Unlike the person for whom no job is good enough (the "coulda-been" from Chapter 10), who also craves acclaim but is so terrified of failure that he or she never tries or steps up to the plate, the home run hitter never hesitates to take the plunge. The home run hitter's obsession is with time—he or she is determined to score a big success in a hurry. And the person swinging for the fence tends to go it alone, seeking applause as he or she makes his or her way—alone—around the bases.

There are, of course, people who become extraordinarily successful at very young ages. This is particularly true in the Internet age, where it seems that new twenty-something billionaires are minted every week. Bill Gates dropped out of Harvard and look at him today. But Gates is a risky role model to follow. The odds overwhelmingly favor those who stick it out and graduate.

Most home run hitters adopt this pattern of behavior at a very young age. But there is a second type of home run hitter who materializes in middle age, during what has come to be called (rather disparagingly) a "midlife crisis." Recognizing that he or she is never going to become president of the company, or be pictured on the cover of *Fortune* or *Business Week*, or become enormously wealthy following the current course, such people become restless. Then, miracle of miracles, they suddenly find themselves with what looks like an opportunity to hit that home run, to make that big score. The opportunity may be far beyond the reach of his or her experience and competence. The person takes a swing and misses, sometimes losing career, house, and retirement savings in the process.

Several years ago we worked with a client who was just about to leave his secure position, as chief operating officer of a company that manufactured electrical supplies such as cable, switches, sockets, and circuit breaker boxes, to "go for it" (his words)—to try to buy a company in a tangentially related industry. Mark was not in a personal financial position to be able to afford failure, and the risk he was considering was high (the first barrier was getting the financial backing to make the deal; he then had to negotiate the sale and successfully take over and turn around the unprofitable business). Why do this? Simply put, at age fifty Mark didn't feel as if he had "made it." He wanted to roll the dice to give himself one last thrilling try. Fortunately we were able to dissuade him from this course of action, but the pull he felt was amazingly strong.

THE ORIGINS OF THE HOME RUN HITTER

What are the origins of a home run hitter's compulsion? There are several seeds from which this pattern grows. Sometimes the person is the progeny of distinguished parents, a member of a family of high achievers. Much is expected of him or her, although it is never clear just how much or what. Is graduating in the top 5 percent of the class enough? The family always *seems* to be expecting an even more impressive feat— and right away. The trajectory has to keep curving upward to some ill-defined "ultimate" success. In fact, of course, the person's parents and other family members may already be enormously proud of his or her achievements. But the individual doesn't know that, or at least is unconvinced of it.

The message the home run hitter hears (whether real or imagined) is that if you're not successful, you just don't measure up. In an example of such a message being communicated in real terms, the father of one of our clients was the chief executive of a major bank in New York. The father made it clear to his son, in just so many words, that his love and respect were directly dependent on his son's achievements. Our client said in his father's defense that his father's requirements were okay and that he himself didn't think he'd love his own son if he were not a high achiever.

Another driving force behind this behavior pattern is the Oedipal dynamic, the desire to defeat and supplant one's father. In a subtle variation, the son seeks to vindicate or redeem his father's own perceived failures, settling scores with those who injured or humiliated his father. Such was the case with our client Warren.

Warren's father had been a high school teacher. As Warren saw it, his father was always treated condescendingly by his contemporaries with more lucrative careers. Even though his father seemed to be dedicated to and challenged by his career, Warren absorbed the community's slights and put-downs and grew up bitterly resentful. He was determined to redeem his father—and his family name—and make himself more successful as it is defined by contemporary American upper-middle-class culture. He dreamed of buying a house for his parents in the best part of town. In this way he would both defeat his father and elevate him. Merely taking an ordinary job would be to be just like his dad, a cog in a machine, looked down on by those above him. He would be at the mercy of the organization. It was this intense (and unconscious) desire that was the engine driving him to start business after business. Warren was determined to create his own kingdom, and create it now.

Another powerful dynamic in the creation of someone who thinks like a home run hitter is narcissism. Contrary to the popular perception of a narcissist as someone who is "full of himself," the narcissistic personality type in fact feels empty inside. He looks in the mirror and sees nothing. The only time he feels alive, as if he truly exists, is when other people applaud his performance, acting as the mirror that he can't see. Without the roar of the crowd he vanishes. He becomes invisible. One client who fit this pattern of swinging too hard, too early, was a classic narcissistic personality. Although he was barely out of business school, this young man wanted us to assure him that he was one of the most interesting, brightest, most memorable clients we'd ever had. What was most memorable about him, in fact, was his need for reassurance.

Other forces that fuel this behavior pattern are societal. One of those forces is largely healthy; the other is not. The healthy force is that American culture, including its business culture, is far more forgiving than most others. In Japan, the recent college graduate who turns down a job with a prestigious insurance company to take an entrepreneurial fling will find it difficult to swim back into the mainstream if he fails. The cost is high, and the risk is high, so the frequency of the behavior is diminished. Not so in America, where a young person can start up a company, for example, take an "at bat," strike out, and still get a second chance (although the probability of a third chance drops dramatically).

Sometimes making the decision *not* to swing for the fences can be the best thing you can do—even in terms of your résumé. One young man we worked with a few years ago was offered the chance to take over a newsletter in a major California city. It seemed a great opportunity to make a name for himself in a hurry and build a chain of newsletters. Local churches had created the newsletter as a movie guide to parents, explaining why particular films had been rated PG-13, R, and so forth. The churches would continue to screen the movies and write the reviews. All the young entrepreneur had to do was sell the newsletter.

The more he researched the project, however, the more discouraged he became. First, the editorial budget of a newsletter is relatively modest, so the churches' contribution was minimal. The greatest cost occurs in the hundreds of mailings it takes to get each handful of subscribers. Newsletters succeed by building masses of subscribers who remain loyal to the publications over time and who buy spin-off newsletters from the same publisher. But very few people have a long-term interest in considering what movies are suitable for young children after their own kids grow up. And there were few obvious opportunities for spin-offs.

Our client backed out of the project before he signed the contract. His question to us was how he could explain on his résumé the months he spent researching a project that was never launched. We advised him to be absolutely honest and unembarrassed about it. Prospective employers would be impressed that he has an entrepreneurial spirit, we told him, but that he didn't allow momentum or his ego to override the dictates of the facts. He followed our advice and soon landed a job that was a plum by anyone's standards.

The clearly *unhealthy* cultural force that drives the home run hitter is the ever-increasing pressure to succeed and make money fast—and an economy that makes it possible to do so. Other societies may honor wealth and position, and even fawn over those who have it, but no other people have as much respect for earned money as Americans. One of *Fortune* magazine's best-selling covers of all time carried the smiling portraits of Warren Buffett and Bill Gates, with the net worth of each emblazoned alongside. It was a cover of two people America both admires and envies.

"Get rich quick" and "Go for the gold" are strong cultural messages in America. Waiting and learning are certainly not seen as being nearly as desirable and "sexy" as racing two-hundred miles an hour across the finish line, as having your net worth go from a few thousand to twenty-five million dollars the day your company's stock goes public. To be fair to the home run hitters among us, a lot of people are telling us that making money the old-fashioned way is for chumps and losers.

Today, young professionals in their twenties are offered as a standard for success the image of a billionaire entrepreneur running his or her own company by age thirty on the new frontier of e-commerce. In an earlier day people served an apprenticeship in trades and in companies, gaining experience in their twenties and thirties and learning from older, more experienced colleagues. By the time you were in your forties you were taking over. You learned how to swing for the fence by developing your skills and experience and waiting for the right pitch and the right situation. In a dot.com organization today the CEO is twenty-eight years old and everybody else is twenty-four. With the news full of stories of twenty- and thirty-somethings worth hundreds of millions of dollars, we feel like losers if we've hit thirty-five or forty and aren't independently wealthy.

Because of his inner need to redeem his father, and the external pressure to make it in a society that celebrates immediate success, Warren, whom we met earlier, swung for the bleachers. His first attempt failed because he had not done his "due diligence" regarding market demand and the competition. As he discovered, he was going after too small a market, one that was already too crowded.

The idea for his next venture was seriously flawed as well. By and large, folks concerned about medical services are the elderly. Today's elderly have not been raised on the computer. They don't automatically turn to the Internet for information, as thirty-year-olds are likely to do. In addition, people with health concerns are less likely to be interested in exotic vacation spots than are people in good health; a connection to good medical treatment was not enough to get them to sign on for trips to Tierra del Fuego. If they were going to need hospital care, they wanted it at home, no matter how good the care might be four-thousand miles away. Warren's business failed again. And about his third business, vineyards and wine, Warren knew nothing other than that he liked wine and that his friends would be impressed.

We had some lengthy meetings with Warren and asked him to read John Kotter's *The General Managers* to learn about what general managers (managers with ultimate profit-and-loss responsibility for their lines of business) really do, day by day and hour by hour. Then we asked him how much he knew of what the general managers in the book had mastered. How much of what they did day to day did he feel competent doing? We had him do an analysis of his assets and deficits. We asked him to find out what his MBA classmates were doing. Were they fabulously successful entrepreneurs? It turned out that the overwhelming majority were still in apprentice jobs.

That was where Warren belonged as well. His mother knew it; his wife knew it; we knew it. And finally he came to know it. First, he had to go through a grieving process over the death of his dream. He was not going to roll into town in a limousine and pick up his father at the high school, whisking him and his mother off to Paris on the Concorde for a long weekend. He was not going to see himself on the cover of *Fortune* with Gates and Buffett ("the other Warren"). He was not going to appear at his fifth-year business school reunion the envy of all of his classmates. He was going to accept a regular job and learn what it takes to run a business, in hopes that one day he would be able to do just that. Fortunately, the treatment worked, and today Warren manages a significant division in a cable television company. Someday he may even hit his home run.

HOW TO BREAK THE PATTERN

First, you should seek out seasoned professionals in your industry to get precisely the same kind of information we just described. How did they get their training? What experiences were most valuable for them? What would they do differently if they could? If they are familiar with your organization and your particular situation, ask for advice about the best next career-building step.

The remedies for most of the other twelve patterns of behavior we've described involve taking a variety of actions aimed at reversing the patterns that are holding people back. The remedy for the mind-set behind swinging for the fences, by contrast, involves *not* doing, *not* acting. The external change we're looking for is like that when you go on a weight-loss diet and have to stop eating high-calorie/high-fat foods. You need to *stop* trying to do too much or going for the big score—*stop* trying to hit those home runs.

One man we worked with several years back had come to us with a résumé that looked like the itinerary for an around-the-world cruise: two years in this port, eighteen months in that, a year here, a year there. No home runs, lots of swings and misses, and when he came to us he was virtually unemployable. He really had been kicked off the team. If you persist in such thinking and act in such a way, you could be, too.

The "work" you need to do to overcome this syndrome is largely psychological. First, you need to understand why you feel as if you have to hit home runs; you need to learn how to battle those demons. What are you trying to prove? Why are you so interested in grandstanding? Why do you feel such a need to be heralded as a star? The father of one of our clients had been enormously successful, in part because he was just in the right place at the right time, and he gave his son a precious gift when he told him (quite truthfully), "Don't try to compete with me, because at least 80 percent of my success was just plain luck."

Are *you* trying to gain someone's approval? Make yourself be seen as someone special? We've worked with many clients who at age forty or fifty are just realizing that for most of their careers they've been trying to get the attention and approval of an important person in their lives. Some of them had so internalized this need that it persisted even though the parent (for example) they sought approval from was no longer living. That parent lived on, however, in the client's emotional memory. Until that time, these clients had never fully acknowledged how much this desire had affected their behavior and life choices. Sometimes you already *have* the approval you're seeking but have never fully accepted or acknowledged it. Alternatively, you may be looking for approval from someone who is simply unable to provide it. By recognizing what you've been doing and why, you can reassess whether or not this is something you want to continue acting on.

We all know people who have done more, and more quickly, than we have. But focusing on other people's needs and successes is a recipe that is likely to lead to misery, if not catastrophe. You need to decide what is best for you, given your own talents, energy, abilities, strengths, and weaknesses. You may get to your destination a little later than some of the others around you, but you're more likely to *get there* if you progress at the speed that makes sense for you.

In order to accomplish this difficult task of developing patience, it is critical to remember that being patient, waiting until you have the right skills and knowledge, and waiting for the right time to put them into play does *not* mean resigning yourself to a life of mediocrity or a life of quiet desperation. It means just what it says: being patient, developing your skills, and developing your career so that when the moment is right you can swing away, knowing it's the time and place to do so. To this end we encourage the home run hitters we work with to change their computer screen savers to read "Less is more!"

MANAGING A HOME RUN HITTER

If you have an employee under you whom you recognize as someone who frequently swings for the fence, ask yourself, "Do they always seem to have 'big eyes' for high-profile projects? Do they have a history of going for the gold when they should be learning how to play the sport? Do they compare themselves unfavorably with those few people who have become high-level executives at an unusually young age? Do they have a work history that includes a string of failures in going after the big score, with fewer more modest successes?"

As a manager, you have the leverage of compensation to help employees attempt to change. You also have the ability to pull back on the type and number of tasks you assign to the person. Although he or she may jump at the chance to take on a new position in on-line sales, you may choose a more seasoned employee, telling the home run hitter that you chose someone else *because* of the person's more extensive experience and demonstrated savvy. You need to make clear that your choosing someone else is not a slight or an insult, nor is it a matter of "waiting your turn." You, as the business leader, have a responsibility to do everything you can to make the business a success, and it is simply a business decision—the home run hitter just isn't ready to take on a job that requires steadier incremental long-term progress.

Point out, as gently as possible, that the employee has a pattern of trying to "work beyond his means" (just as some people live beyond their means). Explain that you want to ensure his future success by applying the brakes just a little. One response you're likely to hear is, "But the only way I can learn is to do it." Well, that's not really true. You can learn a lot by observing closely how other people work and achieve success. And how they fail. Explain to the person that right now they've been failing more than they've been succeeding. Tell them that you occasionally use them as a case in point on how *not* to get ahead. This is almost certain to stop the person in his tracks. "Me, a potential star, being used as an example of someone who is failing?" This is not something anyone wants to hear, but it is especially tough for a would-be home run champ. Look, you might say, if you want to get stronger by lifting weights, and you load four hundred pounds on a barbell for your first bench press, it'll inevitably be your last. Now if I'm your coach, a "personal trainer," I'd be remiss in my duties if I let you do this, right? So let's talk about how to get to the point where you *can* bench-press those four hundred pounds.

The point of this discussion is to try to rationalize career development, to take it out of the realm of the stratospheric accomplishments of the twenty-nine-year-old dot.com millionaires and Bill Gates, and bring it down to earth, to the individual sitting in your office. Point out how important the work is that the employee is doing now and help the person to feel good about what he or she is doing today, and yesterday, and what you want tomorrow. In other words, make it clear that the person is *already* succeeding.

It's important to be as specific as you can about the skill areas the employee needs to develop. Make it clear that the next assignments that you have in mind for him or her are intended to help develop these skills. If possible, give examples of how successful senior executives he or she knows developed *their* abilities with lesser assignments early in their careers. As much as you are able to, give the person a sense of the types of assignments and even the sequence of those assignments that are likely to build the best platform for success in your industry. This doesn't require any commitment to making those opportunities available; the point is to make clear that career *development* is precisely that—something that unfolds in a more or less predictable way over time.

Home run hitters need to remind themselves of what they *have* done—not what they haven't. In Robert Bolt's prize-winning play about Sir Thomas More, *A Man for All Seasons*, a friend who desires to become a part of the court of Henry VIII laments that he feels insignificant, that no one important knows what he does. "Why not be a teacher?" More asks. "You'd be a fine teacher. Perhaps even a great one." "And if I was, who would know it?" he retorts. More responds, "You, your pupils, your friends, God. Not a bad public, that." And not bad advice for those of us who, always focused on the distant fences, miss the joy of the game being played right in front of us.

CHAPTER

EIGHT

WHEN FEAR IS IN THE DRIVER'S SEAT

IN A DECADE IN WHICH THE U.S. ECONOMY HAS GROWN WITHOUT interruption, an age of ebullient optimism in which all things seemed possible, Mike was increasingly out of step with the times. Persistently negative and a chronic worrier, he was someone who could—and did— see the downside of most situations and the upside of few. Terrified of risk and change, he was committed to preserving the status quo at all costs, because he so clearly saw the risks inherent in change, and worried himself and those around him to a state of paralysis.

Mike was what we call a *pessimist-worrier,* a naysayer. If he were identified with a literary character, it would be Eeyore, the woeful donkey in *Winnie-the-Pooh*. Indeed, "Eeyore" is what Mike's colleagues at work nicknamed him, so closely had they come to associate him with negativity over the years.

Mike was in charge of external communications for a world-renowned teaching hospital in New York City. It was his dream job, one of unassailable prestige and security, and Mike was determined to do whatever it took to protect the hospital's name and image. Nothing was more important to him, because in his mind there was no distinction between the hospital and himself. What damaged the hospital threatened him. As he saw it, change within or without the hospital made it vulnerable. So he instinctively resisted any and all change. His fear of change was so great that he almost drove himself out of a job.

THE DYNAMICS OF THE PATTERN

We use the term *pessimist-worrier* to describe his behavior pattern because the pattern really involves two separate but inextricably linked dynamics. First, people who follow this behavior pattern have an essentially pessimistic view of the world and everything in it they encounter. They look at the glass and see it as half-empty. Moreover, they see the level decreasing through evaporation and see the contaminants that might make their way into the glass. All of this has a basis in reality. It's just not what most people think of and worry about first. Robert F. Kennedy, paraphrasing George Bernard Shaw, said in a speech, "Some men see things as they are and ask, 'Why?' I dream things that never were and ask, 'Why not?'" Kennedy's statement is the antithesis of such pessimism. The pessimist imagines all of the possible negative outcomes of any action, of which there are bound to be many, for change of real importance always involves risk.

Moreover, they don't compare the pros and cons of option "A," then the pros and cons of option "B," then the pros and cons of option "C." Instead, they compare the pros of "A" to the cons of "A" *and* "B" *and* "C"; then the pros of "B" to the cons of "B" *and* "A" *and* "C"; and so forth. No wonder, then, that the negative for such people always seems to outweigh the positive. The second dynamic is that the pessimist-worrier fails to consider the possible consequences of *not* changing. As a result, the balance almost always is stacked against change. Under these circumstances, the world begins to look like a pretty scary place.

What is the "worrier" element of the pessimist-worrier pattern? Studies conducted comparing *anxiety* and *excitement* have found that the sole difference between the two is whether the person foresees success or failure. Anxiety, or worry, is the psychological handmaiden of pessimism. If we *think* that something bad may happen, in some way it makes sense then to *feel* anxious about it. The process of worrying at least makes the person feel better, more active and empowered (even if this is not true—worrying about whether a storm is going to hit, or whether our plane is going to stay aloft, for example, will have no effect on the outcomes).

So this behavior pattern has two psychological "engines": seeing the negative and almost nothing *but* the negative; and worrying about it to excess. The behavior itself is simple. But it is capable of causing enormous damage, raising the anxiety level of other people in the organization by bringing to the fore the possible negative consequences of any proposed change.

Pessimist-worriers are often driven by exaggerated feelings of shame and embarrassment. They are extremely sensitive to making mistakes and doing things that would fall short of expectations. This is fueled, in turn, by the acute shame they experience when those mistakes or shortfalls come to light.

To the extent that this avoidance drives one's behavior at work, it will also drive how one is oriented to see the world outside of work. A moderately excessive worrier at work is almost certain to be a moderately excessive worrier at home or in his or her personal relationships. A person who is *intensely* pessimistic and worrisome at work will be just as negative in the outside world. Although many people love to gossip about how bad things are over lunch or a drink after work, most people grow tired of spending time with someone always looking at (and talking about) the negative. Over time it can drive apart a relationship or marriage. Who, after all, wants to spend his or her time (let alone life) with someone who is always forecasting gloom and doom? Moreover, such an outlook on life is frequently contagious. It's easy to pass on your exaggerated concerns and negative outlook on the world to your children and others around you. And to the extent that your own actions are driven by feelings of shame, fear, and a sense of pessimism, your children will learn to feel and fear shame as well.

Like most people, pessimist-worriers project their feelings onto others, imagining and assuming that others feel the same way about things as they do. They assume, for example, that other people are as prone to feeling shame as they are and thus are equally worried about the downside of things. These concerns and assumptions are then played out in their work. As a result, their careers will be compromised unless they can modify this pattern. Pessimist-worriers have a role in certain professional positions, such as risk analysis and quality control. People with that kind of outlook make good proofreaders, information system and software testers, and airplane mechanics—jobs that focus on ensuring nothing will go wrong. However, a sine qua non of leadership is the willingness to take risks, to be wrong, and to take the hit if a decision is wrong. The worst thing a leader can do is to make no decision at all about an important issue, out of fear of making the wrong call. Leadership is not for those who are afraid to take risks. As one moves from sales or production or services to management, where the need for leadership increases, there is an increasingly poor fit between the pessimist-worrier and the position. As a result, people who exhibit such behavior rarely rise above first-line management.

THE CHRONIC WORRIER IN AN ORGANIZATION

Although pessimists usually think of themselves as protectors of an organization or culture, they can easily act as destroyers of innovation and creativity. Their effect is, sadly, toxic. When someone in the organization suggests an initiative—a new product or service, a change in a process or organizational structure, or a new way of marketing old products—the pessimist's response is often, "What if it doesn't work?"

That alone is sometimes enough to chill or kill an idea. We're all capable of feeling anxiety, and when one person starts to worry excessively and publicly—for a good reason or bad—people start to pick up that signal and start to worry themselves. Anxiety, like other emotions, has a "contagious" element, like a *very* fast-acting flu virus. Watch what happens the next time you're in a meeting and one person starts to express anxiety—not simply voice a question about the practicality of whatever is being discussed, but real anxiety and concern. You'll likely see that anxiety spread around the table or room, even if its basis in reality is faint. Psychologists sometimes refer to this as "free-floating anxiety," a chronic sense of unease not caused by a genuine threat. It can quickly attach itself to specific issues (suddenly, the "free-floating" worry becomes a specific worry about whether or not the oven was turned off). If there is a *real* threat, obviously it is adaptive for one person's concern to spread throughout the group. Unfortunately, free-floating anxiety spreads just as easily as legitimate concern, as you'll see.

The pessimist can be especially harmful when he or she is in a position to hire people, because people with this behavior pattern tend first to set exceedingly high thresholds that applicants must clear in order to be hired; and second, such people tend to hire others like themselves. The result? When the pessimist raises the objection "What if it doesn't work?" several people nod in agreement. It amplifies the company's or group's anxiety. It's like turning the old stereotype of hiring a yes-man on its head, and hiring no-men and -women instead.

Of course, every organization needs people willing to speak their minds and offer a reality check to plans or expectations that are unrealistic, people who, because of their long experience, can point out the pitfalls of a new idea or plan. Sometimes such people can remember that the organization has already tried an initiative that colleagues are now considering again and recall the problems that were encountered. This is one aspect of "institutional memory." But it is only one aspect, because there may be ways in which the situation today might be more favorable for implementing the initiative. But when people see *only* the pitfalls, and are unable to suggest constructive ways to proceed with a new plan and avoid them, they become *inhibitors* rather than problem solvers. And the costs they incur by squelching innovation and creativity in the end far outweigh the benefits they provide. That is the way people who exhibit this behavior pattern hurt the group and hurt themselves. They certainly will never be promoted and may, in fact, one day find themselves expendable.

To put it bluntly, no one likes to be around someone who is always a "downer," even if the ostensible reason for each negative comment is to do what's right for the organization. When other people come to see it as a pattern, they begin to think, "Uh-oh, here comes Jack, get ready for bad news." What is worse, though, is when people don't just think it, but begin to say it to one another or seek to protect their new ideas from you so you don't have a chance to shoot them down. This kind of poisonous behavior can have drastic consequences for your career.

These negative consequences are by no means limited to people in mid-career. If you are just starting off on your career and are the person always voicing the gloom and doom "what if" concerning any change, people are going to learn to avoid working with you or having you on their teams. If you are unwilling to embrace change and see the positive opportunities around you, your success is likely to be further limited by your not taking appropriate chances with your own career in terms of new assignments or positions.

Moreover, the same hypersensitivity to feelings of shame that lead the pessimist-worrier to avoid change often lead to procrastination, which can in turn lead to early career failure. Procrastination, as we discuss in "Looking in the Mirror" (Part II), is a function not of laziness or inability but of being overly concerned with whether the outcome of the work is going to be good enough. Pessimist-worriers focus on the possibility—however remote—that their work will be seen as inadequate (and, by extension in their minds, that they personally will be seen as inadequate and will be shamed). They then unconsciously seek to avoid, or at least delay, that event by not completing their projects at all—what isn't seen can't be judged, and some pessimist-worriers prefer to take the blame for not getting things done rather than risk a negative judgment.

This behavior pattern can also be seen when managers micromanage their subordinates' work. In this instance the manager is focused on the "worrier" side of the pessimist-worrier combination, and the worry is that an employee's work will in some way be inadequate and an embarrassment to the manager. In the same way someone might fret about whether they remembered to lock the door when they left, the manager whose behavior fits this pattern frets, worries, sometimes obsesses, about whether the people under them caught all the typos, whether all the figures add up, and so forth. Of course, managers are paid to ensure that the work done by the people in their departments is of high quality—so the line between "just managing" and "micromanaging" isn't easy to define. But if people you manage frequently complain that you go over the line and "micromanage," try not to just dismiss their comments. Think about whether your behavior might be the result of the pessimist-worrier behavior rather than (or, perhaps, in addition to) your simply wanting to be a good manager.

Shooting ideas down doesn't necessarily mean you are a naysayer. One of our clients laughingly told us about her experience working with a group of "high creatives," as she called them. She is a high-energy, high-drive, "get it done" individual who operates with her feet on the ground (although usually only one at a time, since she's constantly on the run). "These guys hated me," she told us. "They thought I was the Grinch that stole Christmas. They'd come up with all these great plans when I was out for a day, and all I'd do was say, 'Great idea, guys! It's just too bad we have gravity on this planet, isn't it?' And they'd all say, 'Rats, gravity! We forgot about that!' But what could I do?" In fact, we found, they didn't really hate her, as irritated as they might be on occasion. She truly was "grounded." If someone had a new concept that didn't have a fatal flaw, she was thrilled. Someone who acts as a reality check is *not* the same as someone who acts out the role of a pessimist-worrier.

But—if you're usually the one who leads the crusade against the new ideas (especially if you're the *only* crusader), you may be in danger. Even if you perceive yourself not as a pessimist-worrier, but rather as a hard-nosed realist—which is how most of the people who fall into this pattern see themselves—take a second look. Perhaps instead of worrying about possible changes you should begin worrying about the effects of your negativity on your career.

The real pessimist-worrier, by his or her very nature, prefers business as usual. But a dynamic economy has no patience with such thinking. Any company in an industry that's doing business the same way today as ten years ago is almost certainly doing business the wrong way. The smartest companies, of course, see change coming and adjust their strategies long before it hits them broadside. The old paradigm "If it ain't broke, don't fix it" has gone by the boards. The new paradigm seems to be "If it ain't broke, break it before somebody else does, and see what else we can make of it." Although this is especially true in high-growth, high-change industries like e-commerce, Web-centric businesses, and other high-tech industries, it holds true now even for what were formerly thought of as traditional industries such as automobile manufacturing, energy, and agribusiness. In an earlier era, people who acted as pessimists or worriers could take refuge in an organization that was hierarchical, based on tradition, and inclined to resist change. These were often the premier organizations in their fields, solidly established in the marketplace and more focused on holding their lead than innovating in order to increase it. No longer. Very few organizations today are leading their sectors so securely that they can afford to avoid change. Those within the company who resist ways of doing things better and less expensively run the serious risk of being pushed aside—or out.

THE ORIGINS OF THE PESSIMIST-WORRIER

There are two very different origins of this pessimist-worrier pattern. One has its roots in a background of privilege, the equivalent of being a runner with the inside track. These are people who were born into "the flow of success" (to borrow a term coined by Sharon Parks in her 1993 book, *Can Ethics Be Taught?* (coauthored with Tom Piper and Mary Gentile). They tend to be from upper-middle-class or upper-class families, are bright, well liked, and articulate, and have typically had the advantage of a good education. They are people who have grown up in environments where their own success was always taken for granted—and expected. Their only experience in life has been success, and the result is a deep concern over whether they will be able to flourish in an environment that is less fertile. They are more concerned with staying within that flow of success than anything else. They work hard and do anything asked of them, as long as they feel certain that they can remain in the flow. A senior managing director in a major strategy consulting firm lamented to us, "The kids [graduates of top MBA programs, law schools, and so on] we're hiring these days will do *anything* we tell them—anything but take chances. All they seem to be concerned with is staying in the comfort zone so they can make sure they get promoted to the next level. The way they manage their careers (at age twenty-eight) is so conservative, it's like watching a pro basketball team play to hold on to a six-point lead—but it's still early in the second quarter!" They want to preserve whatever they have, whether it's position, money, or standing in the community.

One example of this kind of "high born" pessimist was a client of ours who inherited a manufacturing company that made alarm systems. His maternal grandfather had founded the business, and it had thrived well into the 1980s. But when the time came for our client to take over the business, the industry was changing from top to bottom, from the technology to the clientele. Our client was loath to change the business that his grandfather had begun. (It didn't help that his mother kept reminding him what a genius his grandfather had been.) Without consciously doing so, he made the decision to play it conservatively, trying to protect his market share by not taking any chances, by not making any mistakes. As things turned out, this in itself was a fatal mistake. Within five years of taking control of the business, he was forced to choose between selling or closing it down.

The second profile of the pessimist-worrier that we've seen is that of the outsider. This individual often comes from the "wrong side of the tracks" and has been raised, if not in poverty, at least in marginal economic circumstances. These individuals, not surprisingly, yearn for the security and respectability of a venerable institution and the protective shelter of an establishment. (The Great Depression of the 1930s produced an entire generation of people like this.) Through a little bit of luck and a lot of hard work, such people have managed to become insiders, to get positions in an establishment of unquestioned pedigree and impregnable financial strength. What then becomes essential in their thinking is that the institution lose none of its power and prestige, because that is what provides them security. And, of course, they are determined not to lose their positions within that institution. Not having been born into the flow of success, once they've made their way into it they'll do anything to stay there.

This sense of living at the margin can be economic in nature, as described earlier, or it can stem from other forces in a person's life, such as being raised in a nondominant religion within the community, being a member of a less privileged ethnic or racial group, growing up in a divorced or dysfunctional family, or in some other way seeing oneself as an outsider. We are not saying that being a member of a minority group necessarily produces such feelings of marginality. But a number of clients who exhibited this fearful feeling and behavior pattern told us they felt they were not part of the "mainstream," whatever the reason, and that now that they're "in the mainstream," they want to preserve that position at all costs.

WHAT THE PATTERN MEANS TO YOUR CAREER

Regardless of the origins of the behavior pattern, the subsequent dynamics are the same. One is the willingness to fight tooth and nail to retain the position the individual has achieved and an instinctive fear of change. They become naysayers out of fear. The other is an overidentification with the organization that provides the safe, secure identity. "I'm a [name of organization] person" is the message, both metaphorically and frequently literally, the person espouses. This overidentification is the reason the person is so willing to fight—both to hold the connection with the organization and to defend the source of good feeling, of being "inside."

Mike, whom we introduced at the beginning of the chapter, grew up on what he would later see as "the outside," from his vantage point, comparing himself with those who were more affluent. He was born in a small city in upstate New York, where his father was a guard at a correctional institution. Mike felt the family's low social and economic status keenly; he was ashamed of it and hated his background.

Mike was an outsider in an additional way. He was gay, and in his community to "come out" would have meant ridicule and isolation, and likely physical harm as well. Mike worried constantly that someone would discover his secret crushes on his classmates (although no one did). He was always on guard and rarely discussed his feelings with those around him because he was afraid that he might slip. Mike was bright; he got good grades, tested well, and earned an academic scholarship that enabled him to attend the State University of New York, where he majored in communications and graduated with honors.

His first job was with a newspaper in Pennsylvania, where he was respected as a careful and painstaking reporter, although not an inspired writer. He was determined to get a job in the big time in New York City. After he'd held a series of newspaper jobs in the New York suburbs, his solid, careful writing caught the eye of the vice president for public affairs of a major teaching hospital in the city. They were looking for someone to fill the position of director of external communications. Surveys among physicians and other medical professionals invariably ranked the hospital among the top twenty in the world; it was a name *every*one knew. Management was keenly aware that they were in the media spotlight at all times. They wanted to ensure that the light shone where they wanted it to shine and nowhere else; and they thought that Mike could help.

For his part, Mike felt he had finally "made it" into the establishment, and to the top, at least as far as his being a part of such a highly respected organization was concerned. Now he was determined to stay there. Mike's sexual orientation almost certainly would not have caused problems for him at the hospital. Some of his colleagues, including several physicians, were gay; they made no secret of the fact and suffered no negative consequences. Still, Mike's history made him keep his sexual orientation a secret. He had a lover from time to time but never confided the fact in anyone, even to the openly gay members of the hospital staff. He fabricated stories about having dates with women to cover himself. He was ecstatic about being in the flow, and he worried about doing anything outside the accepted norm that might upset his career.

Mike protected the hospital with a zeal that awed his colleagues. Others on the staff might criticize the hospital openly from time to time, and almost everyone occasionally poked fun at its more than occasional pomposity. Not Mike. He loved the hospital and everything about it.

Things went smoothly for Mike until the hospital stumbled into an ugly battle with the local community over construction of a new wing. Several shabby apartment houses in the neighborhood had to be razed to make way for the expansion. That was no loss to architecture, and not even much of a sacrifice by the tenants, who were found better housing nearby. Still, some community leaders felt that the hospital owed the neighborhood something in return. There were pickets and protests.

A dozen or so members of the hospital's executive administrative staff, Mike among them, sat around a conference table every Tuesday afternoon and discussed such issues. Someone suggested that as a payback the hospital offer well-baby care free of charge to all the infants in the neighborhood. Mike immediately spoke up in opposition. It was a dangerous precedent, he argued, the thin edge of the wedge. If the hospital gave away treatment for infants, the protesters might demand free care for the mothers as well and soon free care for everyone. Where would it end? Mike didn't have the authority to kill the idea, even though community relations was within his jurisdiction. But his objection was enough to chill it, and the idea quickly died. Some thought they were missing a great opportunity to foster goodwill at low cost, but they decided to gamble that the protests would gradually lose steam of their own accord, which they eventually did.

In Mike's third year at the hospital the world began to change. All of the city's hospitals were coming under tremendous competitive pressure, a dramatic increase resulting from changes in the entire landscape of the health care industry. The hospital's CEO, who had supported and promoted Mike, retired somewhat sooner than anyone had expected. The board hired a new president who was clearly much more of an activist than his predecessor. He was a great believer in reaching out for business rather than waiting for it to come through the door. He resurrected the idea of free well-baby care. It wouldn't cost the hospital much, he pointed out, and it would put the hospital in good standing with the city's politicians, the news media, and the population at large. Mike repeated his previous concerns. The new president noted Mike's objection, then dismissed it.

At a subsequent Tuesday staff meeting the new president announced that the time had come for the hospital to advertise. He planned to run commercials on local television promoting the hospital's experience and capability in obstetrics and fertility treatment. Mike opined it was undignified for a hospital to advertise. It made him think of personal injury lawyers hawking their wares on billboards outside Houston or Kansas City and might be interpreted by some as an act of desperation. This time the president of the hospital didn't even acknowledge Mike's protest. The commercials ran.

Mike began to suspect that his job was in danger, an opinion buttressed by a couple of his colleagues, so he came to us. We began with lengthy discussions about where he wanted his career to go. What if he did get fired or just decided to leave? What were his options, where did he think he was marketable, and where might he want to go from there? Many people in Mike's position (he was enviably "marketable" in light of his experience at the hospital) might smile at such suggestions and let themselves dream a bit about a future of multiple possibilities. Not Mike. Unsmiling, he made it clear that losing his job at the hospital was not an option. It would be an end to life as he knew it and wanted to know it. It was clear to us that as far as Mike was concerned, he and the hospital were one.

His alternatives were clear. He had to change the president or himself. Turning the president into more of a pessimist like himself was extremely unlikely. Right or wrong, he was a "glass half-full" type, unlikely to (what in Mike's view would be to) "come to his senses and focus on the dangers involved in his initiatives." The president was thoroughly self-confident and seemed to have the complete support of the board.

Mike was probably not going to be able to change his own nature, either, so deep was his conservatism, so pervasive his sense of worrying. But he could at least change his behavior at work. First, we asked him to make a small and simple alteration, but one that had symbolic significance. He created a new screen saver on his computer. In place of the monumental, century-old facade of the hospital, he substituted the initials TPOPT, "The Power of Positive Thinking," a tongue-in-cheek reference to Norman Vincent Peale's famous book of the 1950s. That was easy, but it had real significance to Mike—it meant that he was making the effort to change.

Then we asked Mike if he realized that—without meaning him any harm—his colleagues at the hospital were taking advantage of him. He wasn't the only one who was concerned that a new initiative might backfire and that there might be serious negative consequences. Everyone else was aware there was a downside, too. But why should they bother to make their point when they knew Mike could be depended on to raise the objection and that he—and not they—would be seen as the

Eeyore of the organization? If he were so willing to shoulder that reputation, why should they stand in his way? Mike was, in effect, voluntarily "taking the point" (the lead position in an infantry patrol—the person most likely to be shot); as long as he did that, everyone else got a free ride.

At our urging Mike tried an experiment to see if we were right about this. He kept his mouth shut the next time an initiative came up. Someone at the Tuesday meeting suggested a big Christmas holiday party and open house for people living in the neighborhood. Mike noticed that one or two people turned their eyes toward him. He kept quiet. After a bit someone else pointed out that the entire holiday season was especially busy for the emergency room and for the hospital staff in general. It might be great for the community, but the fear was that it would stress an already overstressed staff. Two or three others seconded that concern and raised their own. The idea collapsed without Mike's help, and he saw that even if he didn't raise the problem, someone else would. He didn't have to take on the role of protector of the institution singlehanded. He could even join the "yeasayers" and still count on someone else to balance things out as a "naysayer."

The next assignment we gave Mike was to break his silence by saying something positive. If someone proposed an initiative, Mike had to find a reason to like the idea, something that even the advocate hadn't thought of. Or, if someone objected to an initiative, Mike's job would be to defend it.

The opportunity came with the approach of the flu season. The hospital was planning to offer free immunization shots to everyone in the neighborhood over sixty-five. Someone at the Tuesday meeting—not Mike—complained that even though the hospital advertised the free shots every year at the local senior citizen clubs and elsewhere, very few old folks took advantage of the offer. Silence. Then Mike spoke up. "Why don't we try sending the message through the schools," he said. "Get the kids to tell their grandparents to get the shots and stay alive. Kids have enormous power over grandparents." More silence. Then someone—Mike isn't sure who—clapped his hands under the conference table. Within seconds Mike heard the sound of two dozen hands applauding.

HOW TO BREAK THE PATTERN

Eliminating or reducing your sense of worry if you are a pessimist-worrier requires reducing the pessimism, the watchful, wary quality with which you approach life every day. No one's basic worldview changes easily, and any changes that are made need to be watched over and protected with great care. If you are a pessimist, it's because you can't help it. Fear is a powerful force in creating and maintaining the seemingly protective hypervigilant concern that is part of the bedrock of such pessimism. Pointing out that nothing has happened will have little effect. "Of course nothing bad has happened," the person responds, "*yet*—but that's only because I've been constantly on guard against possible negatives. If I let down my guard, who knows what will happen!" With the pessimist-worrier the best defense is not a good offense—it's a good defense.

And in trying to help those who suffer from such thinking and behavior, the best strategy is neither defense nor offense—it's to join their team. So we agree with the naysayers that the world is indeed a dangerous place and that there is a real need to be on the alert for hidden dangers and unanticipated problems. We don't want to turn such people into Pollyannas—we just want to make them better at what they do. When scientists are testing the effectiveness of a new drug, they separate errors into two categories. Type I errors result from concluding that a drug is effective when in fact it is not; Type II errors occur when the drug is ruled ineffective when in reality it is effective. Scientists by nature focus on preventing Type I errors, or errors of commission. They want to make sure that nothing is done that is not proven beyond any doubt to be fail-safe. But they allow a multitude of Type II errors of omission, turning down drugs (or ideas) that are good ones. It's *that* behavior we want to change in the office, we say. If you are going to be an error spotter, at least be the best you can, the most productive and effective possible.

The game of chess provides a good metaphor. You need to think several moves ahead, looking out for traps you might not be able to get out of. But you also need to look for opportunities as well. The player who focuses entirely on defense can never become a consistently winning player. We sometimes tell the story of a friend of ours who, as a top-ranked college wrestler, was matched against an opponent from another school in a decisive meet. He considered his opponent to be superior both in strength and experience, and when that opponent fell into a trap early in the match (falling for a fake), our friend failed to capitalize on the opportunity and ultimately lost the match. He later recalled with chagrin that, at the split second the opportunity had presented itself, he had imagined how humiliated he would be if he were wrong, if his opponent weren't *really* falling for it and turned the tables, defeating him only seconds into the match. His focus on avoiding defeat actually caused his defeat.

Make a regular practice of considering the *positive* aspect of the change—the opportunities it presents—as well as the negative, whether in your career, your job, a project, or a strategic direction. Instead of a single list with the negatives of a new idea, draw lists of both the "positives" and the "negatives," as well as the merits and dangers of instituting "change" and "do nothing."

It is important that you realize how the impact of your opinions among your colleagues or managers is diminished if they are too predictable. Not only do you need to be more selective about what you try to raise the alarm about, you need to allow other people to have the opportunity to do so first as well. That way, when there really is a concern, and no one else speaks up, you can do so and be more likely to be heard. Remember, your colleagues are getting a free ride if they never have to step up and express their own concerns. Make *them* shoulder some of the load.

In times of great change, many, perhaps most, people do just the wrong thing: they try to cling to what they have and what they know. They throw their arms desperately around the present (which all too rapidly is becoming the past). The film *The Poseidon Adventure*, cliché-ridden as it may be, provides a vivid scene when, as the ship is turned upside down, those guests in the dining room who clung to their (bolted-down) tables find themselves thirty feet in the air, with no way down. In times of great change we all need to beware of clinging tenaciously to the "old way" of thinking or doing things just because that is what we know—in other words, of acting like pessimist-worriers. In the current business climate and job market, clinging to what used to work may place you at the greatest risk in this regard. Consider a wildebeest in East Africa that should get up and migrate with the others when the dry season comes, but whose water hole lasts a week or two longer than the others. It lasts just long enough for him to ignore the need to change for a time, only to be *really* caught by the draught and perish along the migratory path. When we have no choice but to change, to embrace a new idea or whole new paradigm, we do. Given a choice, though, many of us are tempted to stay with the familiar.

Changing someone's "default option" of the way he or she views and interprets the world is difficult, even if the person agrees that it's in his or her best interest to do so. Fear of the unknown and a negative view of the new and untried are intractable—but not invincible. By taking some of the deliberate steps we have just described, you *can* control your fears sufficiently to allow yourself to be much more effective—and perceived by others as much less negative. In his first inaugural address, Franklin Delano Roosevelt said, "The only thing we have to fear is fear itself." He was paraphrasing Henry David Thoreau, who wrote even more to the point: "Nothing is so much to be feared as fear." The first step toward change for anyone who recognizes this pattern of negativity in his or her thoughts, actions, or behavior is to understand the extraordinarily high cost to one's career when it is consistently grounded in fear. By coming to fear your *fears* more than you fear change, you can change how you approach your job and your life.

CHAPTER
NINE

EMOTIONALLY TONE-DEAF

T ERRY'S EXTRAORDINARY ABILITIES IN THE AREA OF TECH-
nology were vital to the investment bank for which he worked. He was
an information technology guru and had created for the bank an advanced and integrated system for analyzing economic information that
was both far more sophisticated than those of the bank's competitors
and a tremendous leap forward from what the bank had used previously.
The system gave the bank's investment professionals immediate access
to the changing and comparative values of an entire universe of financial instruments, a critical tool in valuing businesses, structuring merg-
ers, and investing for the bank's own account and in a range of the
bank's other activities.

Unfortunately, only a few people at the bank were using this wonderful tool—for one single and fundamental reason: Mastering the system's intricacies was difficult even for technophiles; and the technically
"challenged" found it bewildering. It was not exactly "user-hostile," but
all of Terry's energy had gone into making it faster, more powerful, and
more comprehensive—and none into making it user-friendly. It was like
a stock car designed for speed and handling, with an enormously pow-

erful engine, great transmission, and tight steering, but no sound insulation, air-conditioning, or comfortable seats.

This is not to say that it was impossibly complex, by any means. With either a few modifications or more energy put into training (and perhaps a little hand-holding and patient instruction from Terry), people could have learned the system—as a few of the more skilled and motivated already had. But Terry ignored his "customers." He didn't try to simplify what he could or even go out of his way to make time for those who came to him for help. Those who did manage to make time with him got responses to their questions that ranged from indifference to rudeness. Terry's answers tended to be cold and monosyllabic; there was not a hint of understanding or sympathy in his voice, not even a smiling half apology for the complexities of his system. A couple of the bank's senior managing directors left his office with the clear impression that he thought they were idiots—a fact that did not endear him to them. Most significant, Terry had no idea how his behavior was affecting these important people in his work life. He had not the faintest notion that his indifference to people's feelings of frustration and/or inadequacy was insulting and that by his remoteness and inability to understand their feelings he was stiff-arming himself out of a job that he loved. From his point of view they asked him questions and he answered their questions. He was blind to the questions behind the questions, to the fact that, brilliant though his system was, it was worthless if no one could take advantage of it. Terry could not see that his "just the facts, ma'am" responses were discouraging people from using it.

THE DYNAMICS OF THE PATTERN

We sometimes refer to these *emotionally tone-deaf* people (like Terry) as "Mr. Spock," after the character played by Leonard Nimoy in the television series *Star Trek*. Spock is a native of the planet Vulcan; he and others of his species appear human in most respects other than their superhuman intellect, pointed ears—and inability to either feel emotions themselves or understand them in others. Spock is incapable of deceit (to deceive people would be "illogical," as he would put it), and he is courageous (fear being an emotion he could not feel), the sort of person you would want by your side if your spaceship were hurtling at warp speed into the path of an asteroid belt. He would correct the course in a nanosecond without a fluctuation in his pulse rate. He was also, however, joyless, incapable of love, and of no help whatsoever in understanding human nature.

Our Spocks are, in effect, almost as emotionally tone-deaf and color-blind as the Mr. Spock of the television series. They have a hard time recognizing and understanding fear, love, anger, jealousy, greed, compassion, and other emotions—in themselves or in others. Not only are their own emotions muted, but they have difficulty understanding the feelings and behaviors of other people, because they're blind (relatively speaking) to that whole range of other people's feelings and motivation. Often they are hyper-rational, perceiving problems simply as issues to be resolved, devoid of a flesh-and-blood human component. They see the world, and people in particular, as though they were looking at an X-ray: all bones, without flesh, or nervous system.

Spocks reduce everything to their fundamental structure. They tend to look for the simplest explanations possible. While Occam's razor (which asserts that, all else being equal, the simpler of two explanations is preferable) holds true when seeking to explain natural phenomena, the intricate web of human emotions, thoughts, and actions often does not lend itself to that rule. As a result, those Spocks who are emotionally tone-deaf are caught flat-footed when it comes to synthesizing interpersonal give-and-take and understanding group politics and individual psychology. There is a scene in the film *Annie Hall* in which Woody Allen's character and Annie, having just met, are conversing over a glass of wine. As they stand together discussing photography, the film shows (in text subtitles) what they are really thinking and feeling—and their thoughts have nothing to do with art! The emotionally tone-deaf individual, however, tends to hear nothing but the spoken words that are conveyed and is often unaware of his own feelings, or subtext, much less what the other person is (really) saying, feeling, or thinking. They are oblivious of body language, nuance, shadings, and those things that are left unsaid.

Meritocrats, whom we discuss in Chapter 2, *feel* emotion; they just want to eliminate emotion from the decision-making process. So while meritocrats have trouble functioning in a world that rewards emotions, loyalties, and other non-objective factors—it's not because they don't feel and see those emotions, though they might wish they didn't exist.

The emotionally tone-deaf, on the other hand, have a difficult time recognizing emotions. They have so successfully repressed their own emotions that they often can't hear or see what most of us hear and see. This puts them at an enormous disadvantage in a workplace, where people's emotions and reactions are often as important as—or more important than—the actual work being done. They might walk into a room in which two people are conversing and start talking to one of the two without apologizing for the interruption or even acknowledging the other's presence. If you were to point that out to him, he would be surprised that you brought it up and explain that he didn't speak to her because he had nothing to say to her. They sometimes invade others' space or respond without a trace of empathy when you mention that you're feeling under the weather or overwhelmed on a project you're working on. It's not that they are trying to make you uncomfortable or be unsympathetic—they just don't "get it."

One person we know who fits this pattern routinely takes return calls (the caller having been identified to him by his secretary) without even saying "Hello," let alone "Thanks for calling back." He simply launches into the reason he called in the first place, what he needs. He's not being personally rude or disrespectful. He does that a lot, with *every*body! It just doesn't occur to him to spend a few moments on social niceties—it doesn't matter to him, so why should it matter to anyone else?

And this is the root cause of this behavioral Achilles' heel: a poor ability to take perspective (something we discuss in far greater detail in Chapter 13 of Part II). People who are emotionally tone-deaf are impaired in their ability to hear things or see things from others' frames of reference. They don't acknowledge or value those parts of themselves (emotions), so they don't value them in others, and eventually they come not even to observe them in others.

Talking with someone who is a victim of this kind of behavior is like taking a few turns around the floor with a bad dancer. He or she has no sense of the rhythms needed to move in synch with, and in response to, his or her partner. Such individuals don't hear the beat of the music or the tones of conversation. They often can't distinguish an enthusiastic "yes" from a more hesitant or reluctant "yes" or a sarcastic "yes." Their instinctual reaction upon sensing something about the other response is "off" is to push it down and move on blindly, past the momentary discomfort. As a result, they don't recognize the signals others give off. They aren't attuned to the music (the overall tenor of a meeting, relationship, or situation), and they aren't attuned to the individual dynamics of the other dancer.

Terry, the IT wizard at the investment bank, is an introvert, as is true of many people with this behavior pattern. But some extroverts suffer from this career trap as well. The extroverted Spock will talk at you endlessly without picking up on obvious signals, like facial expressions and body movements, that you are bored or agitated. At times the only easy way to end the conversation is to find an exit as quickly as possible.

One of the clients we worked with is an extreme extrovert and oblivious of others' feelings to an astonishing degree. She would overstay her welcome (even in meetings held within a specific schedule), say things that others might perceive as rude (with total lack of awareness of others' reactions), and generally step on people's feelings with no ill intent, utterly obliviously.

Terry, of course, is an extreme example of someone who suffers from this career Achilles' heel. Most people exhibit symptoms that are milder. Two other clients we've worked with in recent years, Ray and Maureen, while far less attuned to others' feelings than would be optimal for their careers, still recognize how others feel at times. Rather than being tone-deaf, we might describe them as "tone-impaired."

Many Spocks are only selectively impaired. They can recognize and respond to others' *anxiety*, for example, but put up an emotional wall in resistance to sadness, depression, or despair. Many people don't know how to react appropriately to anger or hurt feelings. As a result, they may gain a reputation for being timid or heartless (as a result of an abrupt dismissal of those feelings in the people they work with). One client we worked with cared deeply about those under him but was simply unable to listen to others' tales of tragedy (as when the wife of an employee was diagnosed with cancer). Internally they may feel some emotions and not others. Some people are so uncomfortable with fear, for example, that they effectively react to it by becoming angry, to keep their fear at bay. Others we have worked with are fearful of their own anger, as well as anger in others, and push those emotions down, thus failing to react decisively when an employee or colleague deserves to have an oversight or mistake pointed out. As a consequence, the employee or colleague assumes that the Spock is "easygoing" or doesn't care about the mistakes that occur on his or her watch.

One of our clients, although he was able to see and deal with others' anxieties, sadness, disappointments, embarrassment, and guilt, couldn't handle conflict and anger; as a result, he—through the "miracle" of psychological denial—was able simply to not "see" such feelings. At one point his staff was so angry at him for his inappropriate responses to conflict that their collective anger was almost palpable. But he couldn't see—or feel or hear—it at all, which only served to enrage his staff further.

THE IMPACT OF THE BEHAVIOR

This inability to be responsive to the emotions and feelings of others can present a significant obstacle to success. Some psychologists suggest that you can divide the human experience into three groupings: actions, thoughts, and feelings. All three affect each other: how you act affects how you think and feel, how you think affects how you act and feel, and how you feel affects how you think and act. So if you are unable to hear when people in the workplace are expressing their anxieties about your actions, or a specific proposal, or expressing their anger at a management decision, for example, you're in turn likely to have trouble communicating with them effectively and establishing the kind of relationship that often is the key to success in the workplace. Even if all you suffer from is an emotional blind spot, it may well be a blind spot that those above you recognize and see as an impediment to your advancement.

"Tone deafness" is also certain to have a significant impact on your nonwork life, especially in the formation and maintenance of intimate relations. Being unable to recognize and respond to others' feelings—or to recognize and express your own—presents a tremendous barrier to any close relationship.

Emotionally tone-deaf people can hear only part of the range of "sound frequencies" that most people hear. People with this behavior pattern sometimes—rather adaptively—find their way to positions where they handle numerical data or technical detail with dexterity, sometimes brilliantly. But they are far less adept or comfortable with "soft data." For example, one of our clients held an important position in the marketing research department of a large consumer products company. He performed exceptionally well when it came to analyzing the sales patterns of a range of products, discovering esoteric correlations with weather, employment, and other data. But he was absolutely lost in understanding consumer behavior elicited in focus groups. He would sit behind a one-way mirror with his colleagues and watch consumers handle shampoo bottles, for example, and discuss their feelings about shapes, colors, scents, and such. But because the consumers' reactions were so vague, unfocused, and ambiguous—because it wasn't quantifiable—he simply couldn't grasp this "fuzzy" information and put it to work. Another former consumer goods brand manager we know is "quantitatively challenged"—he just isn't very good with manipulating hard data—but extremely adept at understanding what people in the focus groups were really getting at with their comments.

Another individual we worked with assigned subordinates responsibilities for welcoming and escorting shareholders during the company's weekend-long annual meeting. He handed out the assignments and the hours employees had to be on duty without giving them choices as to which duties they preferred or which hours, and they were furious. Parents who were assigned evening duty had to find baby-sitters for their young children. But he wasn't being despotic. In fact, he was a very nice guy and felt terrible (and terribly embarrassed) by his gaffe. It simply didn't occur to him that people might have preferences, especially based on these human factors.

One widely used personality test based on Carl Jung's theory of psychological type is the Myers-Briggs Type Indicator. In Myers-Briggs terms, the emotionally tone-deaf pattern of behavior describes the archetypal "thinking type," someone who relies entirely on dispassionate analysis for decision making. The polar opposite is the "feeling type," a person who makes decisions based on how he or she and others will feel about them. Here is an example that may help to clarify the distinction.

In a workshop using Myers-Briggs, the group leader separated the feeling types from thinking types and sent them to different rooms. Both groups were told to imagine they were the local board of a national organization that will hold its annual convention in Hawaii in March (typically a cold and miserable month in Boston). Their chapter, they were told, could afford to send only two members to this glamorous meeting, which amounted to a paid vacation.

The group of feeling types first set out to see if there was any way they could send more than two people. Failing that, they evaluated the candidates by measures of compassion: Who might get the most pleasure out of the trip? Who most needed this kind of break in their routine? Who was least appreciated in the organization? They considered taking the money that would have gone to send two people to Hawaii and sending everyone on a more modest trip! The group of thinking types, by contrast, drafted a list of objective criteria: Who had done the most for the organization? Who would be the most impressive representative? Who had the best attendance record? The thinkers established a system of weightings for each category and a means of evaluating the membership. The two candidates who scored highest would be dispatched to Hawaii. No muss, no fuss, no messy feelings to get in the way.

Whether the thinkers' method is more virtuous than the feelers' is beside the point. Clearly there is much to be said in praise of the thinkers' objective analysis. But the point is that they don't see any alternative. They come up with the list of what they feel are objective criteria and then are shocked when some people object to the outcome. The *feeling* types' set of criteria never crosses the thinking types' minds; or, in the case of more mildly impaired individuals, it may cross their minds too late, or only as a kind of background noise that is quickly muffled.

One of the more humorous examples of this behavior pattern involved a client trying to decide between jobs in two cities. He had a list of criteria (options, compensation, growth potential, the people he'd be working with, and so on), with a weighting for each criterion and an assessment for each job. The two were multiplied, all the products summed, and one job was the winner. In showing us his chart, he said, "Of course, my girlfriend lives in Los Angeles. But it's clear from my research that I should take the job in Chicago." What could we say? Obviously numbers don't lie!

THE ORIGIN OF MR. SPOCK

Terry, whom we introduced at the beginning of the chapter, was raised by parents who were much like himself, something we have found to be a typical genesis for the Spock behavior type. In conversations with Terry it became clear that his parents were just as oblivious of the emotional sensibilities of other people as he was. His mother is a woman who thought nothing of asking someone how much her diamond ring cost. When his father learned that a friend's son was about to enroll at the University of Washington, he asked (knowing that the boy had also applied to Stanford) if he had been turned down by Stanford. No malice was intended—mom and dad are just collecting facts and doing so in the most personally inept way possible.

Growing up, Terry rarely heard the kinds of conversations that are familiar to most of us, such as your mother telling your father, "I was really touched when your uncle told me how pretty I looked." Or your father saying, "I don't trust Fred. He's all smiles, but from the tone of his voice and the way he never looks you in the eye, I just can't believe that the guy's sincere." He never learned to listen to what people are *really* saying, the way it was said, the unspoken subtext, the body language. Moreover, he never learned to get outside himself, to rotate the world 180 degrees and look at it from the perspective of another person—to hear himself as others hear him.

The parents of another client with this behavior pattern were not socially obtuse; however, the only thing they rewarded their children for was academic achievement. As a result, both Dawn and her sister came to see grades and what used to be called "book learning" as the be-all and end-all. They studied, they learned, they tested, they got As, and as far as they knew, that was all that counted. Fortunately Dawn proved to be an apt and eager pupil; during our consultation she was able to study and learn about people just as she had once studied and learned about Asian history. She would "upload the files" on human behavior—an unusual way of learning, perhaps, but effective nonetheless.

One of the most interesting, almost baffling, things about the development of this pattern of behavior is that it goes against so much of the momentum of human development. Consider what an evolutionary advantage the ability to "read" other people's emotions provides and how difficult it is to suppress our own feelings. Almost everyone learns to identify their feelings and to recognize at least some of the subtleties of interpersonal interaction, such as body language, for example. The individual who grows up emotionally tone-deaf, then, is swimming against a tremendously strong evolutionary tide by forming and maintaining this pattern.

THE IMPACT OF BEING TONE-DEAF IN AN ORGANIZATION

In earlier times, the Spock affliction was undoubtedly less of a handicap than it is today. There was less of a need for intense interpersonal cooperation and teamwork and less upward mobility. Engineers, accountants, and a host of other specialists only had to worry about their specific responsibilities or expertise. But in the new "service-oriented" economy, everyone has a customer, whether the customer is outside the company or within it, and customers are far less predictable and malleable than numbers. You can't explain something to one person with the same language you use with another. And the same person may be receptive to learning difficult new processes early in the morning but is simply overloaded and not as mentally adaptable later in the day, when his own customers besiege him with demands. More understanding of other people is necessary today than in the past. Most of the Achilles' heels we describe in this book will limit your success, but few are likely to be fatal. But in today's world, being emotionally tone-deaf is a flaw that really *can* be devastating, with results ranging from being passed over for promotions and plum assignments to being fired.

Terry understood none of this. As he saw it, he had developed a brilliant information system for the bank, and whether his colleagues—his customers—could master it wasn't his concern. Terry was a member of the bank's technology committee, a group that met once a week to resolve, among other things, problems that arose from integrating new systems into those the bank already had. Only two or three other members of the committee were techies; the others were executives from bond and equities trading, corporate finance, and various other departments, highly skilled in their disciplines, but not systems analysts or model builders.

It never occurred to Terry when he was designing his new system that it required his "customers" to change patterns of behavior they had been comfortable with for years. People get frustrated, angry, and fearful when they are required to do that, even if they understand that eventually they will be better off for it. Terry didn't take any of this into account. As far as he was concerned, it just wasn't his problem. When one committee member suggested that the bank retain the traditional system as a backup, a security blanket, until everyone felt comfortable with the new system, Terry responded coolly, "That's stupid. It would be a waste of time."

Hostility toward the new system—and toward Terry—grew at a rapid rate. He alienated colleagues of all ranks, including two of the bank's senior partners. The bank was divided into two camps, the minority who understood and swore by Terry's system and the majority who refused to use it. The managing partner didn't want to lose Terry, but he couldn't afford to keep him if the price was civil war within the bank. In the end, he sent Terry to us.

There are few environments in which this pattern of behavior will not cause negative consequences; the severity of the problem the individual has is tied directly to the severity of the behavior pattern. Moreover, there is no stage in one's career—early, mid-, or late—in which it is condoned or accepted. And even at the highest levels in an organization, presidents and CEOs who behave in this way are tremendously disadvantaged. It's unusual for someone with this pattern to rise to that level, but when they do, a good part of their job is to attract and hold the very best and most talented people, as well as to woo analysts, fund managers, and the media. CEOs who are unable to read other people simply can't be as effective as spokespeople, motivators, or leaders.

HOW TO OVERCOME THE PATTERN

We worked with Terry for more than a year, meeting at least once a week. Our first task was to get him to acknowledge that as brilliant as his system was in the abstract, it was worse than useless if only a few people in the bank used it: it was divisive. It would reach its potential as a tool only when everyone, or almost everyone, in the firm was able to use it. Grudgingly he admitted the logic of that statement. Next we asked, "Do you want to design the world's best mousetrap and have it gathering dust, or do you want to get people to use it?" The response was affirmative. We had a student.

What was clear was that Terry had to learn certain skills. We told him we had to scan information into him the way you would enter information into a database. Terry, given who he was, was not offended by the analogy. He had a lot of ego at stake in his information system, but he had almost none when it came to his personal communications skills. He admitted that he was bad at dealing with people—it was something that, given his values, he was almost proud of. Because he wasn't sensitive about his problem, we could be open about the fact that we were coaching him. We interviewed his colleagues and asked them to tell us what Terry did to offend them, and his colleagues didn't hold back.

So we were able to go back to Terry and tell him precisely what it was about him that alienated people, including the words he used, his gestures, his body language. We discovered that among his mannerisms was the habit of never making eye contact with anyone. We sat in on several of the information technology meetings with Terry and took notes on the interplay between him and his colleagues. Then we played it back to him and instructed him on the particulars of what he did—and didn't do—that offended people. Dispassionately he "entered" all of that information into his mental database, creating a series of cross-referenced computer files that he could refer to.

We gave him some rules and guidelines to live by as well. Because he lacked the instinct to know when it was time to listen to what others were saying, we told him point-blank that he was not allowed to speak at a meeting until at least two other people had spoken. It was a rule he was instructed to follow without exception. Similarly, at every meeting he presided over he was required to praise or thank at least two people for something—anything. It might be something substantial, such as a well-done report, or it might be simply for a passing observation. These were tangible signs that he was paying attention to other people. The drill worked. Although it pained him, Terry painstakingly went through step-by-step instructions on using the new information system with even the slow learners, until they were competent with it.

Terry's personality remained the same, and none of his colleagues was fooled into believing that his changed behavior meant he was a completely different person. But he did change his behavior substantially, and they appreciated his efforts. And he made it easier on everyone by developing a sense of humor about his affliction, encouraging those he worked with to call him "Mr. Spock" (in fact, he quite liked the name).

Does our description of the emotionally tone-deaf individual hold a measure of truth for you? If so, we have several suggestions to help you overcome your disability—because careerwise, that is exactly what it is. First, it is essential that you read and study Chapter 13 in Part II, "Taking Others' Perspectives." Learning to pay attention to how other people behave, think, and feel is an essential step in the process of change. In "Taking Others' Perspectives," there is an exercise that takes you through the steps for understanding the psychological perspectives of participants in a hypothetical meeting. Once you're read the chapter, go through this exercise for each of the people you interact with regularly at work. The exercise will help to show you how to think about, evaluate, and appreciate the following for each of your employees, colleagues, and managers:

▲ What types of rewards best motivate that individual?
▲ What general work styles does this person bring to a project?
▲ What are this person's goals in his or her next six months at work?

For some people this type of perspective comes relatively easily. They are aware of these issues, and of their importance, on a day-to-day basis. The closer you are to a genuine Spock profile, the harder it will prove to be. If that is the case for you, you'll need to make a deliberate, conscious effort to understand your fellow workers in a deeper and more subtle way. Empathy is a difficult skill to learn, but it is just that—a skill—and it *can* be learned.

You should also take an "emotional audit" of yourself. This is actually quite a difficult task; you will probably need the help of others who have known you well over a considerable period of time. You need to answer the following questions about yourself. Are there some feelings that you recognize more readily and comfortably than others? Are there some that you are totally blind to? Do you "transmute" one feeling into another? Do you tend to ignore your own feelings in the same way that you ignore the feelings of others? What feedback have you received over the years that you can factor into this change process (both from people you've worked with and from friends, family members, and others)? Where has this pattern gotten you in trouble in the past?

The next step will inevitably require the help of a confidant or confidants from your current work setting or a very recent work setting. You need to gather, as difficult as it may be to hear, examples of your behaviors that others have observed to be insensitive and alienating to others. Ask the person to be as specific as possible with the examples. Then return to those situations in your mind and remember the full context: who was present, what the issues were, how you were feeling that day. Look across the examples given by the person (or people) giving you the feedback. What patterns do you see? What types of behaviors do you tend to repeat? Are there certain people who trigger your dysfunctional behavior more than others? What pattern do you see among those people? Are they younger and less experienced, less educated, of a different gender? Do they share other common characteristics? Can you identify other patterns or themes? Do your behavioral missteps occur more often in group settings or one on one? Do they occur when you're under some kind of stress (either work related or otherwise)? Do they occur not during, but *following*, a conversation with a certain person? By identifying the most significant problem behaviors and the work situations where this behavior pattern is most damaging or dangerous, you can target your efforts for change.

The next step is to identify specific verbal and nonverbal behaviors that you need to work on eliminating. Next, think about specific behavioral antidotes that can serve to correct for your inevitable lapses into old patterns. Consider where you're likely to get the most benefit from your efforts, and decide what needs to be tackled first. In other words, prioritize your efforts at changing your behavior. For example, someone might determine the following:

Top Priority

- ▲ Compliment the three top people under you, or in supporting departments, on their work at least once a week.
- ▲ Make sure to make eye contact in meetings.
- ▲ Don't interrupt when others are talking.
- ▲ Eliminate judgmental phrases such as "You just don't get it" and "Don't you see . . . ?" from your vocabulary.
- ▲ Plan to have lunch with a fellow worker at least once or twice a week. Rotate your lunch partners, being sure not to skip those with whom you find it most difficult to communicate.
- ▲ Ask one fellow worker about a nonwork aspect of his or her life each day.

Second Priority

- ▲ Watch one movie a week that is likely to make you feel something.
- ▲ Talk about it with someone at work.
- ▲ Make a joke at your expense (for example, a mildly self-deprecatory comment).

Remember, you can't entirely remake your personality, nor is that the point. What you should work to do is change how you act toward others and how you think about and perceive them. If you want to be effective in your job and maximize your career success, you *have* to learn to read people. If you had to choose whether to invest an hour a week of your time in this or in virtually any other initiative you could undertake, we would wager that this will have the biggest long-term payoff for your career.

Finally, don't be afraid to make good use of an ally/coach/mentor/ "emotional Seeing Eye dog" (or perhaps we should say "emotional 'hearing ear' dog"). It is almost essential to improvement. The person locked into this pattern of behavior simply does not perceive—indeed, often *can*not perceive—these vital elements of life. And you can't change what you can't recognize or see. You can *learn* to "see," but instruction that is as close as possible to your actual experience (for instance, "Mark, did you notice that the first two times you spoke in that meeting people responded, but after that no one picked up on your comments?") is likely to be the greatest help.

Over the years we've worked with hundreds of business professionals—many of whom are graduates of MBA and engineering programs—who have told us variations of the same thing: "You know, when I was in school the only thing I paid attention to was the 'hard numbers' courses: finance, operations management, accounting, advanced calculus. Now, fifteen or twenty years later I can see that it was the courses I belittled and didn't value (and also didn't study hard enough), like organizational behavior, psychology, group dynamics, and leadership, that made the most difference in my career and success. In the end, I've come to discover it's not my ability to tear apart a balance sheet or production process that counts the most, but rather it's my *people* skills that have made me successful—or been my undoing in certain situations. I just wish I'd known that when I started my career!"

CHAPTER
TEN

WHEN NO JOB IS GOOD ENOUGH

Ann had a résumé that looked like a socialite's passport. She had entry and exit visas from a lot of fashionable places where she had worked for brief periods after college. Her first job was at a city magazine. Then it was off to a publishing house. After that she took a position at a television station, then moved to a job with an international aid group, and then . . . The itinerary went on.

Ann was like a tourist who fancies herself a mountain climber. She arrives in Switzerland with plans to climb the Matterhorn. She can imagine herself on top of the Matterhorn; that's where she belongs—or at least where she expects herself to be. But she never, seriously attempts to climb the mountain, although she may explore the base trails for a few days. She finds a good reason: Her hiking boots aren't right, the mountaineering store doesn't have the ice ax she ordered. So she leaves Switzerland and heads off to Spain or Tanzania. But she could have made it to the top of the Matterhorn if she wanted to, or so she'll tell you.

That was the way that Ann left jobs. She could have become the managing director of that city magazine if she'd wanted to. She could have been editor in chief of the publishing house, or started her own ad agency, or become executive director of the aid agency. She *could* have been if she'd wanted to.

THE DYNAMICS OF THE PATTERN

Ann is a classic example of the behavior pattern we sometimes refer as the *coulda-been* (as in "I coulda been a contender," a line from the classic Marlon Brando movie *On the Waterfront*). Such people have huge eyes for achievement and a very limited tolerance for delay of gratification. Only the top rung of a prestigious organization will do, and only right now. These people have very little tolerance for hard work and little patience—not because they're lazy, but because doing the work to get to the top means that they're not already there. As a mountain climber, Ann really needed not just to get her boots and ax, but to learn how to climb; but the people who exhibit this pattern of business would be embarrassed to be seen taking lessons. They really feel as if they should already be there; to be working their way up is in itself a humiliation. What they seem to be saying is, "No job is good enough." But what they actually *feel* inside is, "*I'm* not good enough for any job."

The coulda-been is paralyzed by fear of shame and failure. The psychological consequences of slogging toward the summit and not making it are so terrible that the person is unable even to start. It's better to stand at the base and tell others (particularly yourself) that you *could* have made it to the top if you had wanted to. A variation of this theme is to "give it a run"—to take a stab at a project or job without any real preparation, so that if you succeed, it will appear effortless (and indeed, the person gives it little effort), but if you fail, you can always say, "Well, it didn't go too badly for not having really put anything into it." The coulda-beens avoid the calamity of failure either by simply not trying or by trying so little as to retain a plausible defense against feelings of shame.

The coulda-been shares some traits with the behavior associated with the home run hitter discussed in Chapter 7. Both expect great accomplishment and recognition at an early age. Hitting just a single or achieving a modest success in the early stages of a career will not do.

That is seen as trivial, laughable, even embarrassing. To learn, to ask for help and advice, would be to let another person see just how inadequate they feel they are. So they pretend to know all that they need to achieve their goals.

Most people derive satisfaction out of mastering the techniques, traditions, and bodies of knowledge of their chosen careers. The disciplined writer experiences real pleasure in learning his or her craft and getting short stories published in a magazine. The sensible psychotherapist gets satisfaction from helping the distressed understand and work through their psychological problems. For both the home run hitter and the coulda-been, the gradual mastery that someday leads to outstanding accomplishment is—at best—tiresome and irrelevant. They feel that they must begin by writing a best-selling novel or unraveling the mind of a serial killer. Naturally, all of us would prefer to have our first book be a best-seller or to scribble on a napkin an idea that contains the solution to successful cold fusion. No one would turn down the chance to leap ahead ten steps to fame and fortune. But unlike the coulda-beens and home run hitters, most of us recognize that we must persevere, hoping that one step at a time we'll eventually get there (or get close enough to there).

It would be easy to think of these types of people in terms of over-entitlement, as spoiled brats, expecting the world to come to them rather than having to work for it the way most people do. But they're not. In fact, the coulda-beens we have worked with are among the most anguished people we know. They deserve not our collective scorn, but our compassion. Regardless of the brave face they may put on things, even the face of arrogant entitlement and bravado, they live every day warding off, consciously or unconsciously, feelings of failure and shame that drive or motivate their behavior.

Coulda-beens bring perfectionism and procrastination to a level most of us could only dream about—or, more accurately, to the level of a waking nightmare. Most people who suffer from the effects of these two psychological siblings are only perfectionistic in certain areas of their lives (their appearance, or the cleanliness of their homes or cars, for example). Likewise, they procrastinate about certain things they have to do (such as preparing a slide presentation or a toast for a wedding). The coulda-been expects his or her whole *life* to be perfect and procrastinates regarding virtually everything it comprises.

Where people who tend to swing for the fences and the coulda-been differ is that the former swings for the bleachers every time he or she comes to the plate. That person almost invariably strikes out, but at least he or she impresses people with courage, and ambition, and occasional solid hits. To be sure, the home run hitter's employer may well encourage the player to move on, given his or her low percentage of success, but the employer usually has praise at least for the individual's drive and determination. If and when the home run hitter starts to swing more intelligently, trying to make contact and get on base or advance the runner rather than hit the applause-winning shot into the bleachers, he or she will have a place on the team. And although not nearly so soon as he or she would like, that person may someday even be a star.

The coulda-beens, by contrast, never step up to the plate, never pick up the bat. They simply tell those around them, "I could have hit it out of the park if I had wanted to." They may even criticize the people around them who are trying, in an attempt to reduce them to the level they feel at themselves. It's often a pretty transparent maneuver, and when people see through it, it is a behavior that is usually considered distasteful. So the coulda-beens often drift away from jobs and relationships, looking for new fields to effortlessly conquer.

In its most pronounced form, this pattern of behavior results in real paralysis; the people who exhibit it either don't start projects at all or start-but-don't-really-start (the series of short-lived jobs such as Ann had). In other people, this avoidance of shame results not in complete paralysis, but rather in never taking any risks and thereby staying well within the "comfort zone." The risk-avoidance pattern becomes evident sporadically, when the individual is presented with an opportunity that entails a degree of risk. The coulda-beens' natural self-protection takes over at this point, and they tend to find a reason to decline the opportunity—confident, as they tell themselves and others, that they "coulda" done it if they had wanted, but for various seemingly justifiable reasons they decided not to.

Mike was an academic whose field of study was applied mathematics. One paper that he published happened to catch the eye of the director of research for the fixed-income investment group of a mutual fund management company. This individual contacted Mike, expressed his interest in what Mike had written about (which had potential application to the firm's investment models), and invited him to lunch. Mike was excited by the prospect, if a little bit intimidated. He accepted, and the two met. The discussion was promising, and Mike's excitement grew. Unfortunately, due to circumstances beyond the control of either Mike or his contact, the relationship failed to grow and Mike's ideas were not put into use. Sadly (and speaking to the issue of the coulda-been), Mike never again ventured forth from the halls of academia to explore other consulting opportunities—although they grew in number over the years. "Oh, I suppose I could have," he would (modestly) say, "but I'm really content to stay where I am and do my work here. I don't need the aggravation, and I'm just not as aggressive as some of my more voracious colleagues." Those who knew him well were not fooled. Mike had been "burned" once, was hurt and embarrassed by the experience, and was not about to risk another similar experience.

THE ORIGINS OF THE COULDA-BEEN

People who suffer from this behavior pattern often come from backgrounds that are similar to those who suffer from the home run hitter syndrome. We think of these two behavior patterns almost as siblings; they result from people reacting in different and distinctive ways to the same set of family circumstances. The family itself is often distinguished by having many high achievers. Ann, for example, was raised in Austin, Texas, where one of her forefathers founded one of the city's first banks; another was once lieutenant governor; two others served in the state legislature.

Obviously the definition of "high achievers" is broad, including far more than just good schools, prestigious pedigrees, and so on. A person whose parents ran the local hardware store and were the most influential members of a small town, for example, may feel this kind of pressure to succeed and succeed big. Whatever the frame of reference, the family expects its children to excel, so much so that the children rarely get any applause for solid but less than spectacular achievement. The parents almost never say, "This report card is wonderful. Let's go out to dinner and celebrate." Instead the atmosphere is one that might be summed up by the comment "You did well enough, but others did better. Are you really doing what you are capable of? What you should be capable of?" This doesn't necessarily get stated at all, and rarely in such blunt terms. Our clients report a much more subtle communication, by way of facial expression, body language, the lukewarm quality of any positive comments that are made, and the juxtaposition of positive ("You ran a really good race, Paula") and critical ("You know, you'd do even better if . . ." and "You know who *really* did well was . . .") comments as well as the always crucial things that *aren't* said. One client told us: "It wasn't even definable enough to see, let alone to confront. It was more like a smell that you get used to. My friends would notice it, but I didn't get it until years later."

The coulda-been grows up under extraordinary pressure to be better, both better than other children and, more important, better than they are and can possibly be. It's bad enough to feel that you always have to be the best relative to your peers, but the people who fall into these behavior patterns typically grew up feeling that they should always be working to beat their previous "personal best." They would be told things such as "You have enormous talent, and it's great that you're number one in your class, but *I* know that you could do better—and I think you do, too." Of course that's true—everyone can do better. But children need acknowledgment and approval of what they *have* accomplished along the way. And isn't it all right sometimes just to do well? It is important that you have an opportunity to feel good about where you are and use these good feelings to motivate you to ascend to new heights. In the eyes of the parents of the coulda-beens, they must always look up to the rungs they have yet to climb on the ladder of life, rather than appreciate and celebrate how far they've come.

In general, the coulda-beens we have worked with seem to have been pushed to learn to do things that were simply inappropriate for whatever their developmental level was at any given time. French psychologist Jean Piaget demonstrated that cognitive development, for example, proceeds along certain very clear lines and cannot be "hurried."

The brightest five-year-old will not grasp the concept of conservation: the understanding that the amount of water, for example, that you have doesn't change when you alter how it's presented (in other words, in one pitcher versus in smaller glasses or in a short, fat glass versus a tall, skinny one). This understanding is perceived by the child's mind at around age seven or eight, but not before; trying to make a young child "get" this fact will be an exercise in frustration for both parent and child—and a source of bad feelings on the part of the child.

The people we have worked with who fit this pattern remember having being pushed too far, too hard, and too early in childhood, in a variety of ways. They were pushed to learn to read before they were ready, to learn arithmetic concepts before they were able, to learn physical skills that another same-age child might be learning but which they, as individuals, weren't ready for. In any number of ways they were what child psychologist David Elkind calls "hurried" not just into adulthood, but hurried to learn to "run before they knew how to walk," figuratively and sometime literally (Elkind's excellent book *The Hurried Child* provides a fuller description of this dynamic). It's as if the child is treated like a pet being taught to do tricks that will then reflect well on the parent if performed well and be an embarrassment if not. As a result, the child learns that there is a lot at stake in every such activity.

People who fall into this behavior pattern learn that there is much more of a downside to failure than there is an upside to success. Success brings a "good, but you could do better" reaction, while failure brings shame on yourself and your family. Understandably, those of us who have gone through this learn the leassons of failure all too well, doing everything we can to avoid failure by refusing, consciously or unconsciously, to accept any risk at all. You can't strike out if you don't bat.

Why the home run hitter reacts by swinging for the bleachers, while the coulda-beens hide in the dugout is not clear. In some instances, it seems, the hitters have somehow incorporated the sense that if they fail in a grand way, people will say, "Well, how can you expect a nine-year-old to succeed in climbing Mt. Everest? But good for you for trying!" On the other hand, if they fail at a more age-appropriate task, they fear other people will look at them critically. As an adult, this kind of thinking translates into "Well, it was a long shot for someone right out of school to try to launch his own restaurant, but good for her for trying." These people have evolved a highly complex and effective psychological defense to protect themselves against shame.

The coulda-been, on the other hand—unlike his shame-armored psychological sibling—tends to be hypersensitive to feelings of shame and embarrassment, and because he or she often feels inadequate, even minor failures reinforce that feeling. Every failure makes the coulda-been feel smaller, which increases his or her vulnerability to future feelings of shame. A reinforcing cycle is put into place, in which any failure "draws down the account" of such an individual's psychic reserves and leaves the person even less able to afford the next failure that inevitably comes along, which further depletes the savings, and so forth.

People often confuse shame and guilt. In light of the fact that the risk-avoidance behavior pattern is driven largely by shame, it's important to clarify the distinction. Shame is a deeper, more persistent, and more *personal* feeling than guilt. Guilt is what you feel about something you have done that was wrong, a transgression of the moral, professional, or legal boundary of what is allowed to be done in our society. When someone steals, or deliberately hurts someone else, or fails to report an accident, or fraudulently files a tax return, for example, he or she feels guilty because such actions are transgressions of that boundary. Shame, on the other hand, is a feeling about who you *are*. Shame is a more intimate, more painful, more enduring feeling than guilt. What I *did* is more distant from me than who I *am*. It's far more difficult to say, "I'm not going to *be* that again," than to say, "I'm not going to *do* that again." Feelings of shame are, for most people, exquisitely painful. Some cultures place great emphasis on allowing others to "save face" (not feel ashamed). In others, the person who has been "disrespected" or shamed may attack the person who caused the feeling. It's not surprising, then, that people who are—regardless of the causes—shame-sensitive will go to extreme lengths to avoid the feeling, even if that means sabotaging themselves and their careers—and even their future happiness—by taking themselves out of the game of life.

ANN (REDUX)

It was clear that some interaction of the dynamics of familial expectations and innate temperament turned Ann into a coulda-been. Ann was not exceptionally talented. Her IQ was likely above average but probably not a great deal so. She had several winning attributes: she had a very animated and engaging personality and was charming and pleasant to be with, except when she would express her frustration over the fact that while her family name might be impressive in Texas, it didn't carry a lot of weight or "name recognition" on the East Coast.

Ann relied on her family name for security, and the realization that it didn't count for much where she lived now was very threatening to her, almost an insult. Beyond that, her great shortcoming was that, like most people trapped in this pattern of thinking and behavior, she rarely put extra effort into her work. Most of us recognize that great achievers who make their efforts look easy in fact put in exhausting weeks, months, or even years of learning, and preparation, and labor. The clichés in this case, such as Edison's "genius is 1 percent inspiration and 99 percent perspiration," are usually right. The journey of a thousand miles begins with a single step. When someone examining one of Picasso's paintings asked him how long it took to produce it, he answered, "Two hours and thirty years." But all of that was lost on Ann.

Like many people whose behaviors are guided by a terrifying fear of failure, Ann believed that success comes easily. Growing up, she never had an example of someone in the family or her immediate world who struggled to succeed. Her father was a born salesman, and that knack, combined with a recognizable family name, was enough to make him one of Austin's most successful businessmen with seemingly little effort. Ann herself was a gifted athlete, who because of her talent and charm was elected captain of the women's soccer team at her university. Because she was a very good athlete, she got away at the high school level with not practicing or training very hard, a habit that held her back from greater success at the collegiate and World Cup level. Because she saw that things came so effortlessly to her father, and because *some* things came so easily to her, when she encountered difficulties, Ann didn't know what to do. She would think, "There's something wrong here;

calculus is *hard* and it shouldn't be. I guess it's just not meant for me."
And she dropped any course of study that was difficult, not out of laziness so much as out of her unconscious fear of failure and her conviction that things should come easily—or not at all.

When Ann graduated from college her family name and connections, backed up by acceptable grades, helped her get a job at a magazine in another Texas city. Ann could imagine herself as the editor, a glamorous and prestigious position. It might have been a long shot given her limited talents, but with hard work she could have risen to a respectably high perch in the magazine. But Ann wasn't willing to "put in her time"—or the effort.

As one of several assistant editors (a starting position despite the semigrand title), her primary assignment was to fact check and read the proofs of contributing writers' articles. It was grueling, thankless work. Writers and higher-ranking editors rarely compliment a fact checker for catching a mistake before it gets to print. But if an error slips by, the fact checker is the one who is reprimanded and has to write up an explanation of his or her oversight. It's a job in which one is noticed only by one's mistakes. But if a fact checker performs well for a year or so, he or she will be given more rewarding work as a reporter who goes out and interviews people the writer wanted to include in a story but had no time to interview personally. A successful reporter will then be given a chance to become a writer of his or her own stories. Ann never found out whether she would have been a good reporter or writer, because eight months into her job she quit.

She told her friends, "I could have been a writer, but why bother? The magazine is so phony, all about pseudocelebrities." It was much the same with her next employer, a publishing house in Atlanta. "They treated me like a slave. What they wanted was a gofer, so I quit," Ann explained to her family and friends (who, unfortunately, bought her story). A very brief stunt with a television station in Dallas followed (where she learned the *real* meaning of "gofer"), then she moved to Seattle, where she worked for just under a year as a program assistant for an agency that was sending medical aid to Thailand.

Ann's pattern was classic for the coulda-been. They rarely seem able to get career "traction." They start a few feet up the rail to the mountaintop, imagining themselves on the top, a powerful image that motivates many of us to keep going even when we want to quit. But in the heart of Ann and others who fall into this pattern, that image is overwhelmed by feelings of shame at not already being at the summit and by an even more powerful image of failure despite one's best efforts. As a result, such people stop climbing, turn around, and start looking for a new mountain, as Ann did.

Coulda-beens are not dilettantes, although the two obviously wander along similar paths. The crucial difference is that dilettantes are happy. They know they're dabbling and are untroubled by that fact. They make a virtue of being jacks- or janes-of-all-trades. Individuals who fall into the coulda-been trap are most definitely *not* happy; and the older they get, the more unhappy they become.

Unlike some of the other patterns we've described, the coulda-been dynamic is not immediately apparent at the start of the person's career. What has been described by others as a prolonged adolescence allows others to see such people through their twenties as still "finding" themselves. For some people that sort of drifting along turns out well. The young woman who finally figures out at the age of thirty where she belongs suddenly soars. She knows she has to make up for lost time, so she works harder than others. Further, the experience she picked up in previous jobs gives her a breadth that her colleagues lack.

But the coulda-beens continue to wander from job to job, career to career, well after others have settled in to something. They are no longer "finding" themselves, regardless of what they might tell other people. *They* know they are desperately lost, and it's obvious to everyone else as well. Ann, for example, went to her fifth college reunion and talked about what she could have been. She doesn't plan on her tenth, because she knows she won't be able to keep up that pretense. Everything in the coulda-been's life tells her that she's been left behind. Sometimes those around her are brutal enough to be explicit. The father of one of our clients told his son, "Your classmates all have great jobs. What's wrong with you?"

Another client began deliberately (if unconsciously) seeking out the company of people twenty years older so that he wouldn't have to compare himself with his same-age peers. There was less need to feel self-conscious around them. Sure, they owned companies or were senior vice presidents of corporations, but they were in their mid-fifties and sixties. In no sense were they rivals; they invited no comparison.

The longer an individual who is a coulda-been drifts without finding help, the deeper his or her anxiety—and frequently depression—grows. Employers lose interest, and who can blame them? Why should they spend energy and money training someone who's obviously not going to go the distance? As the coulda-been's prospects grow dimmer, the status boost he or she needs in order to compensate for a lack of production over the years becomes even greater. As the gap between reality and one's dream grows wider and wider, the flailing becomes more extreme, the pseudoplans become more extreme and grandiose.

HOW TO BREAK THE PATTERN

When she came to us Ann had just turned thirty, and she was frantic. Her family connections were not able to help her find work anymore, and her résumé certainly was of no help; in fact, it was a detriment. She knew that she had to change her life dramatically. We began a series of long and painful conversations with her on how she could do that. If this is a pattern that seems to apply to you, you're going to need to ask yourself some of the same questions and give yourself some of the same advice. We began by examining each job exit in painful detail. We refused to take Ann's superficial explanations at face value and insisted that we dig under the surface to see if there was any theme or pattern to her career stops. We began to discern the pattern of "It just wasn't good enough/worth it" in virtually every one of her decisions to move on. We then explored Ann's life before she entered the workforce and got the family history we outlined earlier.

We made it clear that we weren't judging her. In fact, we felt quite the opposite; we understood how difficult it must have been for her. By talking about some of the other people we had worked with, she was able to see that she was not alone in her problem (which, previously, she had felt—and thus had felt doubly ashamed). After she told about her father and how easy everything seemed to have been for him, we shared a story—identity disguised, of course—of a young man who had consulted us whose father had been a genius (literally) in mathematics. He, too, had grown up assuming that everything was easy (as it was for his father) and had been baffled when he found that some of the things he tried were really difficult.

We understood Ann's similar consternation and her constant feeling in every job that "people" (originally her family, but now a group that included everyone she knew) were shaking their heads sadly as they witnessed her failure. It is hard for some of us to "find our place," especially when it seems to be so easy for some others. We told her about another consultation we had taken on with a client who, constantly comparing himself with his extremely successful businessman father and equally successful orthopedist older brother, could get no "traction" at all for himself. He had chosen a completely different career for himself, as a writer of short stories and humorous essays. He had a number of pieces in his portfolio, some quite good; but he never submitted them to a publisher. He was always revising and polishing them, only to revise them again. Nothing was ever quite ready, it was always just a few days or weeks from completion. And, he told us, he was always in a state of pain (although not, in his mind, in as much pain as he would have been if he had submitted a piece and had it rejected).

Once Ann saw that we weren't judging her, she began to stop judging herself as well and gradually let go of her defensive posture ("It was all their fault that it didn't work out"). We talked a lot about shame, about how hard it is to bear shameful feelings, about how we *all* feel the pain of being ashamed—and about how she felt it all the time. Our meetings were difficult for her, but she never missed an appointment. "This is incredibly painful, coming here," she said at the end of one meeting, "but in some weird way I always feel better when I leave than I did before I got here." *She* knew that *we* knew how she felt; she had never enjoyed that kind of understanding, or the comfort it can give, before.

When we sensed that she was ready to make use of it, we began to talk about the work of D. W. Winnicott, a British child psychoanalyst who wrote about the necessity of having a "good-enough mother" in order for normal child development to take place. (If we had introduced the topic too soon, it would have been, at best, an empty intellectual exercise.) "Why do you think he used the phrase 'good-enough mother'?" we asked. The answer we got to—Winnicott's reason—was that the mother doesn't have to be perfect, just good *enough* to care for and nurture her children. We've found that to be an enormously useful construct in our own lives, to help us control the perfectionism that afflicts everyone from time to time. If we're in a hurry and are having trouble getting a report out, a 'good-enough report' is one that a) tells the reader what our findings are; and b) proves useful in helping to effect change. It doesn't have to be world-class writing. The dark side of word-processing programs is that you can—like our client—keep polishing forever. "Good enough" is something that makes our points, and makes them clearly and well—even if it isn't *War and Peace*. It's often a very reassuring notion.

Ann began to think about her future in terms of work that would be "good enough" and, just as important, good enough *for her*. She came to realize that her best chance for success was in the only field in which she had ever excelled and truly enjoyed—sports. We discussed how she could benefit from continuing her education both by acquiring important knowledge and by getting a fresh start, a new "platform" from which she could launch herself. The past eight or nine years could never be erased, of course, but if she went back to school, future potential employers would at least see her as a new "X" rather than an old "Y" who's been adrift for almost a decade.

Ann got a master's degree in physical education and sports psychology from a good-enough program in a good-enough university and then got a good-enough job as an assistant coach at a good-enough college in the Southeast. She kept in touch, and we held our breath as her contract came up for the second year.

The effects of the coulda-been on an organization are slight, simply because the people in this pattern rarely stay around long enough to accomplish much. They don't have time to do much good or damage. Sadly, although they remember each job in great detail—how they got it, when they started, what it was like, when they left—the organizations they were briefly a part of usually don't remember them at all. If this pattern sounds at all recognizable to you, there are two directions you can go in.

The first (and recommended) option is, as Ann did, to find a qualified counselor with whom you can work. In light of the fact that this behavior pattern is so much driven by feelings of low self-esteem, we recommend looking for help from a therapist or counselor. You don't need someone to give you a career test or two and tell you what direction to shoot at next. You need a counselor with some knowledge of psychology and skill in psychotherapy.

The second option is to sit down with yourself and, as we did with Ann, start digging into your work history and into the years before you started working. Read Chapter 16 ("Looking in the Mirror") in Part II, which explores how people form negative self-images that are so much a part of the coulda-been experience. Look for themes and underlying patterns in your work history and for causes in your early history. This process is usually different, as well as painful (which is why we recommend, if possible, that you work with a counselor). This may take a considerable length of time to work through as well. When you feel that you have as clear a picture as you can get about both how and why your career has taken the course it has to date, begin to look forward and chart your own course. As Ann did, think in terms of a "good-enough job" that will move you in the direction of the career *you* want. Both of these are important. If the job has to be *great,* the process won't be successful. Understand that it is a career move, not the rest of your life. "Good enough" is good enough for now. As Ann also did, make sure it's the direction *you* want to go in, not what some members of your family or other people in your life want for you and are telling you is the right path. We often tell students we speak to that they need to make sure they don't take the perfect job—perfect for their next-door neighbor! This sounds easy, but it isn't. In this regard we also recommend that you carefully read Chapter 12, "Losing the Path," which discusses the importance of fashioning a career from your actual life circumstances rather than from abstractions and from messages received from other people and society at large.

Ann did sign on for a second year—a lifetime first; and in her fifth year at the same college she was appointed director of women's athletics. Sometime afterward we asked Ann what her parents thought of her career. They liked the "director" part best, she said.

When she moved we gave Ann a going-away present as a reminder, a framed favorite quote of ours from the speech John Backus, the original developer of the first computer language, FORTRAN, gave when he accepted the prestigious Draper Prize for his work. He said:

> I myself have had many failures and I've learned that if you are not failing a lot, you are probably not being as creative as you could be. You aren't stretching your imagination enough. So it is important to remember that failure is the partner of success.

CHAPTER

ELEVEN

LACKING A SENSE OF BOUNDARIES

Thao loved her work and felt very close to the people in her office. She thought of them as members of her family. She took their hopes, worries, triumphs, and defeats home with her every night, just as every morning she brought the issues of her household—her baby's earache, her husband's relationship with her mother—to the office, where she spread them out before her colleagues. There was no wall at all between her professional and personal life, between office and home. All that separated the two was a thirty-five minute commute. Thao continued to feel that tight bond to her company and to her co-workers—right up to the day they fired her.

Thao worked for a large travel agency in Minneapolis, where she was a top producer. Her easy interpersonal manner, warmth, approachability and genuine caring for her clients made her an excellent agent. Clients stayed with her and referred others to her as well. Thao managed several of the agency's most important accounts, among them an investment group consisting of several dozen wealthy individuals. Theirs was quiet, discreet money. But one night at a cocktail party, Thao chatted away about how she had just booked first-class airline tickets to Singapore and expensive hotel suites for several of the group's partners.

Someone overheard Thao and later mentioned it in passing to one of the members of the group. He and his partners were furious. For competitive reasons, they had kept their planned trip confidential, or so they had intended. They fired the travel agency—and the agency fired Thao.

It wasn't the first time that Thao had talked too much. Thao *always* talked too much. She wasn't a gossip. Thao never deliberately said anything damaging about anyone. She wasn't malicious. She was generous to a fault, and in fact, the one thing she *wouldn't* talk about was other people's troubles and defeats. Nor was she a braggart. Yes, she gabbed about the commissions on those tickets to Singapore, but she was just as likely to go on about a piece of business they had not landed or about someone else's achievements.

Her compulsion was sharing for the sake of sharing. She couldn't resist an opportunity to pour out her thoughts, feelings, and experiences to whoever was near. When we met Thao we were reminded of the World War II warning made famous in the poster campaign "Loose Lips Sink Ships." The message was intended as a warning to anyone who might innocently pass on damaging information to an enemy agent.

THE DYNAMICS OF THE PATTERN

The person who lacks an appropriate sense of boundaries doesn't understand that some subjects belong in the office and some belong only in certain corners of the office—and definitely not outside. Conversely, he or she doesn't understand that other subjects belong at home; that even if someone in the office *is* interested in your mother's stock portfolio or your marital problems, these topics don't really belong there.

Let us give a hypothetical example. A person who lacks a sense of boundaries overhears Fred in the coffee line complaining in an offhand way about having to work over the weekend; he or she goes to the manager and asks if there is a way to lighten Fred's workload. The intention is genuinely to help out and for Fred to know that someone cares and is looking out for his interests—and for the boss to know that the individual is concerned about company morale. But both Fred and the manager, of course, deeply resent what they see as meddling, and Fred is embarrassed that his boss got wind of his complaining—*and* of the fact that he's behind in his work. The road to hell, as the old saying goes, is paved with good intentions, and people with loose lips lay a lot of the stones.

People who lack boundaries also characteristically feel uncomfortable with—and refuse to honor—the boundary inherent in supervisor-subordinate relationships. They talk "out of school," confiding information to subordinates that they shouldn't know about and shouldn't be expected to keep confidential themselves. In the interest of forging a bond between themselves and their subordinates, they may, for example, prematurely reveal the company's reorganization plans ("But you can't tell a soul!" the person may warn).

What these individuals crave is affiliation and intimacy—not sexual intimacy, but emotional intimacy and closeness. The person with loose lips is the polar opposite of the person who plays his cards close to the vest. People with little sense of boundaries can't wait for an occasion to share inappropriate (although of course they don't think of it as such) information about themselves in the mistaken belief that if they tell everything about themselves, other people will reciprocate, and this will develop a close friendship. They confuse self-disclosure with intimacy.

Indeed, people often do enjoy these individuals—up to a point. When we work as executive coaches we usually interview a dozen or more of the client's colleagues (his or her peers, subordinates, manager, and that individual's manager), asking them to tell us about our client (off the record, of course). On one occasion in which the client suffered from this behavior pattern, the people we interviewed compared our client to a big, friendly, but ultimately overbearing golden retriever. Everyone enjoys seeing that wagging tail and enthusiastic welcome, but when the irrepressible canine jumps up and starts licking faces, most people think companionship has gone too far. Eventually they come to want to put a little more distance between themselves and the individual.

THE ORIGINS OF LOOSE LIPS

What is the etiology of this behavior pattern? In some cases the pattern may be—in part, at least—a function of attention deficit disorder. Experts used to tie the diagnosis of attention deficit disorder with hyperactivity, but today attention deficit disorder is viewed as a separate disorder, sometimes involving hyperactivity, sometimes not. Dr. Edward Hallowell, coauthor of *Driven to Distraction* and a leading expert on the subject, says that these individuals actually have a *surplus* of attention, that the deficit is really in *control* of that attention and its attendant impulses. The child with attention deficit disorder can't control the impulse to jump up from his seat or stop to look at something on her way to practice piano. Similarly, the adult with attention deficit disorder may have trouble controlling the impulse to talk about whatever may be on his or her mind.

Another factor, not mutually exclusive of a possible attention deficit disorder, is the individual's home and broader social environment. Several of the people we have consulted with who suffer from this pattern came from families and ethnic and/or regional cultures in which the self-disclosure of personal information and of sharing feelings was accepted and encouraged. *Not* to talk about what happened at school, at work, or on a date would be seen as odd, either as a sign that something was wrong or as an affront. Secrets are not allowed; privacy is discouraged. There are no psychological "walls."

Such was the case with Thao. Thao was raised in Southern California, where there was less of a tendency to be buttoned-down than is true in other parts of the country. Moreover, Thao's family made "sharing" part of their daily ritual. She grew up in a warm and loving family that in most ways prepared Thao very well for the world. But when it came to boundaries, the family created in Thao an expectation that went far beyond what the business world (or the world in general) would meet or even tolerate. Thao was an only child, and her father was a middle school principal who brought home to dinner all of the disciplinary problems with students, rivalries among teachers and coaches, and concerns about his own job security, pay, and retirement benefits. Her mother debriefed Thao at length every day about what had happened during her hours at school. If Thao looked a bit dejected or upset, her mother would want to know why, asking well before Thao even got a chance to say that she was upset.

Thao was attractive and gregarious, and when she reached high school she had several boyfriends. After every date her mother would ask Thao for a detailed account of the evening. She wasn't concerned about Thao's sexual activity, she just wanted to know all about what they did and if Thao had enjoyed her time. A lot of teenage girls would have resented what they would have seen as prying. Not Thao. She rather enjoyed it, just as she loved to listen to her mother's stories about her own high school days.

In college Thao called her mother almost daily to keep her up-to-date on all that was going on in her life. Thao joined a sorority in which the sisters would sit up all night discussing their classes, dates, family members, dreams, and aspirations—a familiar enough ritual at any college, but one that Thao remembered with particular fondness—along with playing "Truth or Dare" (she always opted for "truth").

After college Thao joined the Peace Corps, a wonderful and rewarding experience and one that reinforced her habit of sharing and experiencing the world as one in which boundaries were, so to say, "permeable." There were no boundaries in the Peace Corps between one's professional life and one's personal life. Exchanging experiences, ideas, and feelings with the villagers was important to the success of the assignment. Other volunteers would arrive at Thao's tiny house to spend the night unannounced, and Thao did the same. The villagers were like family, as were members of the community of Peace Corps volunteers. Thao had gone from one family (her real family) to a family of friends in college and then to another in the Peace Corps.

In our experience, individuals in this pattern are most often college graduates. During those college years they spent time in an educational system that—much more than the average high school—both values their ideas and questions and obscures distinctions between the teachers and the taught. Graduate assistants and teaching assistants are usually only a few years older than the students in their classes and tutorials. Dating between the former and latter is a frequent occurrence. And even freshmen can approach a full professor or a dean with a question or opinion. By way of contrast, an assembly line worker or order taker on an 800 number doesn't expect an immediate audience with the plant manager or business leader. If they have something to say, they're going to do it "by the book" and start with the shop steward or their immediate supervisor—or in some instances they'll have heard the unspoken message that they should just keep their opinions to themselves. For someone already predisposed to ignore boundaries, four years of college only supports their view that just as "rules are made to be broken," boundaries are made to be stepped over.

Thao was not so naive as to think that the world of business was the same as that of the Peace Corps. She understood well enough the difference between the profit motive and the altruistic motive of a nonprofit organization. But after twenty-five years in settings where there were few or no boundaries—family, college, the Peace Corps—she failed to recognize that she was suddenly in a world where there are compartments. Home is one place, the office is another. The office, too, is segmented. The CEO's daily path through the company is very different from that of the clerk's. There are lines as well between the executive level and middle management and between middle management and the "workers."

LOOSE LIPS IN AN ORGANIZATION

In some companies, that segmentation, or stratification, may be very clear and formalized. Top executives eat in a separate dining room and have their own parking places. Their offices are all on "the fourteenth floor," a location subordinates refer to with a mixture of awe, envy, and fear. In other companies the separations may be much more subtle. The organizational chart is "flatter," everyone is on a first-name basis with everyone else, and everyone eats in the same cafeteria.

Still, even in the most relaxed of companies there are boundaries that most employees from top to bottom recognize. A project manager in the research department doesn't wander into the CEO's office and ask him whether he caught the *Nova* special on PBS the night before. Nor does the CEO approach a payroll clerk in the parking lot and start chatting about her golf game. But people who lack a sense of boundaries recognize neither the concrete barriers of the highly structured company nor the subtle signposts of the less formal organization.

One exception here is the world of higher education, where, at least at the lower and middle levels of administration, the "collegial" atmosphere that exists among students and faculty may extend to administration. One of our colleagues, having left the for-profit business world for a position in a university research center, was mildly astonished not only at the informality and looseness of boundaries, but at the "process orientation" that often accompanies those other cultural elements. "I just can't believe it," she said after a month in the position. "They process everything, and I mean *every*thing! We spend so much time making sure that everyone agrees with everyone else and that everybody feels good about it."

Obviously, what is acceptable in one culture may be absolutely taboo in another. This is true in terms of the differences in national culture among countries. There are real differences in the kinds of physical boundaries members of different national cultures prefer and in terms of what is acceptable to talk about. One client company we consulted to was a subsidiary of a South American parent company, and the majority of its employees in its U.S. branch were from the home country. Topics that many members of the firm were quite comfortable discussing among themselves were totally off limits with their American colleagues (conversations and comments about how women dressed, whom they found attractive, who was dating whom—as well as such manners of address as "honey," "gorgeous," and the like). Whatever we might think of such comments, they were a clear violation of boundaries of extreme proportions in the United States.

In addition to variation in how strictly different organizational cultures enforce interpersonal boundaries, the various work functions themselves may present better and worse degrees of fit for someone who has trouble maintaining these boundaries. For example, working in a corporate general counsel's office presents one extreme. Dealing with sensitive legal issues demands the utmost in boundary maintenance. A slip of the tongue could result in a loss of patent rights, the failure of an acquisition, or an insider trading scandal that could result in severe Securities and Exchange Commission penalties—potentially leading to criminal proceedings and prison terms for insider trading. At the other end of the continuum is working on a sales force—but not because, as some people might think, successful salespeople are individuals who talk constantly, "schmoozing" and forming relationships with everyone they meet. The advantage comes from being outside the company, especially selling products that have a short selling cycle. It presents the person whose behavior falls into this pattern with two potentially saving graces. The first has to do with selling products *outside* the company, because he or she is simply not in the office nearly as much, minimizing the potential for the person to talk too much about topics that are inappropriate. Second, the virtue of selling a product with a short selling cycle is that the person calls on a large number of customers for short periods of time—versus, for example, a sales team at Boeing cultivating a dedicated relationship with Japan Air Lines executives that may lead to one sale of several jets—but only after a sales effort that lasts years. By limiting their exposure to each individual customer, people with this pattern limit their potential for doing damage. (This is, in fact, just the role that a few people we know who fit this pattern have gravitated to, with great success.)

People's initial response to someone with this pattern of behavior is sometimes quite positive. The person is often seen as a breath of fresh air, someone whose openness and warmth are attractive. The fact that they are so self-disclosing can elicit a positive reaction and frequently a reciprocal disclosure. These responses can eventually become negative, however, for several reasons. First, it eventually becomes apparent to the co-worker that there is nothing really intimate in the shared disclosure—the person tells all sorts of intimate details to *everyone*. Then comes a feeling of discomfort about anything the co-worker has shared in turn—will that, too, be so openly shared?—and finally a fear to share any similar details as it becomes clear that the person has little or no sense of others' boundaries and desires for privacy.

Frank, one of our clients, for example, had been working for a large consumer goods manufacturer for less than a year, but in that time he seemed to have met *everyone*. He was happy to introduce newcomers around and to share the office scuttlebutt. Frank was a font of information about people and plans: what the management team was thinking about one strategic shift or another, any alliances in the works, whose stars were rising and whose were falling. Given his generally gregarious manner, Frank made many friends in the organization. Predictably, though, things started to unravel when word began to get back to those people he was discussing, describing, and quoting.

True to the pattern, Frank talked too much and too widely about his social life ("Why can't I ever meet someone I really like who likes me?" and so on), his relationship with his mother, his friends, and his therapy. All of this created a sense of intimacy with newcomers to his circle of contacts, until they learned that almost everyone knew about Frank's life and times.

In addition, it came to pass that Frank was as much a font of *mis*information as he was of information. It was true that he had met an unusually large number of senior people in the company (in light of his tenure and junior rank), but he tended to take casual remarks, heard without the benefit of full context, and both magnify them and take them as gospel. The result was that people came to see that his assessments were as often as not flawed and his information incorrect. They also saw that when he was correct, it was most often the most obvious calls.

Ultimately Frank and the company went their separate ways. As is often the case in such circumstances, the parting was generally amicable. Frank was seen as a nice guy with good intentions and someone who worked hard. So people had no hard feelings about him, just a sense that he was someone you couldn't trust not to broadcast any news he got.

Some allowance may be made for the person in this pattern if he or she is young and new to the working world. "They just haven't learned yet," managers and colleagues think. "They'll adjust; in the meantime I'll give them some hints about what is and isn't appropriate to discuss." That kind of allowance goes only so far, however, and lasts for only so long. Several years out of college or graduate school, and the person is expected to know better.

Individuals who fall into this behavior pattern can be very successful in business if they learn to *modulate* their behavior, holding on to that part of their personality that is attractive and engaging while toning down the extreme (and learning something about reading the organization's and other people's "road signs"). Temperamentally, though, they have a serious disadvantage, and the more structured or more hierarchical the company is, the more damaging the handicap. As we discussed earlier, Harvard psychologist David McClelland describes three motivators that account for much of people's behavior in work: the need for power, the need for achievement, and the need for affiliation. People with loose lips are driven almost exclusively by the need for affiliation, the desire to be part of a team, a group, a community. They feel a deep craving to belong and to connect with people on a personal level. By contrast, the predominant motivations of managers and executives in business are first, the need for power; and second, the need for achievement. The need for affiliation tends to finish last. Nevertheless, there is a place in business for people with a high need for affiliation, as long as that need doesn't drive every aspect of their behavior.

Art, for example, struggled mightily with "loose lips." What others experienced initially as boyish enthusiasm and charm wore thin before long, and Art got the message that unless he learned to read other people better and restrained himself, his prospects for advancement into the managerial ranks were negligible. He worked for a large advertising agency, on the "creative" side, where boundaries were generally pretty loose to begin with, but Art managed to push even that envelope. Fortunately his manager made it clear that some topics were taboo, and equally fortunately Art loved his job beyond all measure. The result was a concerted effort on his part (along with continuing feedback on the part of his manager) that continues even now—successfully.

After the Peace Corps, Thao drifted in and out of a couple of corporate jobs. She found the instructors in the management training programs "too stiff" and her managers "unapproachable." (They didn't feel enough like "family.") She was hired to work for the travel agency as she was approaching her thirtieth birthday. In many important respects Thao was perfect for the job. She was smart, articulate, and well traveled; she genuinely cared about people; and, not surprisingly, she learned a lot about her clients very quickly. She knew who was squeamish about certain kinds of food, who had phobias about particular kinds of airplanes, who was snobbish about being put in the sorts of hotels American tourists were supposed to feel comfortable in. She gathered this information easily because as she shared her own tastes and eccentricities with her clients, they gave up theirs as well.

But, as we described earlier, Thao didn't know where to draw the line, where to make the vital separation between the personal and professional, between public and private. Her colleagues, men and women alike, dressed in business suits. Thao would arrive at least twice a week dressed in blue jeans and a turtleneck with her year-old baby in tow. Her child was almost always well behaved, but the sight of Thao making phone calls with a baby pulling on the phone cord was less than professional. The president of the agency, who did her best to accommodate employees, told Thao that it was okay to bring her baby in an emergency, but that she had to find reliable day care. Thao brushed the president off, as though as her boss she had to say that, but she didn't really mean it.

Like an outgoing golden retriever, Thao made it a point to get to know everyone in the office. She brought in homemade cookies and fruit and spread them out on the office coffee table, giving the office a casual, folksy look. A couple of colleagues privately thought it also gave the office an amateurish look and that any clients who came into the office might legitimately wonder if the agents were paying attention to business or having a party.

If someone was depressed or a little out of sorts, Thao did her best to cheer the person up. Colleagues liked and appreciated her for that, up to a point. But she always wanted to know more about what was bothering them than they wanted to tell. Unsolicited, Thao also told them about whatever was bothering her (including her difficulties with her husband)—more than they wanted to hear. Her colleagues felt embarrassed when from time to time her husband would come to the office to pick up the baby. They felt awkward hearing Thao talk about their marriage counseling in the morning and seeing him in the afternoon, obviously pretending to know nothing about their problems.

They also learned more about Thao's conception than they needed or wanted to know. Thao had had trouble conceiving, so she and her husband had gone to a fertility clinic. Thao told her colleagues in detail about the procedures they had gone through before conceiving their daughter. All of this made her colleagues squirm—and more than a little. But because she was so generous in spirit—*and* such a good producer—the boss put up with it.

Then Thao's trespasses became not just discomfiting, but detrimental to the company's business. She began to talk about her clients in front of the other agents. She would hang up the phone after a conversation with a client, for example, and say to no one in particular, "I hope he doesn't get on the plane in that condition," or, "*That* marriage isn't going to last." The president overheard Thao on one occasion, called her into her office, and reprimanded her. Thao insisted that she hadn't done anything wrong, that everyone had problems, herself included, and that it wasn't her fault her clients confided in her. The boss countered that this was simply out of bounds in a place of business. Thao disagreed, but she promised to be more discreet. She broke her promise, of course, when she chatted about her client's Singapore plans at the party. And that was the end for Thao.

HOW TO BREAK THE PATTERN

What can you do if you realize you often behave according to this pattern? One important choice you have to make involves environment. Organizations vary a great deal in terms of their level of formality, whether or not they favor direct or indirect styles of communication, as well as in their tolerance for diversity. (There are many dimensions to diversity, including, among others, ethnic or racial background, sexual orientation, and personality type.) In the interests of making life easier for everyone, someone who exhibits this behavior pattern should avoid employment in organizations with a strong sense of hierarchy and rigid code of dress and behavior. Working for a large, straitlaced New York, Boston, or Philadelphia law firm, for example, is almost certain to be a mistake.

There are some clues any prospective employee with this behavior pattern should pay careful attention to before accepting a job. First, look around the offices of the people interviewing you. Do the employees have pictures of their families on their desks, drawings by their children on the wall? Do the offices "feel" warm, or are they more sterile, as if anyone could be setting up shop in there? How are people dressed? Is there variety in the way people dress? (This is an indicator of the range of self-expression that is tolerated.) How do senior executives talk to their staff assistants and vice versa (familiarly or with distance and def-erence)? How do they talk to their direct reports? If they all go out for a relaxed lunch, what do the executives talk about? Do they discuss per-sonal matters, or is it strictly business? Are there many different types of people in the organization (introverts as well as extroverts, people of different ethnic groups, and so forth)? How much conversation is there in the waiting room and hallways? Pay close attention to all of these in-tangibles. No one is going to define the culture for you ("Well, we're re-ally pretty formal and distant here; the 'human' side of things is kept to a minimum"); the burden is on you to carefully observe and gather data about the culture that you will live in day in and day out should you ac-cept the job.

Even the most relaxed, down-to-earth company has boundaries, borders between the private and public that cannot be crossed. If you fall into the pattern of being unable to properly assess boundaries, you *must* learn to recognize those dividing lines, however difficult that may be. In respect to boundaries, there are two errors individuals with this Achilles' heel tend to make: not recognizing other people's boundaries (taking other people's perspectives into account), and not *respecting* them. In regard to recognizing boundaries, Chapter 13 in Part II, "Tak-ing Others' Perspectives," discusses the importance of learning to see things from other people's points of view. Perspective taking is espe-cially key if you fall into this pattern, in that you probably tend to pay little attention to whether other people *want* to know the personal infor-mation you're giving them—or whether they might even be uncomfort-able knowing it. People with this fatal flaw often fail to consider whether other people might feel intruded upon by personal questions. They fail to recognize that they could be putting a subordinate in an uncomfort-able position by giving information that they shouldn't have. Learning to take the perspective of the listener is critical to learning when to say what—and when not to say anything at all.

Individuals with a "loose lips" syndrome sometimes see honoring boundaries as "bowing to authority." The authority in question may be your manager or the written *and* unwritten organizational culture (for example, in the form of address or in a dress code). It is important, therefore, that you read "Coming to Terms with Authority" in Part II of the book in order to gain a better perspective on the issue of *respecting* boundaries. One analogy we use to better understand the notion of "submitting" to authority is that of dancing. Successful dancing (the old-fashioned "touch dancing" of the fox-trot, tango, and waltz variety) requires both partners to understand where their physical boundaries are and to work together, dancing "as one." Similarly, working with personal and organizational boundaries entails moving fluidly forward, back, and to the side—a bit closer now, then more distant, asking and telling, then silent. It does not really involve submitting per se; it is working together.

People who have problems with this behavior pattern will also, at times, brush aside the matter of boundaries when it is pointed out to them, as if anyone who cares about such things is simply "uptight." Vincent, for example, liked to tell jokes. They were never off-color; they were just inappropriate in the context of his particular working environment. One of his colleagues pointed this out to him, and he responded that this was just what the organization needed—to develop a sense of humor. In effect, Vincent was refusing to acknowledge others' personal authority.

There are two factors that we always address with clients. First, if the person has *any* indications of attention deficit disorder—any at all— we recommend that the person read one of the books available on the topic and that he or she get a medical consultation on the issue. If attention deficit disorder is fueling this impulsive overstepping of boundaries, you will be fighting an unnecessarily difficult battle unless you can bring some kind of help to bear. The other factor we discuss is how well developed the individual's network of friends outside the workplace is. Obvious as this may be, more than a few of the people we've seen with this problem simply don't have enough friends outside their work, so they naturally turn inappropriately to their co-workers to fill that role. They need to find other avenues to make friends and meet their needs for affiliation. As they do so, the "too familiar" behavior often abates.

We provide individuals in this pattern with an array of techniques, "tools" to carry around with them, using whichever is appropriate and appealing at the moment. For example, the television and radio networks have a delay on live broadcasts to allow them to cover any obscenities a guest might utter, and we have our clients think in those same terms. "Think twice, speak once" is one motto for them to live by; "Silence is golden" is another. We remind them always to remember that just as a house is not a home, neither is an office a home or a family. We urge them to remember that once something is said it can *never* be taken back. As we do with several of the other patterns, we have these individuals go into the culture in which they work as if they were anthropologists, observing the customs and rules of the tribe. Then we discuss how they have been violating those norms and what they need to change to fit in. "Meshing gears" is a graphic analogy some find useful as they think about what they've been doing wrong and how they need to change to fit in better.

Having an ally inside the organization to help monitor a problem is crucial, and we urge it especially strongly in the case of this set of behaviors. Because the individuals we have described in this chapter find it so natural to transgress boundaries, and because their actions are frequently met with initial positive reactions, enlisting the aid of someone else to tell them when they are beginning to go too far will be of great help. We recommend that you choose someone you trust and with whom you have a great deal of direct contact so that the person can observe you directly in your daily work. You might even consider agreeing on some kind of signal that this person can make discreetly during meetings or other conversation if he or she sees you overstepping boundaries (a more subtle version of the kick under the table). Thao, unfortunately, was not one of our successes. We met with her for several months after she found another job subsequent to her dismissal from the travel agency. We worked with her to recognize just how little psychological distance she had between herself and her work. We made reference to some of her Peace Corps training, understanding cross-cultural differences (such as in the space people stand apart from each other when talking). We tried to get her to acknowledge the beauties and benefits of silence. We had her put memos to that effect on the dashboard of her car, on her computer screen and elsewhere. But fundamentally Thao wanted the closeness that she had attempted to create at the agency more than she wanted to change. In time, she talked herself out of her new job as well, and we lost contact with her. Her story brings back to mind a variation on the wartime cautionary "Loose lips will sink *your* ship."

If this pattern applies not to you, but rather to someone you work with or who reports to you, one of the things that we hope we've provided you with in this chapter is a deeper and more nuanced understanding of the dynamics of this seemingly simple behavior pattern. At its most superficial level it appears to be no different from the chattering of a five-year-old who hasn't yet quite come to understand that other people might want to talk, too, and that not everyone is interested in every detail about them and what happened during their day. And just as you might want nothing more than to say, "Will you be *quiet?!?*" so you may want to say much the same thing to the person you work with.

Clearly this *is* a pattern that needs management. But if you can help motivate the individual in question to change, educate him or her about the issue and its consequences, and work with the person to overcome the impulse to overstep boundaries, you can salvage an employee who will stay with your organization over the long term. And in an era in which employee retention is one key to any company's success, this is not to be overlooked as a competitive advantage worth the investment.

CHAPTER
TWELVE

LOSING THE PATH

People often seek us out for consultation not because a particular behavior pattern is jeopardizing their careers, but because they feel they have lost, at least for the time being, their sense of direction. Sometimes our client questions whether he or she has been headed in the right direction at all. At other times the issue is a sense of enthusiasm that has diminished or disappeared for reasons that are not immediately clear. Sometimes one of the behavior patterns discussed in earlier chapters are themselves sparked by or exacerbated by the fact that we are in the wrong job or industry. A life crisis, too, can take us to an unexpected turn in the road that leads rapidly into an unfamiliar landscape. The birth of a child, a divorce, the death of a parent, or a business reversal can all deepen our questioning about our work choices in a way that would have been impossible to predict.

This sense of finding oneself in a career desert is not, in its essence, a personal experience, though it always feels like a private problem caused by some personal mistake, inadequacy, or ill fortune. Feeling disconnected and unhappy with our work is a *signal* that it is time for change. It is a sign that the content of our days is out of line with the type of activity we need to feel most engaged. We feel frustration and the need to "dig deeper." Sometimes this digging deeper means a recommitment to our job or a renegotiation of our role, perhaps taking on more or different responsibilities. Sometimes it may mean leaving our job altogether, even changing careers. This feeling of disconnection and frustration can take many forms:

- A sense of powerlessness—that you are not making and acting on the decisions that matter
- Feeling that you are not listened to in meetings and that your ideas are not valued
- A vague sense of lethargy—a reluctance to start projects or push them forward; lack of interest in making calls or widening your network within and outside of the organization
- A sense that your daily efforts have largely become routine, predictable, and lacking in challenge or opportunity for learning
- Feeling that your role is marginalized
- Feeling that you are not compensated adequately or are compensated disproportionately compared with others of similar experience and training
- Consistently feeling high levels of stress or anxiety about performance
- Regularly feeling depressed, cynical, and pessimistic or functioning at low energy
- Feeling that what you are doing doesn't matter beyond immediate business goals, that your work is not making a contribution to the needs of others
- Finding yourself in frequent conflict with co-workers or feeling that most of your initiatives turn into battles
- Feeling that you are "falling behind," that your peers at other organizations or in different careers have more excitement, responsibility, money, and opportunity
- Feeling "burned out," that you no longer care about your responsibilities or about your co-workers and customers

These are the reasons many of our clients come to us for career counseling. Peter Ulani had risen to director level in a university setting.

During the first few years with the school he felt as if he were connected to an important mission that would change the lives of the students in the classes and programs that he administered. Now, four years later, he felt as if his days were becoming routine and his job more that of a bureaucrat. Debbie Chen had excelled as a lending officer at a large commercial bank and enjoyed the autonomy that a successful salesperson earns. Now, returning to her job after a maternity leave, she felt as if the job lacked intellectual challenge and wondered if it was time to go back to school. Ron Lang had entered a start-up with the title of COO. Now, five years later, the job itself had changed radically from a strategy-focused role to that of day-to-day manager of an increasingly complex organization. Not only was he not excited about heading for work on Monday morning, but he was beginning to find that he was letting details slip.

In addition to "first time" clients, we also get a chance to work with people at different times in their career journey, when they return after a period of years to work with us as they face a new challenge. Ray Brautigan was such a client. It had been eight years since we had seen Ray. At that time Ray was thirty-six and in a career crisis. He was working as a communications professional in the marketing department of a large investment management firm in San Francisco. He viewed himself as someone who was primarily artistic in nature, as well as a strong communicator who was highly effective in influencing and persuading others. His personality and life choices contrasted sharply with those of his father, who was a highly analytical, practical, and successful engineer. His father had been disappointed in Ray's decision not to pursue an established, mainstream profession such as engineering. When Ray first came to us he felt that his father may have been right after all. He was stuck in a lower-level staff job, with limited input over the nature of his projects, little authority, and compensation that did not begin to compare with that of his college friends who pursued degrees in law or medicine. By working with us, he was able to move successfully through that difficult time. He married, fathered two children, started his own business with a friend from college, and beautifully renovated a condominium in Palo Alto.

Now Ray was back in our office and feeling stuck again, concerned about his failing interest in work. His business had lately seen new and vigorous competition. Revenue had fallen dramatically and his family was in a difficult situation financially. A redoubled effort and the creation of both new services and a new client base were necessary just to survive. At the same time he felt worn down by ongoing differences of opinion with his business partner, whom he felt was often autocratic and controlling. He didn't know if he had energy to pump into a situation about which he felt so ambivalent. He had already taken a long vacation—but no epiphany was forthcoming. Sitting in our consulting office, he was clearly in pain and at a loss. What he wanted more than anything was to find himself again as he had eight years ago, full of enthusiasm and a large reservoir of energy for work that truly felt right. . . .

We have seen elements of Ray's situation in every person we have counseled, as well as in ourselves and in our closest friends and family members. Ray's story reveals a pattern not unlike the narratives we find in myths and fairy tales: developing a vision; losing the vision and becoming lost; and the search for the way back. In Ray's case it meant learning to make work not ideal, perhaps, but more real and satisfying. Finding a vision, feeling lost, and finding our way back are life stages that we will all traverse many times in our careers.

FINDING A VISION

The way in which we each find our way in our professional lives, and find our way back again and again when motivation and inspiration falter, is different for each of us; there are no formulas, no sages to tell us the answer, no one to do it for us.

One client, Terry Nicolson, a successful investment banker, described to us an early goal that he had held since adolescence—to graduate from a particular business school. He described the discipline and schedule that he had laid out for himself as a teenager to accomplish that goal. "In my junior year in high school," he told us, "I could tell you exactly what my study schedule was and exactly how many repetitions of each type of exercise I had planned for each day between the first day of school and Thanksgiving."

Such a tightly focused career vision is certainly not the only way to success. We have worked with many individuals whose career visions developed at an entirely different pace and unfolded in an entirely different way. One professional we worked with, a management consultant both to the marketing department of a consumer products business and to a not-for-profit agency, changed course at the age of thirty-two and took a major management position in a health management organization. Along the way she seriously considered becoming a psychiatrist. No one who knows her would consider her "unfocused," "drifting," or "lost." In fact, she is the epitome of the efficient, principled, and dedicated business professional. Today she is seen as one of the star senior managers in the organization where she works. Her vision, her career evolution, was quite different from Terry's. Her career rhythm involved experiencing things, questioning herself, seeking new experiences, further questioning, another new experience, and so on. Her way of finding career focus involved more of a willingness to take chances and make mistakes, along with a wish to sample a broader range of life.

The ways in which we find our connection with meaningful work are so nuanced and so individual that most attempts to present models of career decision making, or even describe the process in a convincing way, pale in comparison with the struggle and excitement, the confusion and joy, of the lived experience. Above we related two different kinds of career vision. Both would be labeled "success stories" by the majority of people at most any point in the process. Some, though, wander for years in the desert before finding a road! This is the way they have learned to find what is important. The fact is, there is no single path for each of us to travel. What we call career is a "pathless path" that finds us in a different landscape at each decade of our life, that takes different turns from year to year.

Our first book, *Discovering Your Career in Business*, was about the underlying unique patterns of our life interests that seek expression through our activities. If we think of our day-to-day interests—jazz, cooking, football, soap operas, French literature, gardening, the stock market—it's not always easy to identify an underlying pattern. But the pattern is there. Such patterns are among the most enduring and unique features of human personality. Our interests are, in fact, a "deep structure" of our psychological makeup. During childhood and adolescence, interest patterns are less stable and more difficult to measure. But by the time we are in our early twenties, we each have a unique "signature" of interests that will have remarkable stability for the remainder of our lives. Individual, specific interests may develop later or become less salient as we are introduced to new activities, but the essential pattern of our interests changes very little over time.

Having a career vision is a task of moving continually toward daily work situations that provide for the expression of our inherent patterns of life interests. This "moving toward," however, is not a simple matter. It requires both a "looking in" and a "looking out." We must first become aware of what our deepest enthusiasms are and articulate them in a way that is specific and real for us—"looking in." A lot of this work goes on when we are in our twenties, but it is a task that really continues all of our lives. "Looking out" refers to the task of finding work in the ever-changing landscape of the economy that will allow you to live out what you have discovered about your deepest interests. Knowing exactly what you want is not enough if you don't know where to look for it or how to find it.

These looking-in and looking-out processes go on at the same time. Although patterns of life interests are innate, it takes interaction with the world in order for us to come to knowledge of what interests us most deeply. We have found there is no meaningful distinction between what we call our "self" and our activities in the world. We come to know who we are and what we want only by going into the world and having experiences and then understanding how those experiences affect us. It is as if certain activities "wake up" parts of our selves that were previously unavailable. We have all had the experience of listening to a piece of music that opens up feelings that we have not visited in a long time or reading a book that makes us see or feel in a different way. In doing these things, we do not "discover something new," we *become more of our selves.*

FEELING LOST

In our counseling work we have discovered that the most frequent source of career dissatisfaction is a misalignment between an individual's underlying interest patterns and his or her actual day-to-day work activities. As we move through our twenties and into our thirties, the rising vision of who we are and the work we want gathers intensity. It is a time of exploration, of opening doors, of trial and error. We can sense what we want but can't yet describe it fully. It seems close at hand but mysteriously elusive. The vision is a sense of where enthusiasm lies, of where there is greater likelihood of feeling more alive. This task of vision building lasts a lifetime.

We long to find the circumstances, the organization, the role, the title, the position, the authority, and the place to actually bring our vision more and more into our daily world. In the right job, on many days, we have the sense that we are doing just what we were born for; vision and action are one. At other times we feel far from our calling and are not sure why our workdays have become what they are. We feel lost, out of place, and seemingly less able to act than those around us who appear to have focus and a strong connection to their work and goals. Typically we don't just wake up to this state one day; rather, it's a condition that grows over time until we can no longer deny it. When we are honest with ourselves, we may feel a sense of surprise at how long we have felt this way. Many of the business professionals who come to us for career counseling had been able, at earlier times, to articulate their career vision and had experienced periods of accomplishment and personal satisfaction. When they come to see us, however, they often find themselves alienated and unsure how to retrace their steps to that time when work gave them more energy, not less.

There are few of us who have not experienced, at some point in our work lives, many of the symptoms of alienation listed at the beginning of this chapter. Feeling and experiencing these things is part of the normal process of career development. The great danger during periods of work alienation is that of becoming *identified* with your symptoms. When you are identified with such pessimism, you have no distance from it and feel that you *are* your mood—that the condition you are experiencing is the essence of your true identity. You can become hyper-critical of yourself and taken over by crippling self-doubt. Then you become a problem to yourself, rather than seeing your circumstances as a challenge.

LEARNING FROM ALIENATION AT WORK

Here is an exercise that will help you to learn more about your particular pattern of alienation and frustration at work. It requires focusing on difficult feelings from the past. If at any time during the exercise you should feel uncomfortable, simply discontinue it; you can use the ideas from this chapter without the benefit of the exercise.

Read again the list of symptoms of work alienation that appear at the beginning of this chapter. Think about the images, memories, and associations that come to you as you read them. Now read them again, deliberately and slowly. Pay attention to the images they generate. Do not censor or analyze them. Allow them to develop, these images that arise from words about alienation, frustration, feeling lost at work, and being disconnected from a sense of yourself and your ability to act. Be alert to any specific memories and feelings that they evoke. Pay particular attention to the feelings of alienation, disinterest, and lack of energy. It is impossible to relive such feelings as they were experienced at the time they occurred, but we can catch echoes of them, through our attention and imagination. Stay with these feelings for several minutes if possible. Note where you were and what you were doing at the time. Your tendency will be to cut off and move away from the feelings that emerge. Try to stay with them. Write down, with a few key word reminders, what you are seeing and feeling. Take your time. Allow the images and the memories to develop. Move back in time to when the events took place. Once you are there, look around; try to see, feel, and remember more.

There are three skills you can develop from this exercise. The first is the ability to call up traces of these feelings while in a condition that is not immediately evoking them. This will allow you to work with them with less chance of identifying yourself with them and internalizing them. Working with such painful feelings will allow you to recognize them earlier and not become identified with them when, in the future, they *are* being immediately evoked. It will allow you to stay alert through more of your emotional range, rather than muffling your feelings through denial, repression, rationalization, and the kind of internalization that can lead to depression. You'll become more adept at holding on to these difficult feelings while not getting caught up in them and thereby be able to better tackle the conditions that evoke them.

The second skill that you can develop from the exercise is greater insight into the conditions associated with work alienation. Try to allow the memory images to accumulate. You may want to return to the exercise again after a break. See if you can make the memories stronger by remembering more details of what was going on at that time at work, both for you personally and for the people around you, your business group, and the company as a whole. What was going on outside your work world as well? Can you describe what is so painful about each memory? Does it concern a relationship with someone in authority to you? Your sense of competency? The personalities of specific fellow workers? The scope of your power and authority? The respect that you felt you were not receiving? Are there similarities across memories? How often are certain themes repeated? *Just by giving your focused attention* to the memories, and trying actively to remember more, you begin a process of understanding about what was behind the feelings of alienation and disconnection in you. You need not apply psychological theories or run to an analyst. The attention and focusing alone will initiate understanding. This understanding may not come immediately; it probably won't. It is more likely to take its place quietly, on the periphery of your awareness about yourself and your world.

The third benefit of this exercise is that it builds your stamina. By working consciously with difficult feelings, you build your capacity to experience them and work with them in "real time," as they are happening, without being thrown for a loop. You can become better at catching the first warning signs or whiff of smoke regarding job alienation. You become more confident that you can handle the tough times—not just the tough time of a difficult work problem, but the tougher, less obvious negativity that, if repressed and unnoticed, gathers force only to emerge weeks or months later. You can do a lot more about your work situation if you are fully aware of your withdrawal and negativity earlier on in the process.

This is a subtle exercise, and the skills learned, as we mentioned, may not be immediately obvious. The real payoff comes in moments when we are able to say to ourselves, "I know this feeling I've had since my meeting with the boss this morning. It is the way I felt two years ago when I was given interim responsibility for the northeast sales region when Joanne quit. It took me months to figure out that I experienced the assignment as a lack of respect for the amount of responsibility that I was already handling. I need to do something about it sooner this time." Or, "I am beginning to realize that when I am around Martin I feel the same way about myself that I did when I worked for Audrey. I need to be careful and confront his manipulative requests and behaviors more directly."

The challenge is to be able to say, "These feelings are not me, they are a condition that I am experiencing. Moreover, it can teach me what I need to do next." We all need to become, as psychologist James Hillman suggests, "naturalists of the soul," studying and exploring our psyche's varied terrain. We can't do much serious travel in life without crossing some low-lying areas, swamps, and deserts. We have to learn how to develop the naturalist's keen attention, acute power of disciplined observation, and natural curiosity about even ugly creatures and cultivate a scientific distance from what we are experiencing. Distance does not mean indifference or lack of interest or caring. It refers to the capacity to look and learn from things even when times are tough. This self-observation or self-remembering ("waking up" in the middle of our difficult feelings and thoughts) is what lies at the core of many approaches to meditation. It is a skill that comes naturally to no one. We have to learn it through direct and deliberate experience and practice it patiently. We need to stay with our unease until it speaks to us, until it offers up a clue as to what is *really* missing.

FINDING OUR WAY BACK

Symptoms of alienation, depression, and anger serve as our career development wake-up call. They demand our attention. When we feel them we have to respond, sooner or later. What is going on? Why do I feel shame (inadequacy) or guilt (lack of effort, avoiding growth and challenge), anger, frustration, anxiety, fear, boredom? How long have I been feeling this way? When did it start? Why do I feel it the most around certain people, or at certain meetings, or when I am doing certain tasks and not others? When do I not feel this way? What do I want more of, and what less? Recognizing our alienation is the first step in refinding ourselves in our careers. The next step is to take action that directly addresses the alienation and allows us to grow rather than feel frustrated. In this process of identifying one's alienation and acting to alleviate it, people encounter predictable obstacles. These obstacles fall into three general categories: externalization, egoism, and abstraction.

Externalization

Externalization is a psychological term that refers generally to several types of defensive maneuvers by which, in order to preserve our self-esteem, we blame our own psychological problems on external circumstances. We decide our boss is responsible for giving us tasks that we find boring or uninteresting, when the real issue is negotiating for and building a work role that will realize our potential more fully. We see our organization as bureaucratic or dysfunctional, rather than analyzing the business processes in our area and effecting the necessary change. When we feel alienated, we all have a tendency to externalize to some extent.

When Seth Farber came to see us, he described a work situation that was an unbearable pressure cooker. The Chicago-based investment management firm for which he worked was led by a hard-driving manager who had grown the firm dramatically but, according to Seth, at the expense of the analysts and portfolio managers. Seth described the long hours and intense competition for the attention and favor of the boss. He described the boss's style as manipulative and Machiavellian, playing one employee against another to encourage competition for the best-performing portfolio. Much of our initial counseling session was devoted to the personality of the boss and the atmosphere at the firm. As the counseling unfolded, however, it became clear that the reality of Seth's situation was more complex. He had pushed himself extraordinarily hard through college, through a first job with a Wall Street investment bank and through a top MBA program. In actuality, Seth's current job reflected his personality as much as it did the personality of his boss. Now independently wealthy and the father of two young daughters, Seth was actually facing a crisis in life direction. He felt he no longer had anything to "prove" about his ability, nor was he driven by concern for financial well-being. In essence, his core issue was a very big question: "What's it all about now?"

Seth's descriptions of his workplace no doubt were fairly accurate. But as long as he focused on the problem as an external one, he would never get to the heart of the matter. Eventually he decided to leave the company and start a small firm on his own with partners. But it was possible only after he had thoroughly explored how aspects of his own personality often created the level of stress that he was seeking to escape.

Our level of work satisfaction often seems to change "when we aren't looking." We tend to be more vigilant and proactive about defining and shaping our jobs when we first get them. As time passes we are less likely to notice the effect on our workday as responsibilities are added or subtracted or as larger shifts in our environment or the organization take place. Jobs are like sailboats: unless we are actively trimming the sails and making course adjustments, they tend to drift. Our job can slowly migrate into something that is less attractive. Moreover, at some point we all want to take our skills and interests to a new level by learning more and doing different things. It is important to remember, however, that our capacity to act to change our circumstances rests with ourselves.

Many of the clients we work with come to us asking, "Is this my problem, or is it my job?" They tend to see their career crisis in terms of separating the "inner" from the "outer." But this can be very misleading. It is more useful, and closer to the truth, to understand the external particulars of work as a mirror, of *our* self. Let's say that your boss wants you to be more involved in program planning and less involved in direct customer service. After a while you discover that you really miss regular contact with customers. You were actually quite good at it, you realize, better than at program planning; you also realize that the regular give-and-take of customer contact is energizing and interesting, rather than draining and routine as you sometimes feared.

You realize that you have been growing less and less excited about your job. As you become aware of this, your initial reaction may be to see your boss as arbitrary, overcontrolling, and insensitive to your career development. Or let's say you accurately diagnose the job shift away from your interests and talents and ask for a change in job description. Your boss's response might be, "I am sorry, but I have no need for additional people in direct customer service. The organization really needs your focus on program planning right now." This is still not a problem caused by either your boss or the insensitivity of the organization as a whole. The external circumstances have acted as a mirror, forcing you to think and feel more deeply about what you want. It is now up to you to act on that insight. Your action might entail leaving the organization if there is no place for your interests to be realized. Or you may decide to negotiate, either with your boss or with leaders in other parts of the organization, to create a role that is closer to the work that is right for you. In either case, you are not a passive victim of circumstances. You still have the ability to shape the nature of your career.

Often it is difficult to break through our tendency to externalize. It is almost a reflex. If an organization is going through a difficult change, or if we work for a relatively untalented manager, or if morale is low because of problems with the business, it is all the easier to see our situation as being beyond ourselves. We might find ourselves considering the "geographical cure" of a job change without really understanding why, or becoming further alienated because we feel stuck where we are and are powerless to change it. The key to avoiding this is in asking, "What does this situation say about my psychological makeup and my need to act or change?" Sometimes, of course, jobs become just plain bad jobs due to poor management, high stress, poor morale, or lack of organizational vision. Then it is time to leave. Even when we are the victims of gross injustice or simple misfortune, however, it is worthwhile to consider the situation as a potential mirror on ourselves and explore what we can do to move toward work that is right for us.

Egoism

Another type of externalization that can get in the way of career insight and growth is the tendency we all have to look around and compare ourselves with the person next to us. We want to know where we stand and whether or not we are "winning." Competition has its place in career development, but "career comparison" more often than not leads us into trouble. Our potential is not the potential of anyone else. Our path can be traveled by no one other than ourselves. Yet we spend a great deal of time envying the position, talents, and accomplishments of others. We see our career from their perspectives and imagine how they would judge us. None of this will bring us closer to knowing our unique potential for contribution or our particular genius. Imitation is an important part of learning, but it is an early form of learning that must be internalized and made our own. Early on, we may need heroes, but later on heroes can get in our way.

The ego is that part of our self that needs to be recognized as separate and different. The ego is an important aspect of the self, but the difficulty comes when we experience ourselves only as ego and make our decisions, career or otherwise, accordingly. The ego is fundamentally heroic; it wants to accomplish and be recognized. The ego can be a bully that strong-arms its way at the expense of other aspects of the self, such as love of beauty, spirituality, the needs of the body, the experience of family, romantic love, the need for community, and the experience of being part of the natural world.

Many times in our career counseling we have worked with individuals who have come out of the starting blocks in the race for success with enormous speed and drive, achieving wealth or position early on in life. They have come to us because they feel adrift even amid their success and know that they have left something behind. Ego sees career advancement in terms of some concrete reference point and in comparison with others on a "career ladder." One's place in the corporate hierarchy becomes the primary method of measurement. Its orientation is toward power and the means to its acquisition and use.

Yet the battles of ego that we wage are often not even our own. Our sense of "success" and "accomplishment" is often based on the unconscious and unexamined values and the unlived dreams of others—our parents, our role models, our friends. Several of our clients realize at age thirty-five or forty that most of their career choices have been based on conforming to a parent's spoken or unspoken image of success. Sometimes these images are in accord with the person they are. Other times they are not, as in the law firm partner whose interests would be far better realized as an architect or chef/owner of a quality restaurant. We pass on to our children, both deliberately and unconsciously, our notions of what good work is and what bad work is, about what types of people are more valued than others, and about what the "good life" is.

Kim Whitman, for example, came from a high-achieving Atlanta family where the unwritten rule was that she graduate from the best prep school and enroll in a prestigious private college. This in turn was to lead to a professional education, preferably in law or business. Kim followed the path willingly; not only was she very bright, but she "tested well" and performed best in highly structured environments where expectations were clear-cut. Upon graduating from Stanford Business School, Kim became an associate with the Atlanta office of a leading management consulting firm. After several years she took a leave to have her first child. The leave was extended until, pregnant with her second child, she realized that she had no intention of returning.

For several years Kim consulted with small businesses in the time available amid the demands of her family. When her youngest child entered kindergarten, Kim began to feel a sense of restlessness and anxiety. It was not as if she missed the consulting firm—she was very clear that she did not want to be there. Kim began to question her ability to get the next consulting assignment and to question, as well, her ability to be effective when she got it. This unfamiliar lack of self-confidence was what led Kim to call us and arrange for a consultation. It took her several sessions in career counseling to begin to look more directly at her anxiety and her vague sense of dissatisfaction with her life circumstances.

Kim came to see that her role as a "freelance" mother and consultant was a true departure from the world of structure, explicitly defined achievement, and clearly defined goals that had characterized almost all of her adult life. She found herself keeping track of her colleague and law school classmates' career progress and comparing her accomplishments with theirs. Kim also talked about her mother, a strong presence in her life, who was known for her definite opinions about what defined success, whether it was the right way to host a dinner party, the right private schools, or the right organizations to work for. The extent of her mother's influence on her feelings of self-worth and accomplishment was something that she had explored several years earlier with a therapist. Kim began to realize that her feelings about herself were strongly influenced by the voice of an inner critic that continually compared her life circumstances to her mother's spoken and unspoken expectations and to the accomplishments of her friends and classmates. A large part of Kim's career counseling was focused on helping her separate her own instincts and genuine enthusiasms from the messages she received from her family, peers, and her upbringing about what work was truly meaningful.

The great challenge as a parent is to be as conscious as possible about the messages we give our children and to be both aware and respectful of who our children are and how their paths in life might be quite different from our own. We also inevitably pass on, sometimes consciously, sometimes unconsciously, our own unlived dreams. If there are parts of our self, deep enthusiasms that have not been nourished, the need to live them may somehow be signaled to a child, who may take them up as his or her own. It may be years, if ever, before the adult child realizes the extent to which that parent's unfulfilled dreams have shaped the course of his or her career.

Becoming aware of such hidden influences on our career decisions is not a simple matter. If we make an effort, though, we can learn more about the inner lives of our parents and how they may have affected what we feel we need to do. We suggest that all of our clients ask themselves several questions: What messages, spoken or unspoken, have you received from your mother, father, or other significant adults about work and career? What were each of their ideas about good work and bad work, success, and accomplishment? In what way do you think (each of) your parents feel that they have personally failed in their work and in their lives? What choices do you think they would make if they could do it all again? What are your roles in the family (for example, are you supposed to be the bright one, the responsible one, the under-achiever, the ambitious one, the athlete, the comedian, the one not as smart as your older sister, and so forth?). How do these roles affect your sense of self today? What traits and values do you have in common with each of your parents? In what ways are you fundamentally different from each of your parents? How do you expect that your life will develop differently due to this difference? How do you feel about a life that may be substantially different from that of your parents?

It would be remiss of us not to pay some attention to the topic of money. In the absence of a firm sense of other values, wealth tends to become a least common denominator of accomplishment. The danger here is obvious. To reduce a career decision solely to a process of maximizing compensation, and to design a daily schedule accordingly, is an invitation to alienation and dissatisfaction. On the other hand, not being honest with yourself about the importance of money can also lead you astray. We are surprised by the inability of many of our clients to answer one very simple question: How much money do you want to make? It's as if many of them have never considered the question because they assume the answer is obvious to all: "As much as possible." But this is as much a non-answer as "Money is not important to me" (which we also hear from time to time).

"As much as possible" means that you are willing to sacrifice virtually all other aspects of your daily existence for the effort to maximize income—which, fortunately, few are willing to do. The actual answer for them, conscious or not, is often, "As much as, if not more than, my friends at college or business school are making," or, "More than my father made," or, "As much as or more than the people in my neighborhood make," or, "More than my older sister, with whom I have always been competitive." If you go to a business school with financially successful graduates, or if your older sister is an investment banker, or if your father was in a particularly profitable business, you have set yourself up, probably unconsciously, to put money at the heart of your career decisions. It then becomes an unexamined proxy for ego and for your sense of self-worth. Other aspects of yourself will be slighted *not* for the sake of money, but for the sake of your *unconscious*ness about what money means to you. What *does* money mean for you? What is the cost of the things of value that you would exchange it for? This is a rhetorical question that goes beyond mere financial planning (though that is an important, and often neglected, part of it). Not to attempt an answer is to invite the issue of money to gather psychological energy and operate unconsciously in your decision making.

Abstraction

Business strategy models and the tools of financial analysis are highly abstract. They originate from and speak to only one aspect of human consciousness: that of analytic thinking function. They presuppose that brute thinking can get to the heart of the matter and determine the best course of action. The majority of the people we work with in our consulting practice have a strong tendency to approach life and its problems from an exclusively analytic perspective. But life is not a business problem. When decisions are made that neglect the other aspects of your self, the decision and its consequences will not reflect your full needs and aspirations. This leads to clients who say in surprise, "I thought I got it right this time; why am I unhappy, why is this not working for me?"

Sharon DiGiavonni's career in real estate took off much faster than expected. She was a finance major in business school who also had a natural ability to network and put deals together. The combination made her extraordinarily effective. Yet she would sit in her counseling session with her cell phone by her side and talk about the fact that despite her unusual business success, she felt her life was somehow or other getting away from her. Her husband complained that he rarely saw her, and she had feelings of guilt about the amount of time she spent with her three-year-old son. She was riding the crest of a series of new deals, and the next one always seemed to be so much better than any she had worked on before. She was pleased that her recent efforts to curb the number of hours she spent at the office seemed to be working, but another issue bothered her. Entertaining was a big part of her work, and she did more networking at breakfast, dinner, or on the golf course than anywhere else. Her social life had begun to blur with her pursuit of deals. Many of her friends from business school were now potential business allies. Her problem? She was having difficulty figuring out if she was inviting someone to dinner because she actually wanted to see that person or if there was a possible business advantage to doing so. Sharon was having difficulty remembering what it meant for someone to be *just a friend*.

How do we correct for an overly analytical stance when looking at larger life issues? How do we step outside of our habitual reflex to muscle our way unconsciously forward? Two words act as antidotes for abstraction: *value* and *caring*. *Value* is concerned with what counts, what ultimately matters in our life. There is an exercise that many career counselors use called "the epitaph exercise"—composing your own epitaph or eulogy. It is even better to imagine yourself at your own memorial service. What do you want people to say about you? Do you want to be remembered for what you did and how you were with other people, what you accomplished and how it affected your community, your family, your friends? How will the career decision that you are struggling with right now affect what is said in that room?

Value also refers to passion. What do you cherish? Try to recall those times in your life when you have felt most yourself, most at home in the world, most alive. What was going on then? What types of places do you tend to be in? What other people are you with? What are you doing? Focus on daily values as well. Where do you want to live (country, suburbs, city)? What spaces do you like to inhabit? What do you value in others? Organizations and whole industries tend to have certain cultures and attract larger numbers of certain types of people. Where are you most likely to be around the people you value? Also consider people you want to be with and what it means to be with them. A high-travel, high–time commitment, dual-career lifestyle will work for one partnership but bring another to an end.

Throughout our lives we are given and we build *sources* of value. One example would be a religious tradition given to us by our parents, one that we choose to build through study, participation in ritual, prayer, and meditation. Another example would be the kinds of books we read or music we listen to. For others, connection to the natural world is a major source of value. Climbing a mountain, retreating to a cabin in the woods, or walking the seacoast allows them to reestablish perspective at a time of career decision. For others still, a relationship with another person who is respected for his or her insight and wisdom can become a major value resource.

One of our tasks in life is to identify and cultivate sources of value. We will not have Martin Buber or Henry Thoreau or Lao-tzu available to us in times of crisis if we have not cultivated relationships with them over time (sometimes, though, a crisis can be the cause for discovery of a new value source). At times of career alienation it is important to return to our developed sources of value. The time spent, whether it is on a meditation retreat, reading a favorite author, climbing a mountain, or visiting with a respected mentor is, by its very nature, neo-analytical, non-discursive, and initiated by parts of the psyche other than the ego. We need to pay attention to how what we are "hearing" is affecting us and changing our feelings and attitude about our life and about what needs to be done.

Caring is what you need to do to protect what you value. It takes time and requires sacrifice because we can do only so many things every day. Caring requires attention and listening. Saying "I care about family and will look only at jobs that protect my family lifestyle" is itself an abstraction. What does your son Mark really need? What is required to care for him? Maybe you can work long hours and still care deeply for Mark, or maybe not. If one of your children has a severe learning disability or is a gifted musician, or if your partner suffers from clinical depression, each of these people in your life will need a different type of caring, and you will have to listen and learn what that caring means. To learn about caring requires more observation and attention than it does thinking. That is why it is important to understand what we value and what we need to do to care for what we value while making career decisions.

Many of the business professionals we work with try to determine their next career move "in their head." We often find ourselves urging them to "go and talk with people who are actually doing what you are considering." Move into the information interview process, even if you are ambivalent. Meet people from that organization. Ask questions, talk with current employees and, if you can locate them, former employees.

Pursue several interviews at once and compare your experiences as you proceed. You can always say "No." As you move into action you will be gathering data. You will be experiencing places and having gut responses to people. You will be learning new information that you had not included in your mental calculations.

WORKING WITH YOUR CLAY

Ray, whom we met earlier, considered the possibility that the business he had helped to found was a mistake. Perhaps highly artistic types such as he would do best within the structure of a larger organization after all. Maybe he had gotten it all wrong the last time around. He began to think about the various companies for which he might work. Alternatively, he considered joining a competitor that was doing well. He spent time talking about his marriage. He talked about his father's perspective on his current career crisis, and he worked to prevent his inner critic from swamping his morale completely. He found himself revisiting earlier decisions and opportunities now lost. He followed in his mind the course his career would have taken if he had only . . . He found himself paralyzed from the competing visions that arose before him, unsure of the criteria he would use to decide. Would he move? Was his marriage in jeopardy? What would bring financial security?

Ray spent a lot of time focusing on his business partner's psychological issues and how they interfered with the business. His ego was looking for a means of rescue, any means, that would make him feel less anxious, less ashamed about being at a loss, and more respected in the eyes of his wife, father, and colleagues. He looked around at his colleagues and examined their choices for clues as to what to do next.

In life we can work only with what is given us, and what is given is unique to each of us. What is given, what we are able to find, can be built upon and enlarged, but at any moment in time it is what it is. It is as if we all work as potters and are each given a specific and unique piece of clay to fashion into our careers. Our clay is of a certain color, a certain consistency, a certain composition, and a certain amount. It is what we have, and with it we have a choice. We can look around us and see what others are doing with their clay. We can note that they have different types of clay and different pottery wheels; some of their wheels are seemingly better built and located in more advantageous parts of the studio. Some of our fellow potters in the studio have developed a particular style of pots and clearly established their artistic signature. Others seem to be putting out pot after pot, with an impressive inventory that has built up beside their station. We can imagine what we might do with a different type of clay or figure out how we might get to one of those other stations, perhaps the one over there with the high-speed electric wheel. Or we can pick up our clay, that which has been given us, and examine it closely. Examine it and heft it and let our fingers run through it, being honest about just what we have and what we don't. And then we can place it on our wheel and begin to work with it, looking for the vision that will make our work from our clay.

We asked Ray to pick up the things that were closest at hand for him, the things that really mattered, and to focus his efforts on what he could do with them. He came to see that actually he didn't have many of the choices that tormented him. Some of the company positions he was talking about would entail a significant reduction in income, with less than encouraging paths for career progress. His children loved their home and were established in a good school system with circles of friends. He loved his wife and wanted to make things work. For better or worse, his relationships with his brother-in-law and his wife's family were part of the fabric of his life and had to be acknowledged. He was highly artistic and doubted that he could get the projects that would allow his artistry to flourish in the companies he had been considering. He did want his own business, when he felt deeply about it; having his own business was a meaningful accomplishment in itself.

What Ray needed to do next was not easy, but it was right in front of him. He had to confront his business partner about certain behaviors. He had to develop new clients and make a commitment to a specific number of sales calls each day. He could consider an alliance with a company offering complimentary services. Clearly a big push was required. But even more of a challenge, for Ray, as for most of us, is in remembering his choice, keeping in touch with his vision day after day, even when things are not going well and the doubts begin to surface again. As an artist, Ray could appreciate the image of picking up his clay each day anew and working with what he has been given.

The search for career vision is an ongoing one, cycling unpredictably through the experiences of renewed vision, alienation, and finding our way back. The steely career focus that seems to characterize successful business professionals does not come once and for all. Genuine career change and progress begins not with a flash of insight or with a great idea; it begins with a sense of alienation and discomfort, and a period of frustration and uncertainty, with no guarantees as to the outcome. But it also provides an opportunity for learning, if we can give it attention and let it speak to us. It can tell us of the hidden potential in us that has been shut out because there is no way for it to act in our current world of work. We may get frightened, because there is no obvious path in sight and we are afraid of losing ground and esteem in the eyes of others. We have trouble recognizing and connecting with what our heart of hearts says about our life and our work at that moment. But rescue can come only from determined attention to our unique circumstances and with the bit of courage necessary to act.

PART
I I

THE PSYCHOLOGICAL ISSUES
BEHIND THE
12 BEHAVIOR PATTERNS

INTRODUCTION

People don't simply fall at random into one or another of the twelve behavior patterns we've just described. There are four fundamental *underlying* psychological issues that contribute to each of the behavior patterns. The peacekeeper behaviors of Chapter 4 result from one combination of these dynamics, the bulldozer behavior of Chapter 5 will be characterized by another psychodynamic "recipe." The hero of Chapter 3 will have still another. In Part II of the book we're going to discuss what those dynamics are—*and what you can do about them if you find that any of them are limiting* your *career success.*

We began to identify the twelve behavior patterns discussed in Part I of the book over the course of many years working as consultants and executive coaches. Each pattern came into view gradually, almost in the way a latent image appears on a piece of photographic paper when it is placed in the developer—shadowy at first, then slowly, over months or years, becoming more and more distinct.

As those twelve images clarified themselves, so did our understanding of what underlies them. Eventually we were able to piece together the psychological processes that operate in the various patterns. Those four primary causal elements are as follows:

▲ Having a negatively distorted self-image
▲ Not being able to understand the world from other people's perspectives
▲ Not having come to terms with authority
▲ Having an inability to use power comfortably, skillfully, and effectively

These are the fundamental concerns that, in varying combinations, are at the root of each individual behavior pattern. One pattern may result in large measure from negative self-image along with, to a lesser extent, difficulty in dealing with authority. Another pattern may be characterized by more or less equal degrees of these two elements, as well as difficulty using power. Each of the twelve behavior patterns we identify that can hamstring your career success has its own makeup. Of course, other variables can come into play in any of the behaviors. Some are specific to each individual (level of intelligence, for example), while others are external forces (such as economic boom or bust times, having siblings who are enormously successful—or who are failures). But in our work we've found that these four are the primary causes of the patterns we described in Part I.

If you saw yourself—or someone with whom you work closely—in one or more of the behavior patterns you just read about, it is important to study this section carefully. Each of the four chapters that follow includes not just a description of the core psychological issue, but tools you can use to assess yourself in each area and exercises that you can do to strengthen those weaker psychological "muscles." Learning all you can about how to use power effectively, or see things from other people's points of view, for example, is bound to make you more effective in any organizational setting. Simply put, you can't know too much about these dynamics and how they affect people. Moreover, even if one of the four affects *you* very little, it likely *does* affect someone you work closely with.

As executive coaches (albeit with Ph.D.'s and advanced training as psychotherapists), we are called in by the highest levels of management in our client companies to work with two kinds of individuals. The first is the person who is being groomed for significant advancement in the

company and who needs his or her "people skills" brought from an A−
or B+ level to an A+. The other kind of person we are called on to work
with is someone who is in trouble, who may even be in danger of being
fired or demoted because of one of the patterns described in Part I. In
some of these instances there is an urgency to the situation bordering on
an emergency room procedure—the individual client has *one last
chance*. Regardless of the level of urgency and of whether the task is to
save the person from self-destruction or to groom a client for a move
into the senior executive ranks, our focus is on clear and definitive
change in his or her behavior in the workplace, and our understanding
of these four dynamics is what informs our consultations (and makes us
effective in our work).

Of course, we do not claim that these four chapters are full explica-
tions of the various issues they describe. Numerous books have been
written on each, and many more will undoubtedly be written in the future. Nevertheless, knowing how these dynamics drive the behaviors
described in Part I—your own and those of your peers, subordinates,
and managers—should prove invaluable in your attempts to change
your own behavior and manage and work with others.

CHAPTER

THIRTEEN

TAKING OTHERS' PERSPECTIVES

VIRTUALLY ALL BUSINESS WORK IS ACCOMPLISHED *THROUGH* *other people.* Having the right knowledge and a will to succeed are not enough. You must also be able to *take perspective:* consider any given business situation from the point of view of the other individuals involved.

In our executive coaching and career consultations we have often worked with unusually bright and determined individuals who, nonetheless, were failing or stalling in their organizations because they didn't understand and respond to the perspectives of fellow workers. It is the single most common skill deficit we observe among the executives with whom we work. Successful people in business know that there is no such thing as an autonomous career. People can achieve maximum success in their careers only by working effectively with other individuals, individuals who have their own needs, goals, and agendas. They learn that they must achieve their goals within organizations that, similarly, have their own objectives.

Perspective taking requires "stepping outside of your own skin" and experiencing the world from someone else's point of view. Businesspeople who are skilled in this area have excellent "psychological peripheral vision." Like the greatest basketball players, they work with a good sense of the full court, of where each player is, of what each needs to—and can—do, of the flow of the game, and of what needs to be done to score. All the players develop their own "games" and will be judged by their own scoring and rebounding statistics, but they'll never be judged *great* if they can't make things happen with and for the team.

Taking perspective and using empathy doesn't necessarily mean being excessively nice or compromising. In fact, perspective taking and empathy are *completely* value-neutral. Machiavelli, the fifteenth-century master of political intrigue, is famous for his insight into the motivations and perspectives of others for the purpose of using power effectively. "All men will see what you seem to be," he wrote in his classic *The Prince,* but "only a few will know what you are." In other words, empathy, then, not only leads to insight and greater appreciation for others, but is a competitive advantage as well.

Understanding others' points of view can help you to use whatever power you have with greater reserve, precision, and finesse. The ability to restrain yourself is just as important as taking action directly and strongly (in the same way that a car's brakes are just as important as its engine). Similarly, taking action with subtlety and deftness can both conserve your "power reserves" and accomplish your goals more effectively (like using the car's steering mechanism). A skilled tennis player or fencer, by "reading" his or her opponent and using that insight into the person's playing style to anticipate the next move, makes his or her own efforts much more economical, thereby scoring points with seeming effortlessness. Taking perspective in a business setting allows you to achieve your goals with more ease, "spending" less of your "capital" in the process. The greatest victories, after all, come not by using brute force, but through being able to persuade your opponents to join your side.

Some people have a "head start" in perspective taking. Early on in life they developed a greater capacity for psychological mindedness and empathy and developed a social, and later a work style that makes use of that ability. Perspective taking *can* be learned or cultivated, but it takes careful and consistent attention and intervention.

This chapter is a primer on how to take the perspective of people you work with—in whatever capacity—and use the knowledge you acquire to maximize your effectiveness in your job or career.

Imagine that you're sitting around a conference table with your boss and three colleagues. You're making a proposal for a project that excites you. It involves adding a new feature to a service that your organization delivers. This new feature is your idea; you've been thinking about it, working out the details for a long time, and you've written what amounts to a mini-business plan, in which you would manage the development and launch of the new feature. Your presentation will be experienced differently by each person in the room. One may be interested in the novelty and actual potential of your project. Another may be worried about its impact on the budget. Someone else will be concerned about the impact of your proposal on his or her own projects. You're going to need the help of everyone there to make this project go, and one or two people will actually have to work on it directly with you. They may see it as in their best interest to do so, or they may not. It might mean a significant sacrifice for one, drawing time away from existing projects or forcing him or her to stay at work a bit later a few days each week to get your idea off the ground.

One person at the table may be a highly detail-oriented operations director, who's thinking through exactly what your project will mean for the front-line employees that he supervises. He knows process flow and the interface with the schedules of the larger organization better than you do.

Another member of the team has her own proposal that will not be ready for another month. She's concerned that there won't be sufficient resources to launch both ideas. She's friendly and a good team player, but there's been an unacknowledged sense of competition between you since you joined the company at about the same time.

Still another member of the team is known as something of a hothead, and if he weren't so good at what he does, he might have been asked to leave years ago. He can be counted on to be totally thumbs-up or totally thumbs-down. He's either with you or against you, and when he's against you, his style is to ask tough, specific questions about virtually any problem that might arise.

Finally, your boss is concerned about the budget for the overall division or business area. She's already looking at a 5 percent overrun. She knows that new revenues generated by your idea in the last two quarters could put her ahead of the game by the end of the year. She also knows that she's up for promotion. Should she play it safe and not risk the failure of a new idea, or would supporting a winner be what pushes her up into the next level? (*Her* boss's psychology, then, is also a presence in the room.) If you're going to be successful, you need to get all, or virtually all, of these people both to agree that your proposal is a good one and to change some aspect of their day-to-day lives to see that it actually gets implemented. More to the point, if you haven't thought about all of this before you enter that room, you and your proposal are in serious trouble.

It is very unlikely that you'll be able to present your project in such a way that it will be accepted if you haven't considered your proposal through the eyes of each of the people involved. The same process is true for anything you want to accomplish at work, whether it entails taking on a new responsibility or suggesting a new way of doing things. If you don't cultivate your relationships with the people involved and learn about their interests, motivations, values, goals, and personalities, it's unlikely that whatever you want to accomplish will have the full "buy-in" that you need. You should have a sense of the following for each person involved in whatever you hope to accomplish:

- ▲ What type of work makes the person enthusiastic and excited
- ▲ What rewards motivate him or her
- ▲ What general work style the person brings to the table
- ▲ What is most important on this person's personal work agenda for the next six months

"But I'm not qualified to be a psychologist," you might say. "I'm a marketing manager." Or a telecommunications sales rep. Or an account manager. This is a concern that we hear from many of our consulting clients. It's as if they fear that thinking in a deliberate way about co-workers' motivations and personalities and putting their insights to work might constitute practicing medicine without a license. But *every* business professional needs to be a psychologist. Every employee and manager *is* a psychologist. Business is done with and through people, and each person is different. Moreover, the relationships we experience at work are a big part of what many of us find valuable and stimulating about how we spend our days. The question is not whether or not you want to be a psychologist—the question is how to be a good one.

The biggest obstacle to effective workplace psychology is *projection*. This refers to the process whereby we typically see our own psychology (wishes, values, interests, feelings) reflected in others, rather than seeing those people for who they actually are. We need to be able to recognize that their experience of a situation may be essentially different from our own. The fact of the matter is that the same situation, and the experience of work itself, *means* different things to different people. We are not all in the game for the same reasons!

We all project; it is part of human nature to understand the world first from our own point of view. To actually focus on the experience of another person from his or her perspective requires a conscious and deliberate effort; it is a skill that is acquired through study and practice. Some people employ their "intuition" when it comes to understanding other people's points of view. Intuition, however, can be misleading. It combines our observations and subjective experience, and as a result it can be right on target or really off base. When the latter is the case, projection has probably outweighed accurate observation and disciplined reflection.

Nor can we assume that fellow workers will always act and make decisions based on their best business or career interests. Sometimes people don't know what their best interests are, and at other times people act unconsciously in self-destructive ways. If we're really going to understand our colleagues and customers, we're going to need tools that augment our "gut" intuition and analysis of what appears to be in their best interest.

There are no formulas for understanding the human psyche. Thinking about human behavior and individual differences is an art that we learn over many years. Nevertheless, there are some useful frameworks for thinking about individual differences and how they affect behavior and attitudes in work situations. We will present two models for thinking about the personality and behavior of one's fellow workers. But no model can be of help without good data.

GATHERING INFORMATION

Our "data" or knowledge of other people comes from three sources: observation, listening, and disciplined imagination. Good *observation* takes time. You have to spend time with a co-worker in different contexts (meetings, crisis, conflict, leisure, and so on) before you really know him or her. Good observation also takes objectivity and something of a scientific attitude. People tend to be too quick to rationalize the behavior of a friend and judge harshly the same behavior of a supposed foe.

Listening—active, deliberate listening with no preconceptions—is the greatest tool of psychology and business alike. How else can we possibly understand the world and the needs of a customer or the unseen, inner perspective of a boss? Real listening is hard. We typically enter conversations with "momentum"—that is, an agenda, a goal, and a biased point of view. Of course, there are times to argue forcibly and there are times when you know that the person you're talking with is simply wrong about the facts of a certain situation. But this is beside the point when you're focused on trying to understand the other person's point of view. To do so, you need to practice the art of pure listening, whether in the service of making a sale, being a better collaborator, or managing an employee, colleague, or boss more effectively.

Imagination is the process by which we put together all our knowledge of another person, knowledge that comes from observation, conversation, memory, intuition, feeling response, and analysis. We form this imagination, a kind of inner picture of other people, and carry it with us, to be retrieved when we want to develop our understanding of or connection with them. It is only through this imagination, hopefully formed with (and informed by) skilled and disciplined observation and listening, that we can enter the world of another person and come to understand his or her point of view. Active imagination is a process whereby we can bring together and integrate what we know about another person, thus deepening our understanding of her or his perspective. Before turning to our psychological models, why not practice what we've just prescribed: gathering and integrating information about one or more people in your work life? You can begin by trying an imagination exercise for bringing together all that you know about a person that is important to you in your work life.

Think about the three or four most important people in your work. For the moment, select the people you either interact with the most on a day-to-day basis or who, through positions of authority or power, have the largest impact on your success or failure. You can return to others later and expand your list as well. From this initial list of three or four people, select one person to start with, perhaps someone who puzzles you with his or her behavior or attitude toward you. Call to mind a picture or memory of the person you selected. Allow this image to grow into other images and memories of this person.

Stay focused. If your attention wanders to other events or memories, try to bring it back to an image of the person in question. Notice how you feel as you observe these images. Notice the content of the images and the specific memories that are attached to these images. Don't try to analyze the person or come to any conclusions, just pay attention to the images, memories, and feelings that arise as you direct your attention toward this person. After you have observed your feelings, imagination, and memories, write down brief impressions or key-word reminders. Write five adjectives that you think best describe this person. Be careful with your choices—remember, Shakespeare used many thousands of different words in his plays; we're limiting you to just five. Take your time and choose carefully the words that most accurately capture your impression of the person in question.

Next, pay attention to your general feeling or attitude toward this person. Every relationship is characterized both by complexity and ambivalence. It's never true that you completely "hate" or "idolize" someone. Relationships and feelings are far more complicated than that. Pay attention to all your varied feelings. What do you admire about this person? What quality of hers do you most wish you had? What quality are you happiest that you don't? What would you like to tell this person but don't, and why not? What advantages has he had that you envy most? What quality of hers repels you most?

After paying attention to your feelings and actions, allow your reflections to become more analytical. What do you see as the person's most significant weakness in his work? Would your fellow workers agree? What is the biggest obstacle that this person has had to overcome? In what work situations is this person most, and least, effective? Where does this person want his career to be in five years? In two years? What's the most important thing for her to accomplish in the next two months at work? Who are her strongest allies in your immediate business area and in the whole organization? What is the quality and extent of his network in your organization and in the industry or in his professional field? What is her relationship like with her boss? In what ways are his values (more on this later) and styles like or unlike those of his boss? What do you imagine this person's general attitude toward *you* to be? How are you most alike and most different?

Now that you've allowed your *imagination* of this person to become "full-bodied," nuanced, and three-dimensional, we want to give you two formal models that we have found to be useful in taking people's perspectives. We want to teach you how to assess someone's work-reward values and general work mode.

ASSESSING THE REWARD VALUES OF OTHERS

All people work for rewards. When someone mentions the word *reward*, the first thing that comes to most people's minds is compensation, whether it's salary, bonus, or equity of some sort. Money, however, is only one reward for work. In our research we studied work rewards and how people value them, and we came away with two interesting insights. The first is that despite the common perception that we basically all work for the same reasons, we don't. How people value the various rewards for their work varies substantially from person to person, even among business professionals. A common response from our clients when they discuss their work-reward values is, "Of course that's what I want. But doesn't everybody?" Projection at work again.

Another important observation we made was that, unlike some other aspects of personality that have great stability over time (one's interest patterns, for example), some—although not all—work-reward values may change as life circumstances change. A good example of this is the young, unmarried new graduate who places a low value on the reward security (security is one of the business reward values that we identified in our research). Ten years later, if this student has married, is a homeowner, and is the father or mother of several children, we might expect to see this value increase. (By contrast, a very high value for autonomy is unlikely to shift due to life changes.)

In taking the perspective of fellow workers or customers, it's crucial that you think about and factor in their work motivation. What do they want to get back from work? Security? Money? Prestige? Intellectual challenge? Work hours that protect other aspects of their lifestyle? You *cannot* assume that they are working for the same reasons you are. Their stake in a project or an organizational change at work may be radically different from yours if their work-reward values are different. We've identified thirteen basic work-reward values that came up repeatedly when people in business talked about what they wanted from work. As you read each of the definitions, think about how important it is to you.

Financial Gain

This reward value dimension is not concerned with making money generally—everyone wants to make a comfortable living. It is concerned with exceptional financial reward. If you value this reward highly, you're saying that the opportunity for compensation that is unusually high is a strong source of motivation for you. The actual sum of the compensation is irrelevant: at an early stage in your career it might be a sum that's large compared only with the salaries of those around you in the same age bracket; later on it may be a significantly higher salary or an equity position in the company itself. For some people, the accumulation of wealth is a central purpose of their careers; for others, compensation beyond a certain desired level adds little meaningful value.

Power and Influence

People with high scores in this area find it rewarding to make things happen. They want to have an impact on their work team, their business group, or an entire organization. They want to be "players" whose input is sought out before a decision is made. For people who highly value the *power and influence* reward, staff roles providing information and analyses for the real decision makers are unlikely to be satisfying (although they may be a useful step to a position of more authority and visibility). During the early stages of a career, people who highly value this dimension often have to settle for less *power and influence* than they want, accepting a position that allows learning, skill building, and the development of a network that will lead to a later role with more power.

Variety

For some people boredom, sameness of task, and predictable routine are among the biggest threats to job satisfaction. They look for work roles that require different types of activities during the course of a typical day. They usually prefer project-oriented work environments rather than "steady-state" work environments.

Lifestyle

This reward value represents the importance of aspects of life other than work and career. An individual with a high *lifestyle* score is essentially saying, "There are some things that are as important as, if not more important than, my job; a good job will allow me the time for them." The most frequent issue here is time for one's family. In other cases the need to place a limit on employment time demands is driven by a particularly meaningful activity such as an artistic pursuit, a contribution to social welfare, avocational study, or dedication to a sport. A high value of *lifestyle* is often in conflict with other reward dimensions, particularly *financial gain* and *power and influence*.

Autonomy

People who value this dimension highly are likely to be dissatisfied with positions that are closely supervised or managed. There are many different paths to autonomy in the workplace. Individual contributor roles typically offer more autonomy at earlier stages of a career, while management roles progressively acquire greater autonomy (as a result of greater power) over time, with promotion. Sales roles often provide a great deal of autonomy even at the earliest stages of career development (as long as you're meeting your target numbers). Many research studies have demonstrated that the vast majority of entrepreneurs have an unusually high desire for autonomy.

Intellectual Challenge

People who value *intellectual challenge* highly are saying that they look to work to provide them with challenges that stimulate their thinking. They are problem solvers and most enjoy work that provides them with a steady diet of problems that require analytical reasoning.

Altruism

Those who most value this reward derive significant satisfaction from knowing that their job directly benefits others. Altruism can be realized in terms of both type of job and kind of industry. People with high *altruism* needs may also meet them avocationally through volunteer activities. It is important to note that people who assign a low ranking to this reward value are typically not *lacking* in altruistic orientation but express their altruism primarily in nonwork pursuits and value other rewards more highly when making career choices.

Security

People with high *security* scores are usually extremely conscious of financial obligations in making their next career moves. This score is likely to elevate when new financial responsibilities, such as the arrival of children, bring the issue of security to the foreground. A high *security* score is saying, "I don't want to have to worry about whether I have enough financial resources to meet my needs," whereas a high *financial gain* score is saying, "Irrespective of necessity, building up wealth is an important goal to me." When both *security* and *financial gain* are elevated, it's a sign that the person has "money on the mind" and is very focused on the financial aspects of career choices.

Prestige

People who value *prestige* highly look to their work to provide a sense of status and pride based on their affiliation with an industry-leading or otherwise prominent organization. They value the connection with an outstanding institution and with the "brand equity" value of working with a prestigious company.

Affiliation

This typically refers to friendship generally, but in this context it has a more specific meaning, referring to the importance of working with people who share similar interests, values, enthusiasms, and frames of reference. Having a group of colleagues with whom one can easily relate is a vital ingredient of enjoying work for those who value this dimension highly. If you assign a high value to this dimension, you'll want to take your time during a hiring process and try to meet as many of your potential co-workers as possible. You'll want to get as thorough a sense as possible of the organizational culture and the day-to-day social environment of the workplace.

Positioning

A person with a high valuing of this dimension is essentially saying, "I'm at point A and want to get to point C. I know I can't go there immediately because I lack the required credentials, experience, knowledge, or connections. I'm going to evaluate my next job, point B, in terms of its potential for providing me with what I need to get to point

C." If you value positioning highly, ask yourself what your ultimate goal is, how clear that goal is, and how clear you are regarding what's required to get there. Do you have a good understanding of how this next move will help you toward your goal? This dimension may also be highly valued when one is worried about making a wrong career choice. Sometimes people who change jobs in midcareer place higher value on this dimension precisely for this reason; they're concerned about a misstep at a time when they see themselves as being vulnerable and so are approaching their next job choice thinking several moves ahead.

Managing People

This dimension is concerned specifically with the interpersonal aspects of the management role. People who place a high value on this enjoy the interpersonal aspects of leading and directing the activities of others. They enjoy the personal relationships with subordinates and often find fulfillment in the role of mentor. This dimension is concerned with the "people" aspects (vs. the "power" aspect) of being a manager, supervisor, or leader.

Recognition

This reward value measures the importance of a work environment that provides explicit personal recognition for work that is well done. Some organizations rely on compensation to be the exclusive, or nearly exclusive, vehicle for recognizing good performance. Others are managed with a philosophy that people work for more than money and that the explicit acknowledgment of contributions is essential for building the spirit and dedication of the working community. If you value this dimension highly, you'll want to work for the latter type of organization. You desire clear signs that your work is noticed and appreciated. If this value is highly important to you, you should take your time during any job interview process and try to meet as many of your potential co-workers and managers as possible to get a thorough sense of the organizational culture and the day-to-day social environment.

Below is a "value priority" exercise that you'll be able to use in taking the perspective of other people. Your first subject, however, is going to be yourself. Create a deck of index cards with one reward value written on each card. Next, sort the cards on a flat surface in front of you in a column, placing the cards representing the most valued rewards at the top. Continue until you have the sequence of cards arranged from most valued to least valued. Now think through the cards. If you feel comfortable about the general order, focus on the top three cards, the cards that represent your most dominant work-reward values. Create a new column with just these three cards, this time making the space between each card represent the difference in importance to you of the two reward values being compared. For example, let's say that you value *lifestyle* above all other rewards and that it is significantly more important to you than your number two choice, *variety.* Place the *lifestyle* card at the top of the column and at a significant distance from the *variety* card. If your third most important reward is valued very closely to *variety,* it would be placed below it, separated by a short gap. Take your time with this exercise. At the end, you should have in front of you a visual representation of the three most important work rewards, as well as a visual sense of their relative value to each other.

Let's say that your third most valued work-reward value is *intellectual challenge.* We might read the above sorting like this: "This person values *lifestyle* significantly above all other rewards. She derives much of her meaning and satisfaction in life from commitments and activities that occur outside of the workplace. A choice of career must take this into account, and any job with consistently exceptional or unpredictable time requirements, or travel, will be inappropriate. This dimension is so dominant over all other reward values that it needs to have an almost exclusive focus in considering a career or job. After a job satisfies this requirement fully, it should ideally provide for *variety* in daily tasks and consistent intellectual challenge of problem solving."

If you had these same three reward values at the top of your list but with no strong preference for one over the other, the "read" would be quite different: "This person values *lifestyle* and *intellectual challenge* equally. As a result, the person should look for a job or career that provides for enough time to participate in avocational activities, that offers a steady supply of problems to analyze and solve, and that is not characterized by a high degree of routine." The point we want to make here is that the *degree* to which one dimension is valued over another needs to be factored into your analysis, not merely the rank ordering. Look at your cards and think about how these reward values have affected your most recent work choices (either the company you chose to work for or the job or assignments you've taken on internally). Is your current position allowing for fulfillment of this profile? What types of assignments would enhance the realization of this profile?

Once you've performed this analysis of your own motivational values, you can do the same for your colleagues, bosses, or employees. You can do this formally, by sorting the cards, or informally, simply by thinking about which work-reward values seem dominant for the person. Once you've analyzed his or her work motivation, think about what this information tells you. Given this person's reward profile, is he or she likely to remain satisfied in his or her current position for much longer? What types of assignments would offer more of these rewards? If you're the person's manager, can you restructure the position the person holds, or change his or her project assignment, or change the "mix" of the rewards you personally control? Given this profile, is this person likely to be particularly motivated to work on any projects you're planning? Could you link the person's support for your project to helping him or her get access to a position that would better fit the reward profile? If you were concerned about the organization losing this person, how would you restructure the person's work? How similar or dissimilar is this person's profile in comparison with your own? (This is important to consider in guarding against "projecting" your own values onto that person.) Make notes on your thoughts before moving on.

ASSESSING THE WORK MODE OF OTHERS

Swiss psychologist Carl Jung developed a now widely used road map of human consciousness that can be helpful in thinking about an individual's overall orientation toward work, or *"work mode."* Jung wrote about three dimensions of human personality: *judgment, perception,* and *attitude.* In analyzing a person's work mode, we use two of these dimensions, *perception* and *attitude*. With regard to perception, at one end of the scale are individuals with a *sensing* orientation, while at the other end are those with an *intuition* orientation. With regard to attitude, at one extreme are those who are *extroverted,* while at the other end are those who are *introverted.* There are four possible combinations of these two dimensions (*introverted sensing, introverted intuition, extroverted sensing,* and *extroverted intuition*).

In the Appendix we provide a brief introduction to Jung's model and an approach to analyzing your work mode in these terms. The next step is learning how to assess someone else's work mode. By knowing a person's work mode, you will be better able to appreciate how he or she approaches a business situation.

After learning more about the dimensions in the Appendix, take a look at each of the modes. As you read the descriptions, pay particular attention to the mode that represents your own combination of orientations on the perception and attitude dimensions (from your assessment in the Appendix). If the description doesn't seem accurate, return to your earlier analysis with the help of the mode description below that seems to describe you most accurately.

People with an *extroverted sensing* orientation are pragmatic doers. They prefer tasks that have practical goals that are measurable and make a clearly demonstrable contribution to a business effort. This is the sleeves-rolled-up, get-it-done activist. This is the statistically most common mode among business managers in the United States and is also the most common mode in sales jobs or careers. The rallying cry of someone who thinks via extroverted sensing is "There's a job to be done, we all know what it is, now let's do it." This mode sees analysis, models, and strategies in the service of action and implementation. Individuals who operate in this mode see the "real work" and see the most motivating challenges as those that turn strategy and analysis into actual business results.

If you determine fellow workers or bosses or employees to have this style, you can count on them to focus on the bottom line: what it's going to take to get the job done right. You can anticipate practical questions about implementation and questions about details as well. This type, as well as the introverted senser, will try to "pull your ideas down to earth" and make sure that they are going to work before signing up for the project. It's important in working with them to make sure you've thought through the details and potential obstacles to implementing what needs to be done. Try to anticipate the challenges you'll get from the pragmatists in your group.

People who operate in the *extroverted intuition* mode are innovative implementers. They aren't content with carrying out an established plan to achieve a business result. They want to find a new and better way to do business. They want to turn the assumptions of the existing business model on end and make sure there isn't a whole new perspective that makes more sense. These people like to identify *possibilities* (the hallmark of the intuitive function) and then *act* (the hallmark of the extroverted attitude) on them. Both innovation and implementation are important for the individual who operates in this manner. Extroverted intuitive people aren't interested in theory and strategy for their own sake, nor are they interested in carrying out someone else's established routine, as profitable as it may be. In our experience, the extroverted intuitive mode is by far the most common of the modes among entrepreneurs.

If you're trying to influence or persuade someone whose work mode is extroverted intuition, be prepared for your ideas to be met not with resistance, but with more ideas. The extroverted intuitive type wants to innovate when given the opportunity. So it is vital that you have these individuals innovating *with* you rather than generating alternative projects to accomplish similar ends. It's a good idea to involve them earlier in your planning process, so that they can feel—and be—a part of the project and see that their ideas are being included in your thinking. (This is much better than watching them start their own brainstorming process in front of the group during your big presentation.) Their energy and imagination can be a big boot to your efforts; just make sure that they feel there is room in your project for their imagination.

People who operate from an *introverted intuition* mode tend toward the visionary. They are interested in theory, strategy, and concepts and in what lies "over the horizon," and they thrive in the world of ideas and imagination. Business problems are interesting in and of themselves—not just for their practical application. The focus of this person's interest at any given time might be the business implications of an emerging technology, or it could be a new way to structure a sales force, or perhaps a new model of customer behavior, or a new way of thinking about a business supply chain. The implications of his or her vision may be immediately practical for the business effort, but what draws out the enthusiasm of the person with an introverted intuition mode isn't the day-to-day carrying out of the vision. It's in coming up with the answer that this person finds the fun, rather than what can be done with it. This combination of orientations is well represented in roles such as management consulting, advertising, marketing, strategic planning, business development, and new product development.

Like extroverted intuitives, introverted intuitive people like to be in on things from the beginning, so include them early on in your projects and ideas. They'll want to think about the "big picture" implications of your proposal, and they'll be most attracted to aspects of your projects that are yet to be worked out. They like to think big thoughts and dream, and they may present you with alternatives that you hadn't considered. If you involve them early enough, you'll have time to respond to, and perhaps incorporate, their ideas. They may want to take things deeper and broader than you think is necessary, but don't be impatient with their seemingly academic approach. You have nothing to lose by being a good listener, and potentially a lot to gain.

People who operate in the *introverted sensing* work mode are drawn to pragmatic intellectual challenge. They want to solve problems that require a depth of focus; the problems are more interesting if they have immediate consequences for the business at hand. These individuals are "hands on" thinkers rather than theorists. They are often good with details and methodical in their approach to problem solving. This combination of orientations is found frequently among engineers and is also the most frequent work mode among accountants.

Like the extroverted sensing individual, the introverted sensing person is going to give you "push-back" on details. Have you run the numbers? Are your budget and timeline realistic? Can you really meet your deadlines? Have you thought about how your project will affect program X and program Y? Imagine presenting your plan to a roomful of accountants and detail-oriented project engineers, and this will give you some idea of how your ideas will be received by the introverted sensing types in your group. Don't take their challenges and questions personally; they are not bringing up "nitpicking" details for the sake of making your proposal look bad. They'll probably only be trying to help—this is just the way they think about getting things done.

Step back now and think about the four work modes. Who in your organization do you think has the same work mode? Whose work mode is opposite to yours?

Now think about the person or people you've been focusing on throughout this section. Which of the four work modes do you think best fits? Who else in your organization has the same work mode? Who in your organization has a work mode opposite to his or hers? In light of what you have determined, do you think this person's current position likely to remain satisfying? What types of assignments would be a better fit? If you're the person's manager, can you restructure the position the person holds or change his or her project assignment to make a better match? How will his or her work mode affect the way he or she responds to your ideas? Given this profile, is this person likely to be interested in working on projects you're planning? Could the person's support for your project help him or her in their goals? How similar or dissimilar is this person's profile compared with your own? (This is important to consider in guarding against "projecting" your own values onto that person.) Make notes on your thoughts before moving on.

TAKING OTHER FACTORS INTO ACCOUNT

People are complex, and any one person's motivation is going to be affected by more factors than even the best psychological model can take into account. In addition to the models we just introduced, you should add an "existential" factor—namely, what are the unique elements about a person that affect the perspective he or she takes? Does one of your colleagues always seem to need recognition of his or her intellectual ability and because of that feel compelled to challenge your ideas and suggest changes to them? Are the decisions and work habits of another heavily influenced by anxiety about finances because he or she recently assumed a large mortgage? Can you predict that one fellow worker will react positively to a proposal in order to feel "a part of the group," regardless of the issue? Will a recent setback by another colleague make that person feel a need to reestablish his or her position in the group by asserting dominance and control? In addition to the more formal analysis that you've already done, ask: "What do I know about this person from both past experience and intuition? What's going on in his or her life right now? And given these considerations, what is the one thing that he or she will want most from this situation right now?"

PUTTING IT ALL TOGETHER

Think again, one at a time, about each individual you focused on in the exercises we presented. Consider the information you've gathered on each individual's reward values and work modes. Think first about the results of each analysis separately. Now try to see a current business situation that you are facing from the perspective of this person, with this orientation. You should be able to think, feel, sense, and intuit the differences between his or her point of view and your own. Add in any existential factors, as previously discussed. Then step back and let your analyses merge into a complete portrait of the individual. The portrait you now have is probably very much like your earlier impressions of this person, but drawn with more subtlety and much finer detail. Your work has probably brought you some new knowledge of this person and aspects of his or her personality, outlook, and behavior that you hadn't considered before.

Now think back to our hypothetical conference room at the beginning of the chapter with your manager and co-workers. Assume that one of your peers has *affiliation* and *recognition* as her two highest reward values. Her work mode is introverted intuitive. Another peer's two highest reward values are *power and influence* and *prestige,* and his work mode is extroverted sensing. Imagine how differently each of these two people thinks about your proposal and what it would require from them.

To better imagine, think back to a recent proposal or initiative of your own and see it through the eyes of these two hypothetical colleagues.

Now, extend this analysis to your own day-to-day colleagues. Recall their reponses to a recent development at work, possibly some crisis or an innovation. Try to take the perspective of each one in that particular situation. Finally, as you prepare for an upcoming meeting, take five minutes and do this analysis for the key people who'll be present. During the meeting itself, pay attention to how your analysis and hypotheses about their various behaviors actually play out. Does what you observe change your original analysis?

At this point, your reaction probably is, "But this is a lot of work! Who has time for all of this?" There are two answers to this. The first is that this *is* your work—it's a vital part of the work of anyone who works in any organization. You can't afford *not* to do it. The second is that you're *already* doing this work, but perhaps not doing it very well. You cannot escape being a business psychologist. It's part of business life. You do have the opportunity, however, to become a better one. By using the models presented in this chapter, you will. Over time, you'll become more and more efficient in your perspective-taking analyses and better able to do a "quick study" of newly met colleagues and business partners (which is particularly useful, for example, in negotiating with suppliers and customers).

Business, in its essence, is a social enterprise; commerce is an exchange between *people.* The fascinating variations in human personality can be one of the enduring attractions of a career in business. For some people *the* greatest attraction of business is its interpersonal aspect. Regardless of our reward values and work modes, business can be done only with other people. You will never achieve your maximum potential or success if you don't gain some insight into those individuals who work together to achieve a business goal or "do business" as buyer and seller. Over time, organizations themselves seem to develop "personalities," and these too can be analyzed productively.

This chapter could have accurately been titled "How to Be a Business Psychologist." However, business psychology is not about learning to label people and put them in boxes or to reduce them to a set of predictable behaviors. Business psychology is about seeing and acting—

about *seeing* better and *using* that "sight" *productively.* It is the ongoing process of stepping outside yourself to look from another's perspective; to *see* the world through the eyes of your employees and colleagues, your managers, your customers, and other business allies; and to *use* that knowledge to be more effective at what you do.

CHAPTER
FOURTEEN

COMING TO TERMS WITH AUTHORITY

UNDERSTANDING YOUR OWN CONSCIOUS AND UNCONSCIOUS attitudes toward authority is essential to being effective in any organization. *Everyone* has a boss: every worker, every manager, every entrepreneur, every CEO, and every chairman of the board. They all have people to whom they are responsible and without whom their businesses or departments would fail. When we consult with business professionals they often spend a lot of time and energy discussing their relationships with their bosses, current and previous. We hear tales of tyrants and heroes; we hear anger at exploiters and adulation expressed for wise mentors. We hear fantasies of "not having to have any boss to screw up my work." Sometimes people acknowledge this as wishful thinking inspired by recent frustrations at work. Other people make it clear that working *under* someone who has authority *over* them is so distasteful that they have, consciously or not, organized their career thinking around the fantasy of an escape from a relationship with a manager—*any* manager.

For some people the theme is the search for a mentor, a "Great Father" or "Mother" figure who will guide them. For others it's the escape from all authority. The archetype of "the boss" carries enormous psychological energy for many people. You need only look at the tremendous success of the Dilbert comic empire for evidence. In fact, it's so pervasive that we almost take it for granted. But why *do* so many of us struggle so much with the dynamics of authority at work? To answer this question we need to look at the nature of authority itself and at the origins of our ambivalent relationship toward it.

AUTHORITY AS PERMISSION TO ACT

Authority is closely related to power, but the two are not the same. Power, as we discuss in the next chapter, is often confused with dominance or status, but at its root it is neither of these. Power, defined most succinctly by Aristotle, is the capacity to act. Authority, on the other hand, is the right or *permission* to act. No one can grant us *power;* but authority, by its nature, *must* be granted. Authority is a social concept: it has to do with a right or a *permission* granted within the context of a group, organization, or other political entity. A CEO is authorized by the board of directors to exercise her personal power and acumen as an expert businessperson. Before being hired, this CEO possessed power, or the potential to use her knowledge and experience to make effective business decisions. After she was hired she had the authority to do so in that particular organization.

The word *authority* derives from the Latin *auctor,* "author"; authority is, so to say, "authorized." By implication, authority is written, codified, authored, by whatever group is in turn authorized to grant that authority. Authority, with its permission to do something within a particular organization or group, is permission to exercise our power; it carries an acknowledgment of our place in the hierarchy, our status, "weight," "substance," and "presence." This begins to explain why authority is such an explosive psychological issue. Authority is permission to express our self, to act in the world, to be an acknowledged and respected person. If you have no authority or if your authority is withdrawn or diminished, it leads to feeling isolated and alienated. This applies as much to the most recently hired staff assistant who is on the verge of being put on probation as it does to the most experienced senior manager whose ideas have lost favor and who has been removed from the senior operating group.

Loss of authority does not mean a loss in personal power—a diminishment in our own capacity or reality. Imprisoned, neither Gandhi nor Socrates appears to have experienced a loss of personal power. Nor did Nelson Mandela or Martin Luther King Jr. But most of us are not Gandhi, or Socrates, Mandela or King. When we believe that we are being denied the authority to act, most of us feel slighted; our egos are "bruised." If we examine this bruise carefully, what we find can more accurately be described as a diminishment of our sense of ourselves: we feel psychologically "smaller."

POWER AND AUTHORITY THROUGH THE EYES OF A CHILD

This "feeling smaller" is a clue to why problems with authority bedevil every business organization. The desire to be psychologically big rather than small is archetypal. The phrase *the big boys* in reference to an organization's senior managers or partners suggests that authority struggles have their beginnings in the family setting. We all grow up in families with parents (big people) and children (little people). Feeling small and less powerful and wanting to be bigger and more powerful is a fundamental aspect of human development. Freud, in his exposition of the Greek myth of Oedipus, pointed out that children experience the big-small dynamic in the family as essentially a zero-sum game: "As long as you're so big I'm always going to feel small." This fantasy is then compounded, according to Freud, by the child's sense that the parent is in fact threatened by the personal power or attractiveness of the child. In other words, the child believes that the parent wants to suppress the child's natural expression of power and effectiveness. The problem of power thus becomes a problem with authority. Someone else has authority to act in a "big" way, and I don't. I haven't been given permission to be fully myself.

A child's perspective on authority is further complicated by his or her dependence—and desire *to be* dependent—on the parent. There is always a part of the child that wants to be taken care of by Mom and Dad, even when angry at them. This leads to an ambivalence toward authority, the wish to be dependent and at the same time to establish one's authority. This ambivalence is evidenced both during the "terrible twos" of the toddler and then again during adolescence. For many people it is not fully resolved and is carried into adulthood as both a wish for and a rebellion against strong leadership. We want to have a strong, protective parent, but we resent what we experience as the suppression of our own authority and autonomy. The outcome of these early struggles, resentments, and ambivalence toward authority is affected by our individual temperaments and personalities, by the child-raising skill of our parents, and by our experiences with other early authority figures outside the family setting.

Whether or not we agree with the details of Freud's analysis, it is clear that we enter early adulthood and the world of work with definite attitudes toward authority. At that age, our young lives are already full of wishes, longings, resentments, and hopes when it comes to what we expect from a "boss," often mostly forgotten and unconscious. Over time, those seeds of childhood experience with authority grow into distinct attitudes toward authority that we tend to carry with us from one work situation to another. These attitudes interact with the personalities and styles of our individual bosses to produce a variety of different experiences. From a distance, our feelings about authority are evident by virtue of their stability from job to job. Insight into those feelings and patterns of attitudes is the essential first step in coming to terms with the drama of authority relationships that seems to be inseparable from the experience of work in organizations.

RECOGNIZING YOUR ATTITUDES TOWARD AUTHORITY

Collecting Data

Before examining the various patterns of relationship with authority, it's important to gather some data from your own experience. Write down the names of your last three managers. You are going to do a series of exercises, considering each manager separately. The exercise using your current boss will be the easiest; for the others you will have to put yourself back into the world you inhabited at the time.

Let's start with your current boss or manager. Try to remember specific interactions between the two of you and the places at work where they occurred. Try to picture him or her in different settings: with you alone, with others at meetings, speaking to a large group, interacting with his or her boss. Allow these images to develop. Don't analyze them, just *watch* them.

Where is the action taking place? What is your boss doing: sitting, standing, talking, yelling, gesturing, listening? Where are you in the picture? What is your posture? What are *you* doing? What time of day is it? Allow the images to develop and evolve into other images of your work life. When your boss appears in these images, pay close attention. Try to recall a specific painful or difficult incident involving your boss. Remember as fully as possible what the experience was like. Try to recall a particularly pleasurable or rewarding experience. Remember as fully as possible how you thought and felt at that time. In this exercise you are "reminding" yourself with your emotions and intuition and sensory perceptions of what it was like to be with your boss.

Once you've observed many images and recalled as much as you can about your experience with your manager, you can begin to think and analyze. How would you sum it up? (Take brief key-word notes.) What is your *first* memory of your manager? What did you hope the relationship would be like? How does the reality of it match, and not match, that hope? Do you look forward to continuing it? How could it be different? What do you miss or have you not taken advantage of in the relationship? How were you feeling about yourself generally throughout your relationship together? How do you now feel about your decisions and behavior? What would you have done differently? How do you think your boss experienced you? How would he describe you if someone called him for a job reference? Again, take brief, key-word notes. Pick four adjectives that best describe this boss. Pick four adjectives that he or she would use to describe you. Pick four adjectives that an objective observer would use to describe your relationship with your supervisor.

When you have remembered, observed, reflected, and recorded, put down your pen and leave the exercise. Allow some time to pass before returning to the same exercise using a previous boss as the focus. Go through the exercise three times, once for each of your three most recent bosses.

After completing the three sections of this exercise, go through the exercise again for your parent(s) or primary caregivers. This part of the exercise may be more difficult. Most of us aren't used to analyzing our relationships with our parents in an objective fashion—nor are we accustomed to looking at them exclusively in terms of their role as authority figures. We're looking here for clues about your parents' influence on your relationship with authority.

When you've finished these exercises, put aside your notes and adjective lists. Before returning to them, we want to discuss a model that will help you analyze themes in your relationship with people in authority.

Different Stances Toward Authority

Each of us brings to our adult relationships with authority a unique personality and temperament and a unique set of emotional experiences with earlier authority figures. Of course, our emotional reaction to being managed is also affected greatly by the personality and style of our manager. But we all have a tendency to repeat underlying attitudes and patterns of behavior. To the extent that we can become aware of these patterns, we have an opportunity to change them if we need to. Your pattern of feeling and attitudes will be far more specific and nuanced than the broad categories indicated by the models we are about to offer, so take them as a starting point, modifying them to fit you better. The real goal is to recognize your patterns and attitudes *as you experience them,* when they're actually unfolding.

There are three general stances toward authority: *engaged, reactive,* and *laissez-faire.* These stances or attitudes don't have any value attached—one isn't any better than the others in and of itself. Each has the potential for being productive or dysfunctional depending on the individual's level of development, the personality of the authority figure, and the organizational environment. Your actual response to authority at any given moment is determined both by your own psychological conditioning and by the behavior of your manager. But by looking at their past relationships, most people can identify a tendency to characteristically adopt one stance.

Someone with an *engaged* attitude tends to seek out and welcome a relationship with someone in authority. This person sees a boss as a potential mentor, teacher, protector, and/or nurturer. He or she welcomes the vision and direction provided by a strong leader and looks for ways to spend time with that person. This individual holds the perspective, consciously or not, that power flowing through a hierarchy of managers is the most effective route to accomplishment and success. Many of the individuals described in "Doing Too Much, Pushing Too Hard," "Always Swinging for the Fence," and "Running Roughshod over the Opposition" have an engaged stance toward authority. People with an engaged stance have often had positive, nurturing, and collaborative experiences with past authority figures (or, conversely, a strong appetite for a relationship like that based on past experience with distant, absent, or weak authority figures).

In its most mature and productive mode, the engaged stance represents a high level of commitment and willingness to dedicate a great deal of personal energy to the goals of the organization or business unit. It can also, however, be the posture toward authority adopted by overly dependent individuals who are uncertain about their own ability and purpose. This dark side of the engaged stance is seen, in its extreme, in an abdication of personal power and a projection of that power onto the leader. The common element in both manifestations of the engaged stance is the strong orientation toward and engagement with formal structures of power and authority.

The *reactive* stance is similar to the engaged stance in that the individual with this attitude is strongly oriented toward authority and toward the person who holds it. But these people stand and behave in a *reaction* to the directives of the person in authority (as in, "for every action there is an equal *and opposite* reaction"). They see the issue of authority as a developing dialectic worked out between individuals who are equals despite the fact that one of them is currently in authority. In its most positive mode, the individual with a reactive stance is highly vigilant about the mission of an organization or business area and challenges peers and superiors alike to think more deeply or differently about the problems and opportunities facing the group.

In its most destructive mode, the person with the reactive stance is the chronic rebel, with unresolved issues toward authority generally. We have talked about this pattern in the chapter "Rebel Looking for a Cause." These people see the directives of the manager as attempts to restrain their creativity and autonomy. Their relationships with superiors are often conflicted and intense in a way that undermines the morale of the larger group. The reactive stance toward authority brings intensity and focus to the issue of power and its use in an organization or work group. This intensity has the potential to be either a creative stimulus or a dysfunctional challenge to the legitimacy of a leader, expressed in ways that can either enhance or undermine a group's goals.

Entrepreneurs often exhibit some of the features of the reactive stance, but rather than engaging with authority, and defining themselves in opposition to it, they act outside of established organizational boundaries because no other arrangement makes sense to them. They're not attracted to having *authority* as much as to having *autonomy:* the freedom to pursue their own ideas and act on their own initiative without oversight. Most successful entrepreneurs are not rebels as much as they are pioneers, heading for the frontier so they can establish themselves on their own terms. A dysfunctional variation of the true entrepreneur is those people whose reaction to authority is so strong that their only solution is to set up their own company, whether or not they feel either prepared or genuinely interested in doing so. These are really pseudo-entrepreneurs.

The laissez-faire stance toward authority is characterized by an essential indifference toward formal authority. This is not a rebellion, but rather a stance adopted by people with a strong sense of themselves and an equally strong sense of competence and mission. They view a leader as a coordinator of the activities of fellow professionals, almost like an air traffic controller. They're willing to follow the manager's lead as long as they think it makes sense and doesn't impinge too much on their professional enthusiasm and mission. People with this stance often become individual contributors of some sort. The laissez-faire stance is frequently found among academics, physicians in a medical center or research facility, and partners in a law or other professional services firm. In its most positive mode, this stance can be the core of an egalitarian model of professionalism founded on mutual respect and rational compromise.

More negatively, the laissez-faire stance can drift toward indifference to the overall direction of the organization and to the need for unified action. Dysfunctional manifestations of this stance are sometimes seen in behavior patterns described in the earlier chapters "Seeing the World in Black and White," "Emotionally Tone-Deaf" and "Lacking a Sense of Boundaries."

Identifying Your Dominant Stance Toward Authority

It's important to realize that the three stances toward authority just described are not personality types. Rather, they are a way of looking at different *dynamics* of relationships to authority. The personality and behavior of both the person being managed *and* the manager determine the relationship dynamic. A highly skilled manager who has an appreciation for the unique ability and potential of each of his or her subordinates might be able to evoke an engaged stance even from someone with a history of negative relationships with managers and a reactive stance toward authority. On the other hand, an authoritarian manager with no appreciation of the diversity of skills and perspectives of his or her subordinates can alienate and force into a reactive stance even the most typically engaged worker.

We all, however, have a typical stance toward authority, a "default option" of sorts. To determine whether your stance is engaged, reactive, or laissez-faire, return to the data from the exercise you did earlier. Review the material, this time keeping in mind the model of three stances toward authority. You'll almost certainly find periods where you adopted each of the three stances. But you'll also find that one occurs more often and could be described as your "default" stance. Seeing this pattern may require extending your analysis back beyond your three most recent bosses. Take your time. Think about how those people who know you best at work would characterize your relationships with authority. Which stance would they see as most characteristic of you? To help with your analysis, following are some behavioral markers that are associated with each of the three stances:

Engaged Stance

▲ You've worked for several managers whom you strongly admire.
▲ You look to your relationship with a manager as a major source of learning.
▲ You believe that organizations work best when there's a strong leader who isn't afraid to assert his or her authority.
▲ You have a high *recognition* work-reward value (see Chapter 13).
▲ It is your observation that ability and hard work really are what get people to the top levels of organizations.
▲ You'd like to be the general manager of your organization someday.

Reactive Stance

▲ You have a history, extending back to childhood and adolescence, of being a "free thinker" with an often unique point of view.
▲ Your list of personal heroes includes many people known for their strong individuality and tendency to challenge formal authority or established customs.
▲ You believe that the performance of an organization relies more directly on the talent of its members than on the quality of its management.
▲ You're known as someone who speaks your mind in meetings, whether or not you agree with either the consensus or the opinions of superiors.
▲ You appreciate managers who invite "push-back" and challenges to their point of view.
▲ You frequently disagree with your manager's perspective and judgment.
▲ You see yourself as being essentially an innovator or entrepreneur—inside or outside the organization.
▲ You often think about having your own business.

Laissez-Faire Stance

▲ You see your career developing essentially as that of an expert individual contributor.

▲ You learn more from professional peers than from your managers.

▲ You turn to colleagues more often than to managers when faced with challenging situations at work.

▲ You don't aspire to the role of general manager or to any management role at all.

▲ You tend either to be critical of people who actively seek positions of power within organizations or to simply not be able to understand them.

Recognizing Your Authority Stance Blind Spot

Every stance has a potential for dysfunction that is self-defeating. What do you know about your own self-defeating behaviors in relationship to authority? Your personal self-defeating patterns may be variations on the major dysfunctional aspect associated with each of the three dominant stances that we have discussed. Let us consider each of these dysfunctional tendencies.

It can be argued that the *engaged* stance is generally the most productive and adaptive style in most organizations, particularly in those that offer workers experienced and committed leadership. People with an engaged stance will easily be able to align their personal talents and goals with the mission of the organization and the goals of the business unit. Relationships with supervisors are likely to be positive and unconflicted. Morale and commitment would be expected to be high within an organization where most of the workers adopt this stance toward authority. The dysfunctional potential of this stance, however, lies in the area of personal initiative.

Senior managers are paid to take initiative and lead the organization in carrying out the initiatives. But every business professional has to take responsibility for identifying opportunities and taking initiative on their own. No one can rely solely on the vision and directives of his or her manager to understand how the current business situation is developing and to see what creative responses are required. Every manager needs to be challenged and needs to see the developing situation through the eyes of subordinates.

Good managers want the best thinking and insights from their subordinates, even if they contradict their own perspective, and they want them expressed when and where they add value to decisions that are being made. Some managers invite this type of participation more explicitly than others. It's the job of every business professional to adopt an independent stance vis-à-vis authority when they think the business situation calls for it. The person who usually adopts an engaged stance and is uncritical and unquestioning of the direction set by those in authority is likely to be deficient in this regard.

If you usually have an engaged stance, you should consider whether or not you also have a pattern of avoiding disagreement and conflict with your superiors. Do you speak up in meetings against the consensus perspective or against the perspective of your manager if you need to? Do you often talk about your thoughts and feelings, or criticize management's plans to others, *after* the meeting? (These are behaviors that can often better be assessed by someone you work with who has known you in a variety of work situations.)

You are the one ultimately responsible for your career. People with a positive, engaged attitude toward authority are more likely to see their managers as wise and powerful because they *want* to see them that way. We see this even in very mature individuals. This is always accompanied by a subtle abrogation of responsibility for personal choice and career direction, which is then left in the hands of the person with authority. Mentors can be helpful in the development of any career, but you cannot rely on them to know what you should do. For one thing, your best next career move might well be outside your current business unit or organization and thus in conflict with the interests of your manager. Even when this isn't the case, no one can know the path that will bring you the greatest career satisfaction.

The reactive stance toward authority, in its most dysfunctional manifestation, can lead to a series of authority relationships characterized by chronic conflict. It's one thing to be the "loyal opposition" at times and play the "devil's advocate." At times. It's quite another to constantly and consistently oppose or be angry, frustrated, and disappointed with your superiors. After a while this ceases to be a source of creative give-and-take and becomes something close to its opposite: a drain on energy and morale for you, your boss, and the group. There is a big difference between the rebel who is a reformer and the rebel who is always acting from a stance of negativity. In this latter case the "revolution" never gets converted to the new order; it stays as a permanent undercurrent of criticism that can turn to resentment and bitterness.

Over time, as creative disagreement and an independent point of view turn into a predictable pattern of negativity to new initiatives from above, the person's identity within the organization as a non-team-playing rebel begins to form. Once formed, it's hard to change, and it becomes a serious threat to an individual's credibility. A consistently negative and disruptive attitude toward authority is almost always an in-dication that the person in question is struggling with unconscious con-flicts with authority rooted in earlier life situations. The potential for career damage is very high in this pattern.

If your review of your relationships with authority over a span of time suggests that you frequently take on the role of negative rebel, we advise you to get counseling or coaching help. We are *not* saying that this is a sign of deep psychological problems. Each of us has weak-nesses, dynamic personality tensions, and self-defeating behaviors, just as we have our strengths. But the issues associated with the negative rebel are poorly tolerated by most organizations and lead to a career-threatening reputation as someone who is always at odds with the orga-nization. You need to find help changing that pattern of behavior.

The potential blind spot of people with a basically laissez-faire atti-tude toward authority lies in their indifference to power. Power is a fact. It is social energy. It cannot be ignored. The individual contributor who is so caught up in his own projects that he loses track of organizational dynamics and politics is in danger of being marginalized within the or-ganization. The professor in her department, the doctor in his hospital, the law partner in her firm, may all at times be tempted to leave the "ad-ministration" to others so that they can focus exclusively on research or a client's needs. And they can do so, for periods of time. But not indefi-nitely. Power in an organization is concerned with the allocation of resources and setting the direction for the organization. If you want the resources to do your work, you have to participate in the power dynamics of your workplace. If you want to have any say in where the organization goes and what it becomes, you have to participate in organizational politics. This doesn't mean that you have to become a manager. But you do have to engage management and be part of the power dynamic and decision making.

Authority, as we have seen, is a loaded psychological issue for most of us. It carries an emotional charge that was formed in childhood, and you operate from attitudes that were being formed well before you took your first job. Because all work in organizations is carried out with and through authority, you need the capacity to be flexible and creative, as well as alert and self-protective in your relationships with superiors. This is one of the fundamental tenets of career success. Conflicts in this area are among the most common causes of career disruption.

The first step in coming to terms with authority is insight. You need to understand your feelings about authority and how they both contribute to your effectiveness and get in your way. You need to bring your unconscious habits into conscious awareness—a process that is neither quick nor easy. We consult with successful senior executives who are still working on their "authority issues." The insight process involves paying attention when attention is most difficult to come by, in situations where you are caught up in strong emotional reactions or when you have to respond to very complex problems involving many different personalities. The guiding principle, as always, is "Know thyself." By being aware of your stance and attitudes, you gain the ability to make your own decisions about how you engage with authority, rather than letting your history dictate your future.

CHAPTER
FIFTEEN

USING POWER

Not believing in power is the same as not believing in gravity.
—LEON TROTSKY

Susan Meyer was bright, personable, hardworking, capable, and willing to make personal sacrifices to achieve the objectives of her business—the kind of woman you expect to find one day in *Fortune* magazine's "Fifty Most Powerful Women" list. Susan's career was a steady series of ascents—more responsibility, more people, more budget, bigger operation. She was, so to speak, *on her way.*

From her beginning as an assistant brand manager in a large consumer-oriented packaged goods company Susan had excelled, displaying the kind of creativity and insight into consumer psychology—backed by "hard data" analysis—that the firm prized most highly. She worked well with other members of her team, with her manager, and with the pre-MBA associates assigned to the brand she worked on.

Susan attracted the attention of top management, who saw in her a potential general manager for one of their divisions. She was picked for an assignment that in many ways was a "plum," taking over a mildly troubled manufacturing facility in an area where their principal competitor had been crippled by a strike and lost a tremendous amount of its market share. It was an assignment that held a high probability of success and had the eye of the president and CEO. Susan accepted the challenge gladly, eager for the opportunity to prove herself capable of taking on general management responsibility in a situation where she could hit a home run for her company—with top management all watching in the box seats.

At considerable personal sacrifice, Susan arranged to move herself and her family to Dallas, and just after Christmas she arrived on the scene, ready for action. Prior to the move she had met the other members of her management team, most of whom seemed friendly enough, "despite your being a Yankee" (Susan was a native New Yorker), as one of them joked. Susan knew that there were some hard feelings about the previous GM's having been told that it was time to step aside, but people seemed to understand that this was not her doing—and some seemed to agree that Jonathan, her predecessor, was standing in the way of the growth of the business. Susan was surprised, then, when she was greeted with a polite but rather aloof manner by some of her new staff when she arrived to go to work.

The behavior of the head of sales, Steve, was particularly puzzling and troubling. He called late to tell her that he wouldn't be able to make it to the first meeting they had scheduled, because he needed to go with a sales rep to visit an important customer. He took days to respond to her voice mail messages and never got back to her on e-mails she sent. When they did talk he was curt, implying that he thought the company had made a mistake bringing her down there to solve problems they could have taken care of on their own. He'd been in this business for almost thirty years, he told her, and didn't need her help (he stopped just short of reminding her that he was at least ten years older than she was).

Throughout this time Susan was determined to win the respect and cooperation of the group, which she attempted to do by redoubling her efforts to prove herself a trustworthy and competent leader and manager. She refused to take the bait and engage in battles with Steve, even going out of her way to get his input—as someone with long and deep institutional knowledge—in key decisions. Susan made it a point to meet with not only her direct reports, but other members of the organization. And she "outworked" anyone and everyone, doing a more thorough strategic analysis of the business and its position in the marketplace in her first two months than had been done in the previous twenty years.

Sad to say, Susan failed in her efforts. In the end, she was unable to gain the support of a "critical mass" of her staff. Steve continued to resist her leadership passively—and to undermine her efforts to establish herself as the group's leader. Ultimately it proved a Pyrrhic victory for him; he was forced out of the company at the same time Susan was reassigned to corporate headquarters. In the process of a lengthy "postmortem" of the eighteen months she spent in Dallas, we were able to draw several conclusions about Susan's failure. The first was that she had simply been blindsided by Steve, not having known that he had considered himself the heir apparent after Jonathan—and not "getting it" for almost four crucial months. But then, even after it became clear that she had an enemy in him, Susan failed to react effectively to Steve's challenge to her leadership. She tried to make friends, to take him into her confidence, to "talk it through." She tried to work around him. She tried to win over his allies. She tried to prove her worth to the members of her staff by working diligently and intelligently.

But she never "pulled rank." She never called Steve into her office after a meeting in which he was marginally disrespectful (he was too smart to challenge her directly) and say to him, "Look, Steve, I've tried my best to work with you, but you don't seem to be interested. So I just want to say two things. First, don't mess with me, ever again. And second, I think it's time you started looking for another job, because you clearly don't want to work for [not 'with'] me." Nor did she fight back in the same kind of bare-knuckled, no-holds-barred way in which Steve was going after her (gathering "dirt" on him, setting him up to fail, embarrassing him in front of others, forcing him out of the organization). In short, Susan never wielded her *power* to dispose of Steve or to put him in his place.

In talking with her about what had happened (and what had *not* happened) we noted that Susan reacted in a telling way to the word *power:* her head recoiled reactively, and she said that she really had a hard time imagining herself *using* her power over someone else, actually commanding them to do something. "Intellectually I know it's not necessarily bad, using power for a good cause. But personally, I have a really

negative gut reaction to it. It feels like I'd be beating up on somebody."
(Some five years later, Susan tells me that she frequently reminds herself
that "power is value-neutral"—one of her maxims that emerged out of
our work together.)

FEELINGS ABOUT POWER

The discomfort with power that Susan expressed is both more common
and more problematic than one might expect. Many people's relationship with power is one of the most deeply ambivalent aspects of their
lives. Even the word itself—"power"—stirs up feelings of strong desire
and deep fear in people.

Power is good. We have the "power of righteousness," the "powers
of office," "power hitters," the "power of concentration," "power to the
people," "powerful novels," and "powerful engines." "Potency"—from
the Latin *potis* (powerful)—is good, while being impotent (in both the
sexual sense and otherwise) is bad. Managers vow to "empower" their
subordinates. (Empowerment has become such a buzzword that James
Hillman, writing in his book *Kinds of Power,* refers derisively to "empowerment" as "the major catchword for barking people into the self-
help and recovery booths at the therapeutic carnival.") Jack Welch,
CEO of General Electric, widely admired as one of the great business
leaders and managers of the twentieth century, used his power effectively to revive and grow the company.

Power is bad. There are "power trips," "power mongers," "power
games," "power brokers," and the "abuse of power." The word *despot*
(tyrant) derives from the term used by Greek slaves for their masters:
despotes (from *dems* [house] and *poti* [power]). Power can be abused just
as easily as it is used. Most people *don't* admire people like "Chainsaw
Al" Dunlap, known for his ruthlessness in closing plants and laying people off in companies he was brought in to manage.

Most of us are wary of someone having *too much* power, since the
greater the amount of power a person, organization, or nation has, the
greater the amount of damage if that power is abused. Both semiauto-
matic rifles and baseball bats can be used wisely or abused—but the

damage that can be done with the rifle is much greater than what can be done with the bat, if they are abused. Before there were laws in the country protecting the rights of workers to unionize, powerful corporations hired thugs to brutalize and intimidate labor organizers and strikers. Even a cursory glance at the Constitution of the United States, with its "checks and balances" of power among the three branches of government, shows that this was very much on the minds of the Constitution's framers back in the 1700s.

Our feelings toward power, then, range from attraction (to being strong and potent) to repulsion (out of fear of abuse and of despotism). Remember that we're focusing on our *feelings*, not a rational analysis of what power is and is not. Because power can instill both reactions, there is a natural *tension* to our feelings about it, like the tension in a rubber band being pulled apart (although *we* are the rubber band being stretched!).

People experience other deep psychological tensions as well. One is the impulse toward altruism versus the impulse toward self-gratification. Altruism simply means concern for others. Humans are social beings and act out of concern for the greater good on a regular basis. At the same time, we all want to take care of ourselves, to act at times in ways that are not best for society or a particular group—cutting ahead in the line to exit a turnpike, for example. Yet as individuals we're able to hold on to the knowledge that if *everyone* cut in line, anarchy and chaos would rule. We somehow learn to manage that tension.

Some people, in the face of such tension, attempt to deal with it simply by slipping the metaphorical rubber band off one of their fingers. Thus one person chooses a life of selfless service to the poor, while another (likely without any conscious deliberation at all) chooses to become wholly selfish in his or her approach to life, taking care of number one. Still another lives life as a kind of Peter Pan, never acknowledging responsibility to anyone else, while his or her neighbor becomes a "young fogy."

When it comes to power, a large number of people (Susan Meyer being one example) disown the part of themselves that wants to have and wield power. Their stated reason for doing so may be that they believe power can never be used fairly (but then, why not gain and use power in an attempt to ensure that it is used as fairly as possible?). They may aspire to play in an arena where all is fair and the best man/woman/team/idea wins—where "politics" and "power games" play no role—which is fine, of course, as long as the people around are all interested in playing by those rules. (There are, in fact, very few such realms—although professional sports and investment portfolio management come to mind.) Often these people express disdain, even contempt, for people who "play the power game." Frequently, these feelings are a function of what psychologists refer to as "reaction formation"—a psychological defense through which unacceptable impulses are denied by going to the opposite extreme. They may want power but do not feel as if they *should* want it, and so they disavow their desires.

Other people slip that metaphorical rubber band off the other finger, becoming totally focused on (in some cases obsessed with) gaining and using power. Robert Moses, for example, who was responsible for building many of New York City's bridges, tunnels, expressways, parkways, parks, and airports, was famous for his ruthless use of power and his relentless pursuit of it. This complete disavowal of one element (fear of power) and total embrace of the other (desire for power) causes problems of its own.

But in our experience the more common problem is those people who disavow power. This can have serious consequences for those people who enter the business arena with neither shield nor sword and find themselves competing with colleagues who are more comfortable with acquiring and using power. Such was the case with Susan, and it has been the case with a large number of our executive coaching clients.

Understanding your feelings about power, your life stance in relation to it, is critical to success. Like it or not, power is a fact of business life, and each of us needs to be keenly aware of the feelings it elicits in us (both conscious and unconscious) and of our characteristic actions in response to it. However, before further discussing power and why people feel the way they do about it, we would like you to take some time and go through the brief exercises that follow. They will help you understand more about what part power plays in your own psychological life.

EXPLORING YOUR FEELINGS ABOUT POWER

First, take a moment and focus in your mind on two groups of people, those who have very little power and the very powerful. The powerless group could comprise poor, indebted nations, the poorest people, those living under the oppression of a totalitarian regime, people laboring in low-paying jobs under poor working conditions, and so on. The very powerful group could comprise any combination of nations, governmental leaders, people of great wealth, religious leaders, business executives, authors and people of intellectual influence, members of the news media, and so on. Now anyone with any heart will sympathize and feel sorry for the former group. But we want you to focus for a moment on your feelings about the powerful group.

Do you identify with them? Aspire to be one of them? Resent them? Blame them for the suffering of the powerless? Do you wish you had that kind of power? Or does it make you uneasy? ("I wouldn't know what to do if I had a billion dollars—I think I'd give it all to someone else to deal with!") Do you think, "I'm not willing to do what it takes to get there (work one hundred hours a week, travel 90 percent of the time, put myself through the electoral process), but if I were magically put into that position, I would *love* it." Does your list of personal heroes lean toward the Churchills, Edisons, Eisenhowers, Gateses, and Henry Fords of the world or toward the Mother Teresas and Gandhis?

Now consider people you have known—either in a work context or outside work—who have significantly more power than you do (as seen by you). Would you like to have their *power* (rather than just the personal wealth that they may have acquired as a result of their power)? Would you like the authority for assigning the work? For having the final say on the design? Would you want to have the final say in a negotiation? In deciding whom to hire and fire? In determining the direction of your division or company?

Think back over the last year: How have you behaved with regard to power—your own and that of other people? Do you recall instances of having been anxious about power? Of having felt envious of people with more power? Have you had dreams (either sleeping or waking) involving power? If you can remember them, what was the context, the feeling tone? (Whether or not you can recall any dreams, if this notion of having and using power holds much psychological "charge" for you, you may find yourself having such dreams sometime in the near future; if you do, pay careful attention to them. They may provide you with some very helpful, even surprising information about yourself.) Compare how you feel about power now with how you felt about it five and ten years ago, respectively. Have you changed in any way? How, and what do you think accounts for the change?

How would your closest co-workers and managers, past and present, describe you in regard to power? In thinking about this question, be sure to include people who may not be your biggest fans as well as your confidants. Would people in the two groups see you differently? Have you been accused (rightly or wrongly, in your view) of wanting too much power, of engaging in "turf battles" just for the sake of your own position, of empire building? Are you seen as somebody who needs to stand up for him- or herself more, someone too easy to push around with no push-back?

Have your reactions to power caused you any trouble in work? Have you used power ineptly and failed in your attempts to achieve your goals? Have you let other people make the choices just to avoid "power struggles" and then regretted it? Have you pushed too hard for your agenda or engaged in ill-conceived "power plays" in an attempt to take over another group or project (when, being honest with yourself, your real goal was not to do what was best for the company, but to get more power for yourself)? Have you been comfortable around some types of people with power and not with others? Do you see any pattern of fluctuation in your level of comfort with your own power (more comfortable using power with some people than with others, in some settings or for some objectives than others, when you have formal authority to use it, and so forth)?

If the attraction to power is one finger, and discomfort with power is the other, and your psyche is the rubber band being stretched between the two, how tight is that rubber band being pulled? Do you experience a very strong attraction to *and* a very strong discomfort, resulting in a lot of internal tension? A weak attraction without much discomfort either ("It'd be okay if I had it, but it's okay if I don't")? Or is that rubber band unhooked from one or the other of your fingers (all attraction or all avoidance)? In the final analysis, are you more drawn to power or do you shy away from it? Do you trust people with power or mistrust them? Would you trust yourself with power, or are you afraid that you might misuse, abuse, or squander it? Do you seek to acquire power or insulate yourself from it?

Your feelings about power may be relatively straightforward, or they may be quite complex. Take this time to explore them and think about how they affect your career. Try to paint as clear and nuanced a picture of yourself and power as you can. Once you've got your self-portrait clearly in mind, move to the next section, where we present an overview of the principal factors underlying people's misgivings about power.

THE ORIGINS OF THE FEAR OF POWER

Power may be value-neutral, but we, the authors, are not. We do have a point of view and place a value judgment on the use of power. This comes from having seen people damage their careers by being too strongly enamored of acquiring and using power and having seen other people undone by their refusal to attend to issues of power. In both instances the people are being driven by some internal complex of feelings and have been unable to get the psychological distance and perspective necessary to be able to deal with power effectively. In order to maximize your success in your career and to be as effective as possible in whatever role you have, you must be—or become—comfortable having and using power. You have to learn to be *comfortable enough,* just as you need to be a good enough swimmer to be safe in the water or a good enough driver to be trusted on the road. That doesn't mean you have to be an Olympic-class swimmer or Grand Prix racer—or the most skillful wielder of power. You only need to be "good enough" to function effectively in your job.

The American Heritage Dictionary's first four definitions for power are "1. The ability or capacity to perform or act effectively. 2. A specific capacity, faculty or aptitude: *her powers of concentration.* 3. Strength or force exerted or capable of being exerted. 4. The ability or official capacity to exercise control; authority." The dictionary goes on to provide twelve more definitions, not one of which implies anything even slightly negative about power.

Power, then, is neither linked with domination or abuse nor presented as something one should work ceaselessly to acquire. So why are some people so frightened of it and others so obsessed with it? While we can't undertake an exhaustive discussion of these issues, it is important to be familiar with the reasons people go emotionally overboard in each direction, both to understand ourselves better and to better understand the people we work with.

Fear of the Power of Others

With good reason, both rationally and more instinctually, we fear being injured by groups and individuals with greater power than we have. In the last fifty years this planet has seen a world war of devastating destructiveness as well as countless smaller but no less savage conflicts, not to mention the "police states" created by various dictators. The fear of institutionalized power has obvious and easily identifiable roots. Personal physical violence has existed since the beginning of time, with the smaller usually being defeated by the larger and more powerful. Fear of other people's personal power has equally obvious roots. In most of us this instinctual fear is, over time, balanced and outweighed by our personal experience of other people using their greater power to advance just and worthwhile goals and protect and comfort us. But in some people that balance tips, and remains tipped, toward fear.

Martin, for example, worked as a Web designer for a client company of ours. He had worked for this firm for four years when we met him, always as an independent consultant, and always at his insistence, despite the fact that if he'd taken a permanent job with them, he could have had a significantly better compensation package (including paid medical and dental insurance, retirement benefits, and paid vacation). He was an excellent designer, and the company was anxious to "secure" his services. Martin refused all offers and entreaties. He had escaped from East Germany as an adult and made his way to the United States and was leery of any relationship with an organization in which they would have a claim on him. He simply didn't trust them to use their power fairly. Based on his experience with the East German government and its secret police, the Stasi, who could blame him?

Individuals who were abused as children, too—whether psychologically, physically, or sexually (or any combination of the three)—learn to fear those with power. They learn early in life that people with power are not to be trusted; that they may be rational and kind one minute, cruel and hurtful the next. Because as children they are less powerful than adults or older children, they feel they are at their mercy. As adults they are sometimes overly deferential to those in power, out of fear (they become the good workers who will do whatever you tell them—except think independently). Some become overtly or covertly rebellious, mistrustful of those in power but electing to fight rather than cower (they often either quit or get fired in fairly short order from the jobs they have). Others become abusers themselves, perpetuating the cycle of abuse. For example, one of our clients had been referred because he was too hard on people who worked for him, shredding their work and humiliating them in the process. When we talked with him about his life history, he initially described his father as "strict but fair," but on further elaboration it appeared that his father ran the household like a drill sergeant, strictly and rather brutally. His son, in turn, was treating the professionals who reported to him in much the same way.

Fear of Our Own Power

For some people, the root cause of discomfort with *possessing* and *using* power lies in a deeply unconscious fear of their capacity for destructiveness. This fear of the "shadow," or darker aspect of ourselves that we fear and deny, is universal, but it is more pronounced in some people than it is in others. On an individual level, this "shadow" aspect of ourselves, as Carl Jung identified it, may have to do with our feelings of sexual desire, our desire for fame, our anxieties about the future, even our compassion. Suppose my shadow side loves power so much that part of me would like to rule the world—making everyone do things my way or else.

A glance at the newspapers is enough to remind us that the veneer of civilization is thin, whether in East Timor, the Balkans, Southeast Asia, or the United States. We can't insulate ourselves from the fact that human beings can be moved to abuse power relatively easily. Some of the people we've worked with fear power because they're so frightened of their own potential for abusing any power they might have. They defer and give up power rather than risk awakening that part of themselves they fear would—by virtue of its unbridled rage, insatiable appetite for more power, or lust for those things that power can obtain—be stimulated by having a bit of power.

One of our clients had almost totally shunned acquiring and using power throughout his life. When confronted with a situation that required him to deal with his need to use it, as well as his desire to have it, he told us, "But you see, I'm afraid of getting carried away, of becoming some sort of ogre. I not only want to defeat [a rival], I want to annihilate him, and I'm afraid that this side of me will just take over." When people deny or suppress a part of themselves, the longer they keep it locked away in their psychological closet, the more frightened they become of it. This is true of feelings of anger, sexual desire, aggression, even of joy and of fear itself. Our client had been so estranged from this part of himself for so long that he was terrified he would be carried away by it. And when he did have occasion to use power, he was so uncomfortable in doing so that he was awkward and clumsy, which only added to his discomfort.

One source of this "shadow" self for some people is left over from their childhood years, when they (like everyone else) experienced a desire to depose their fathers or mothers and take over his or her role in the family. Because of that, they experience guilt (for wanting to get rid of Dad or Mom) and fear (that, sensing their desires, the parent will retaliate)—what Freud identified as the Oedipus complex. When these feelings are resolved in childhood, there may be little residual feeling carried on in life. But when they are not, the result may be a fear of one's own desire for power, fear of anger (originally toward the parent standing in the way), and guilt over wanting power. This is another dynamic that in some people leads them to be frightened of having and using power and locking it away as we described.

Cultural expectations concerning gender roles can also influence our feelings about appropriate and inappropriate power. Many women over countless generations have been socialized to see power as unfeminine. In fact, until relatively recently, strong, independent women were ostracized and at times labeled as witches. Prior to the suffragette movement and later the feminist movement in the United States, women were unable to vote, have independent careers, or receive advanced education—and in many cultures even today, they are not allowed to own or inherit property or wealth. These are all forms of power.

If you are fearful of power—others' or your own—it is critically important to understand why and to work to overcome that fear. This fear often comes to the fore in the meritocrat ("Seeing the World in Black and White") and in the Mr. Spock ("Emotionally Tone-Deaf") patterns described in Part I, as well as in the pessimist/worrier ("When Fear Is in the Driver's Seat") pattern. Such fear can at minimum inhibit career success or even cause severe career damage.

OBSESSION WITH POWER

Why are certain people—far from being timid and fearful with regard to power—destructively obsessed with *gaining* power? Let's say that as an average person doing white-collar work and living in a city or suburb, you may need enough strength to pick up thirty pounds. Any more strength is, in some sense, wasted, so compulsive strength-building exercise is a waste of time. Similarly, to accomplish your career goals let's say you need to control an organization of x number of people and y size budget. Why, then, do some people spend their time fighting for more and more people and dollars—in other words, for more "power" than they need? Why does *anyone* become what people would call "power-mad," "power-hungry," or "power-crazy?" Thinking about power objectively, that makes just as little sense as shying away from power out of the fear that you would misuse it. But some people, such as the bulldozer ("Running Roughshod over the Opposition") and the hero ("Doing Too Much, Pushing Too Hard"), *are* obsessed with it.

In our work we've seen several roots for this kind of behavior. First, just as some people are more driven by, more drawn to, power, some people*s* (plural) and cultures are more interested in power. America, for example, is not only a powerful nation but a nation whose culture celebrates power, especially the power of the individual. Even a casual look at American movies and television makes it clear that power is *the* dominant theme. The rate of violent crime in America, the number of handguns held by individuals, and the prison population on a per capita basis echo what we see in theaters and on television. We celebrate the powerful (Bill Gates, Michael Jordan and Mark McGwire, Billy Graham) and ignore or even disparage the weak (the poor, the working class, teachers, *non*televangelists). America, in the eyes of much of the rest of the world, is like one big power theme park; we can't help being affected by that cultural surround. The result is that people who are personally inclined toward power are moved even further in that psychological direction by our culture. Similarly, we have seen people whose leanings toward personal power were inhibited when they lived in cultures that looked *un*favorably on the purposeful acquisition and use of personal power.

Some of our clients have an almost compulsive need to compete for power and status and money, vying constantly for the position of "alpha" male or female in their given group. They seem unable to stop competing even when it is quite inappropriate in a work context. Some individuals we have worked with seem impelled to "go for it" (more power) even when they themselves know they should hold back, and their careers are the worse for it.

Ralph, for example, worked as a high-level administrator in a teaching hospital. He had an MBA from a top school and prior to that had graduated with high honors from Stanford. Working in the medical establishment, however, he was, in a subtle way, a "second-class" citizen to physicians, and his routes to power were limited. Ralph was so enamored of having power and status ("behind the scenes" influence did not suffice for him) that he insisted on challenging the heads of services. He was finally told to find work elsewhere.

In other people the drive for accumulating more and more power seems to stem from never having felt love(d). As Jung put it: "Where love reigns, there is no will to power; and where the will to power is paramount, love is lacking." Many of the people we have worked with who were truly obsessed with power (versus simply being ambitious and having an agenda that required power to carry it out) were individuals who came from families or childhood circumstances where love was in short supply or, at least, rarely demonstrated. As adults, they were often quite reserved in their expression of love. It is as if they have substituted power for love, perhaps because power is more easily acquired and controlled than feelings of love.

Death is the ultimate loss of control. If, as Hillman says in *Kinds of Power*, "power stands behind our fear of loss and desire for control," it's easy to see how some people could be spurred on in the chase for power by their (unconscious) desire for immortality. In one of his films Woody Allen says, "I don't want to achieve immortality through my work, I want to achieve immortality by not dying!" This is an obviously absurd (yet understandable) desire, and it appears to be a force behind some of our clients' compulsive acquisition of power. Like the character in Ingmar Bergman's *The Seventh Seal* who plays chess against Death, we all dream of some way to "cheat death." With age, or after a health crisis, some people say, "This has really helped me set my priorities straight. I want to work less and spend more time with my friends and family, and smell the roses." Others have a different response: "I may [*may?*] die," they say, "but my company will live on (bearing my good name) forever." They unconsciously imagine that if they are heroic *enough,* they will, like Hercules who was taken to Mount Olympus and made immortal when he died, be spared the trip to Hades and the underworld and live forever with the gods. One of our clients, well into his late sixties, took on a new position and set of responsibilities just when people expected him to retire. Those who had known him over a period of years were not surprised, though, having seen his appetite for power increase steadily with age.

We commonly see people who are obsessed with power seeking to compensate for some inner sense of inadequacy, shoring up their shaky sense of self-worth. Alfred Adler, for example, described what he called the "inferiority complex," born from our infantile sense of helplessness. Healthy individuals "compensate" for these feelings of inferiority by seeking to improve their skills, achieve their goals, and express themselves—all in the service of feeling good about themselves. Others "overcompensate" and become overly competitive and aggressive, striving to acquire power of one kind to erase those early feelings of powerlessness. Power here is used in the same way some people acquire "status symbols" such as expensive cars and jewelry. The car and more may come as part of the package, but these individuals are interested not so much in those trappings as in the genuine power they are garnering, proving that they really *are* somebody! They want to be recognized by others only insofar as that recognition provides a "mirror" for themselves to ratify their existence and worth. And they seek power for the same reason. For such people, René Descartes's axiom *Cogito, ergo sum* ("I think, therefore I exist") could be more accurately rephrased, "I have and use power, therefore I exist." A graphic example is an individual we worked with who would cycle between berating his colleagues and smoothing out the little hair remaining on his head, then more berating followed by a statement to the effect that he really *could* have gone to law school if he'd wanted to, and so forth.

Of course, a few people want power because they want ruthlessly to use and abuse it. History gives us plenty of examples of such dictators and despots. Perhaps you know examples of people who acted in this fashion in your life, people who used power to undermine and humiliate. Often, in our experience, these individuals suffered from some sort of early childhood abuse or neglect, although not always. The psychology of such tyrants is complex and at times unfathomable. The social nature of organizations tends to ensure that eventually such people are "expelled from the ant colony" for their antisocial behavior, but often they are clever enough to find another company to move into, where they can again abuse their power. If you find yourself at some point either reporting to someone or having someone report to you who fits this description, their prognosis is poor; we suggest professional counseling or coaching for the individual.

This, of course, is something that you can recommend if the person reports to you. If the relationship is reversed, you have three likely options. The first is simply to move on. If you report to a true tyrant, you have no leverage over your manager and the situation is unlikely to change. Second, you can go to your human resources representative. This is the recommended move if the tyrannical behavior includes any reference to people's gender, age, sexual preference, and so on—all being grounds for legal action against the company. Even if this is not the case, the HR department may be able to help (although in some instances—such as when HR is closely controlled by the tyrant—this move carries some risk). Your third—and riskiest by far—option is to skillfully and stealthily engineer circumstances in which your manager's unprofessional behavior is seen firsthand by his or her own manager. By and large, organizational tyrants hide that behavior from those above them in the organization—they know that what they are doing is wrong and are smart enough to conceal it. So if you can put into place a scenario in which your manager is witnessed berating and humiliating you or others (or displaying other grossly inappropriate behavior), the result may be the tyrant's dismissal. The risk, of course, is that this is not the result, so you would be wise not to have left your fingerprints on the effort.

USING POWER

There is an essential paradox to power: *Having* more power does not necessarily equate with *being* more powerful. Whether the holder of the power is an individual, a company, or a nation is irrelevant. The "weaker" power holder, if it is more willing to actually use the power it possesses, may be more powerful than a reluctant but more powerful other party. An individual with a gun in his hand who is frightened to actually shoot an attacker is likely to be overpowered by someone who only has a club. His unwillingness to *use* his power renders him less powerful. Although the United States possessed nuclear weapons during the Vietnam War, it was unwilling to use them. As a result, the United States was defeated by a nation that was objectively (in terms of military strength) weaker.

Just as force equals mass multiplied by its velocity, the *effect* of power equals its magnitude multiplied by the degree to which it is used.

No use of power, no power. In Tracy Kidder's *The Soul of a New Machine*, Herb Richman (one of the founders of Data General) recalls that their lawyer insisted that each founder put aside enough money to be able to walk away from any negotiation without fear of personally losing everything. If the objectively weaker of two parties in a negotiation is willing to quit it—*really* willing to walk away—that party's power is increased immeasurably. If you are willing to quit a job, the company's "power" vis-à-vis yours is drastically reduced.

In this sense, the urge to acquire power that is not used is a fool's errand. Power simply stored away is like money never spent; it becomes nothing more than paper with ink on it. Yet many people spend their lives gaining—or attempting to gain—power and then simply hoarding it.

They do so most often out of a fear of losing—the essence of the definition of risk. Although power is something you have to risk losing or forget about using, those who are afraid to fail are paralyzed into inaction and powerlessness—regardless of how much "potential power" they have. One of our clients had, through his years of good service and good judgments, amassed a large "credit" that he could have used for any number of purposes. He could have stood up and championed an unpopular cause or used the CEO's faith in him to launch a new venture or change a corporate direction. But his fear of not succeeding or of being proved wrong (and suffering shame and loss of face) prevented him from using his power, to the detriment of his career development—and at a loss to the organization. He will likely go to his grave with a huge balance in the "favor bank."

THE POWER ANALYSIS

Determining how much power and what kind of power you need at any given time is an essential beginning step on the way to getting and using power. First you need to identify what your goal is. We use the singular "goal" purposely, because you need to be thinking not in terms of overarching "goals" (eventually to become CEO or managing director or head of sales, for example). Focus on a specific goal that is achievable in the short term: to reduce cycle time on this product by at least 15 percent, to get your group's computer network operating system upgraded, to hire three qualified people in customer service. You can go through this analysis several times for each of several goals you have, but for the moment concentrate on only one goal.

Then think about what resources and/or authority you *need* to accomplish your goal. Don't be greedy; if you only need "x" don't say you need "3x." In this exercise, less *is* more. If every time you go to your manager with a request for resources that is "inflated," he or she will soon learn to cut your budget. If you are right on target, your manager will learn to trust you and even add a little. Resources flow naturally to people who demonstrate good sense and good use of the power they are given. Empires are expensive to build and maintain, so build one only if you need it.

Now look at your organization and think about its power structure, both formal and informal. Who really has power? What kind do they have? How many people need to be behind an idea for it to be accepted? Who are they? What is your relationship with each of these people? What do you have to offer to those who must give you resources if you have a project that is to succeed or some other goal that you are to achieve? Most new initiatives are, in fact, power "stretches." The very act of proposing them means that you're bidding for a position of greater power in your organization. Think about what your increased power will mean to your colleagues. In some cases it will enhance their own status due to their relationship with you. In others it may be perceived as potential competition in what your colleagues may see as a zero-sum race to acquire status and resources. Someone may not have the power to enable your goal but have the power to disable it, so think about who may have "veto" power. Think about why those individuals kill things (see Chapter 13 on taking perspective in Part II). Work to ensure that they have no reason to veto your initiative or to passively ensure that your project fails.

Of course, initiating a new project is not the only reason you might need to acquire and use power. Simply defending your department or business from being swallowed up by another may demand skillful garnering and using power. Similarly, proposing and implementing a new organizational structure involve power, as does changing the strategic direction of your line of business. Whether on a personal level or the level of a department, business unit, or entire corporation; and whether the goal is to build something new, to make a change of some other kind, or simply to stay on course, not allowing outside forces to move you—in any combination of these circumstances, power is going to be required.

You also need to factor into this analysis how much (and what kind of) power you already have, both within the organization and personally. What is the base of your power—skills that are in high demand? Is there a strong network of people who trust your work within the company and the industry? An undeniable track record of success? Are you willing to cash in many "chips" and ask for support that entails risk to others? Are you willing to leave your organization if resources are not available?

There are times when power grows by giving it away. By doing so, you accomplish several things. If your goal is to build a village and you lend others the tools you are not using at a particular time, your objective may be met sooner—you are using your power with greater leverage and thus more efficiently. You are also helping the village (company) as a whole by giving others what they need to develop their skills as leaders and managers. Finally, by virtue of having "granted" power to someone else, that person is in your debt. As his or her individual power grows, then so does yours by extension.

In summary, then:

▲ To be most effective and successful in any career and in any organization, you have to be able to gain, hold, and use power effectively.

▲ If you are either uncomfortable with or unhealthily attracted to power, it is important to explore, understand, and work through those feelings so that they don't interfere with your use of power.

▲ Think about how much power you need to achieve any particular goal—don't acquire (or expend) power needlessly.

▲ If you are overly concerned with losing power, failing, or making wrong decisions, you must learn to overcome those fears so they don't impede your using the power you have.

▲ For every business and personal career objective, do a "power analysis" of how much and what kinds of power you need and of how power is held and used in your organization.

Understanding the power we hold and becoming more comfortable with its use are fundamental tasks of career development. Ultimately the use of power is highly personal. The power held by a CEO of a Fortune 500 company is different from the power wielded by Gandhi or the power of Einstein's ideas. The power derived from possessing leading-edge technical knowledge is different from the power of a master communicator or superb teacher. Each of us can develop our own power—power that is particular to the specific way we make decisions and act in the world. Seeing this clearly is the first step toward understanding what must be done if we are to effect change in our work and our lives.

CHAPTER
SIXTEEN

LOOKING IN THE MIRROR:
EXAMINING YOUR SELF-IMAGE

W<small>E HAVE DISCUSSED COMING TO TERMS WITH POWER, AU-</small>thority, and other people as skills that are crucial to maximizing your potential. In this chapter we turn to coming to terms with your *self.*

Each of us carries within us deep, often unexamined beliefs about who we are and what we're capable of doing. These beliefs, or inner "images" (which are not necessarily "seen"—they are often unconscious), can be sources of energy and conviction that convey messages that allow us to experience ourselves as capable, confident, and resilient. They can also carry messages of perceived failure or shame from earlier, even very early, times in our life. These messages can, in turn, act to diminish our sense of power and capacity for initiative and risk taking. This fourth essential career development step involves bringing any disabling elements of our self-images into full consciousness so that we can understand them and thereby diminish the corrosive effect they have on our ability to develop ambition, be effective, and enjoy our accomplishments. The first step in doing this is to understand how self-images are formed and how they develop into influential forces in our psychological world.

OUR TWO MIRRORS

We go through most of life with two mirrors. We begin life with one, the mirror presented to us by our parents and the others who attend to us from our birth and during infancy. Observe an infant and the adults watching him or her and you will see those adults "mirror" the expressions on the infant's face. If the infant frowns, so will the adults; if she smiles, so will the adults; if he yawns, so will the adults. Over time, given normal development, children internalize that parental function and develop their own "mirroring" of themselves. One mirror (the adults around us) becomes two (other people and our internal mirror). From that point forward, throughout the rest of our lives, we have two distinct mirrors—that formed by other people and our internal mirror (the "*self*-image")—that "faithfully reflect and give a true picture of ourselves." Unless, of course, they don't—unless those mirrors contain distortions, which they seem to do all too frequently.

For the most part, the external mirror tends to be more or less accurate. Of course, that external mirror, comprising all of the people around us, can *at times* be grossly inaccurate and can, *in parts,* be *consistently* grossly inaccurate (my parents always think I'm the smartest, best, and so forth). But with enough people forming the mirror, over a long period, that mirror tends to provide a reasonably accurate picture. Our internal mirrors, by contrast, can be wildly inaccurate over long periods of time. For example, anorexics truly see themselves as fat when objectively they are not; people suffering from depression see themselves as incompetent while others see them as highly competent.

We resolve the differences between the two mirrors quite differently depending on whether the internal mirror's image is more positive than the external mirror's or the inverse. If I think I'm very funny but no one laughs, or if I think I'm much more intelligent than most people but I get below average grades, I will quite likely be forced to adjust my overly positive image of myself downward a bit to become more accurate. It's hard to hold on to the idea that you're the fastest runner when you keep coming in last. But when people's internal images are more negative than the external, they can dismiss the positive image from the outside with relative ease. "I was just lucky," they say, or, "They don't really mean that, they're just being nice." People are able, and for various reasons willing, to discount quite easily and effectively external mirroring that is positive and to hold on to their negative (and distorted) internally mirrored self-images.

They are equally able to "project" their feelings about themselves onto other people, imagining that those people see them and feel toward them exactly as they see themselves. The consequence of this phenomenon is that in the absence of feedback people create their own—often of a negative variety. This is evident in group settings where, if one person is silent, other people in the group will make up their own notions of why the person is silent and will frequently attribute the silence to the "fact" that the person dislikes them. Given the opportunity to make up their own external mirrors, many people will create mirrors that produce a negative image. Such is the power of the human psyche, and such is the power of the negative self-image.

THE NEGATIVE SELF-IMAGE

For the purposes of this book, we are going to confine our discussion to having a negatively distorted self-image. (If you believe you are smarter, better looking, and so forth than you actually are, you are unlikely to fall into one of the behavior patterns in Part I.) One way of thinking about negative self-image is that it is the *degree of difference between a person's self-image and the external mirror* of the world around. In other words, if I am in fact a terrible basketball player (I can't dribble, shoot, rebound, or defend) and I know and acknowledge it freely, that does not signify a negative self-image. On the other hand, if I am in fact good (in the eyes of my teammates, players on other teams, and my coach) and think I'm lousy, *that* variance constitutes an element of negative self-image. Similarly, if I'm a lousy financial analyst (I'm innumerate and can't tell one side of a balance sheet from the other) and I know it, there's no variance and no sign of a negative self-image.

Another important point to make in thinking about negative self-image: It has to do with who we *are* vis-à-vis what we *do*. To clarify this distinction, consider the difference between the feelings of shame and guilt discussed in the chapter "When No Job Is Good Enough." Guilt is the feeling we have when we transgress acceptable behavior. When you steal, or break the law, or commit adultery, you feel guilt over your *actions*. Shame is what you feel about *your self*. People experience shame and embarrassment when they feel others see inadequacies in their makeup. If you do something for which you feel guilty, you may feel remorse and guilt, but not damage your self-image. On the other hand, even if you have *done* nothing wrong, if you have a negative self-image, you may feel that you are inadequate and feel ashamed. Negative self-image, then, involves the sense of who you are as a person; you experience *shame* and embarrassment when you sense others perceive these inadequacies.

A client of ours named Patrick was below average in height. However, it was not his height but his negative self-image that led him to feel that other men viewed him with contempt, and women with disdain. He imagined that other people's first thought on meeting him was, "What a short guy!" and they completely ignored the fact that he was a bright, witty, caring, and attractive individual with much to offer.

The person learning a new skill who feels fine about the difference between his or her skill level and genuine mastery *perceives* that difference in skill levels but doesn't attribute it to inadequacy and suffers no negative distortion to his or her self-image as a result. Another person, at the same skill level after the same amount of time, might perceive that variance, attribute it to inadequacy, and feel bad *about him- or herself*. The former may be spurred on to greater efforts. The latter individual often gives up in despair—and, in the act of giving up, suffers further damage to his or her self-image ("I'm a quitter"). This raises the question: "Why are some people 'shame hardy,' recognizing the areas where they are deficient but not devaluing their self-image in the process, while others go through life with a negatively distorted self-image?"

FLAWS IN THE MIRROR

People form and hold on to negative self-images over long periods of time for reasons that may be classified into two groups: those created and/or reinforced by factors that are a result of the individual and his or her unique development and history; and those created and/or reinforced by common social and cultural forces.

Individual Causes

In his seminal work, *Childhood and Society*, psychiatrist Erik Erikson described eight developmental stages that people pass through, each involving a developmental "crisis" or challenge. If the individual fails to successfully resolve the challenge, the result is a distortion in the person's formation of what Erikson called "ego identity." As a result, some distortion in the individual's self-image is almost certain to take place.

The first developmental stage takes place in the first year of life (approximately) and has as its focus the formation of trust in the world and, more specifically, in other people. If the infant's caregivers are loving and responsive, "basic trust" is developed. Alternately, if they are unloving and neglectful—or inconsistent in their love and responsiveness to the infant's needs, the result is "basic mistrust." Years later the results of this mistrust can be seen, both in a continuing lack of trust that others will be responsive to that person's basic needs and in the belief that he or she is fundamentally unworthy of love. It's important to note that Erikson does not claim adults consciously remember that first year of life—conscious awareness is not necessary for either the successful or the unsuccessful resolution of the developmental stage. However, Erikson argues, failure to emerge from that first developmental challenge with establishment of a basic sense of trust *will* result in a distorted identity—in a negative self-image, causing the adult, for example, possibly to be rebellious, mistrusting of authority, and suffering from low self-esteem.

Erikson's second developmental stage occurs roughly during the second and third years of the child's life. No longer helpless and immobile, toddlers set out with their newfound locomotion to explore the world around them and master a variety of other challenges. They push their parents away to do it themselves, sometimes wanting to do things that their parents do *not* want them to do. If all goes well, the result of this "challenge" is a child who is autonomous and confident in his or her ability to learn and achieve mastery in a variety of fields. During this stage the child needs the parent to set outer boundaries for the sake of the child's safety and to help the child learn new things by demonstrating and instructing. But if the child's parents are *overly* protective or overly critical, the outcome of this stage is self-doubt and feelings of shame. ("Otherwise," the toddler wonders unconsciously, "why would my parents be so anxious, so critical, of how I do things?") This lack of confidence and feeling of shame, of not being good enough, result in a long-lived and significant distortion of the person's self-image. Adults who did not successfully resolve the challenge of this stage as children tend to be passive and dependent on authority figures for instruction, lacking the confidence to make autonomous decisions.

The third stage, corresponding roughly to ages four and five, holds the challenge of learning to feel good about taking initiative (versus feeling guilty about your fantasies and actions). Children at this age want to "be big" and to do big things. They have powerful emotions, including feelings of anger that can frighten their parents, their siblings—and themselves. They have powerful fantasies (including wholly age-appropriate notions of getting rid of Dad, Mom, brother, or sister—or any combination thereof). And they are capable of powerful actions, including throwing things and hitting other children (and adults). When parents accept and explore the child's feelings and fantasies ("Sure, we all feel that way sometimes" and "That's some story! What happens next?"), the child learns that taking the initiative and expressing his or her feelings and ideas is all right—in fact, it is a good thing. When parents limit the child's actions appropriately but without shame or chastisement, the child learns to control his or her behaviors while still showing initiative. But if the response is overly punitive and critical, the child learns to feel guilty about his or her feelings and fantasies and to withhold them. The enduring damage to the person's self-image is a distortion in how the individual looks upon his or her desires, feelings, fantasies, and impulses, seeing them as bad, deserving of punishment, and needing to be restricted and hidden from view. In adulthood such feelings might impair creativity and general initiative taking, causing conflict-avoidant behavior.

Erikson's fourth developmental challenge is what he refers to as "industry vs. inferiority." This evolution takes place over several years, during what Freud called the "latency stage," from about age six until the child enters adolescence. During this time the typical child is in school and a student of increasingly academic material and/or is learning about the non-academic world in greater depth than ever before. These are exciting and challenging years for a child, and the positive results of this stage are an image of oneself as competent, confidence in one's ability to tolerate the frustration of the early stage of learning a new subject, and the ability to fit into a nonfamilial environment, learning and obeying the rules of the organization. The outcome of having met this developmental challenge unsuccessfully is a feeling of inferiority vis-à-vis one's peers. ("They can . . . and I can't. What's wrong with me?" and "I'm not as good as they are, I must be stupid.") Obviously any individual will not be as capable as his or her peers along some dimensions. Some students, though, seem to be able to recognize that they are not as good at something and yet avoid feeling a sense of general inferiority. Those who do see their inability to measure up in a skill as a sign of general inferiority, or who have difficulty fitting into the process of organized learning, emerge with a negative self-image. Their picture of themselves as less competent, less bright, or less creative can have a wide range of effects later in life. These individuals may not pursue further education or more challenging work (see Chapter 10, "When No Job Is Good Enough") or engage in the self-absorbing behavior of the acrophobe.

Adolescence brings its own challenges. The fifth developmental crisis focuses on the struggle between the desire to form one's own identity and the wish to identify with, and remain a part of, the group. In its benign form this group identity (which Erikson called "role confusion") results in adolescents dressing alike, idolizing the same pop music and movie stars, using common (to the group) slang expressions, and so on. More negatively, there can be peer pressure to use alcohol, tobacco, and other drugs, engage in sexual activity, join a gang, eschew studying in school, choose the same college as other members of the group, even choose a "group-approved" career. These are all, in effect, the "price of admission," and the price obviously can be quite high. The desire to separate from parents and the rest of the family is matched only by the fear of being alone in the world. So the identity that the group provides (ironically, replacing one's family of origin with another kind of family) makes an appealing, if sometimes costly, alternative. The outcome for most is a gradual separation both from the family and from the group. But others remain in this state of role confusion even well into adulthood, and this can affect their career choice. Erikson states, "It is the inability to settle on an occupational identity which [most often] disturbs individual young people" who fail to clear this developmental hurdle. We have consulted with people who in their mid- and even late twenties were still preoccupied with choosing careers that would meet with others' approval—the "others" being not parents, but their peers. Many of them have come for help three or four years later, only then recognizing the mistake they had made.

The subsequent developmental stages described by Erikson, which occur during adulthood, are less relevant to the formation of negative self-images and the effect they have on people's ability to be effective and successful at work. You can see, however, what a significant role children's development plays in how we as adults feel about ourselves and, ultimately, in how we see ourselves as capable and effective in the world of work.

There is another cause of a long-term negative self-image: depression. This topic is the subject of hundreds of books and thousands of articles, and we do not pretend to offer anything more than a snapshot of the topic. In the context of this book, we are able to give it only a brief look; nonetheless, we would be remiss if we did not discuss it—however briefly. People often describe their feelings of depression as being like perpetually cloudy weather—with the only variation being in how dense the clouds are. Negative self-image is one of those clouds and one of the hallmark signs of depression. The causes of depression itself are complex, and an individual's depression may stem from multiple causes. There is evidence, for example, of a hereditary element that predisposes some people to depression. An individual's biochemistry may be a significant factor (one of the reasons antidepressant medications are often effective in treating the problem). In fact, in the last ten or fifteen years the field of public health has seen dramatic success in the use of psychotherapy and medication to effectively treat depression. If you suspect that you might be suffering from depression, you need to get medical help for this problem. We recommend that you consult your primary care physician or some other knowledgeable source for referral to a counselor or speak directly with a psychotherapist (at the end of this chapter we present some advice for how to choose a counselor to work with). Effective treatments *are* available for depression, and there is no reason to suffer through those feelings—or with the negative self-image that depression often causes.

Social/Cultural Causes

As noted earlier, the other general cause of a negative self-image is the variety of social and cultural elements of modern life that can play upon our vulnerabilities.

Let's offer a hypothetical story, about a boy named John, the third of eight children and the first son. John's father was a farmer, as his grandfather had been before him. The family farm supplied enough to feed John's family and his aging grandparents, with a small surplus left over to barter and sell. Their clothes were handmade and hand-me-downs, and there was very little money for "extras" and little luxuries. John, his brothers and sisters, and their friends who lived on farms nearby made their own games, explored the woods adjacent to the farm fields, and swam in a nearby pond.

Then one day when John was fourteen, he and his father traveled to a city several hundred miles away. When they arrived, John was amazed by the towering buildings, the expensive clothes and jewelry worn by the wealthier citizens he saw. Even the doormen, servants of the wealthy few, were better dressed than he and his father were! He was amazed, envious, and suddenly ashamed of how little he himself had in comparison. He now saw, with startling and painful clarity, the gap between what he had and what people "of means" had.

If John were living in the 1930s on a farm in central Illinois and had traveled to Chicago with his father, this could be the beginning of a "great American dream" story, something by Horatio Alger, perhaps. John, having seen the big city, determines to make it there and become one of those people with wealth. But what if we were to add the fact that John was a peasant in the 1630s, not the 1930s, and that he and his father had traveled to Paris and seen cathedrals and members of royalty—not successful businessmen in fine cars? Then there is a jarring clash. First, what is the probability that John and his father would have traveled several hundred miles at all? Transportation being what it was in the 1630s, it is unlikely that John would ever have traveled more than a few miles from home. And the possibility that John would have aspired to join the ranks of those privileged few he had seen in Paris? Zero. The wealthy individuals he had seen would have been members of nobility, and no peasant seriously entertained the notion that he could cross that divide. John, then, almost certainly would never have left his village on such a trip; and if he had, he would not have compared himself with the people he saw. They were noble men and ladies, so no comparison was possible.

Today, on the other hand, we do travel extensively. And there are two additional and equally fundamental differences between life even as recently as fifty years ago and life today. Fifty years ago the great majority of the world's population lived in small towns and villages, not in cities. And fifty years ago there was no television. Those two facts, along with the growth of democracy throughout the world, have had an enormous impact on the "standard" to which people compare themselves. In 1950 a girl living in a small town in Texas or a village in Chile or in India might *know* about people who were very successful and wealthy—but she would not *see* them and be able to (forced to) compare herself and her life with them and theirs in a direct way. Today this young girl lives in Dallas or Santiago or Bombay and *sees* the Mercedes, the BMW, and the Jaguar and can't help but compare herself. These feelings are in turn heightened by the fact that most people on this planet are now exposed to television. Television is populated by people who are more of everything: more handsome and beautiful, more fit, better dressed, and younger (if you are thirty-five or older); they live more exciting lives, drive better cars (always clean and shining), and own homes that make ours look drab by comparison. In short, ease of travel, urbanization, and the mass media (especially television) encourage a comparison between oneself (and all aspects of one's life) with an unrealistic benchmark. The result is that as the definition of "should be" rises, the self-images of people who are vulnerable to comparison with others become increasingly distorted.

One additional factor pushes people in some cultures toward viewing themselves negatively: the pace of life, and the increasing acceleration of that pace. That ever-faster pace results in longer work hours for many and more pleasure. It also, however, results in greater impatience, both in how long it takes for things to happen and in *how long it takes people to succeed* (however they define personal success). Again, a hundred years ago no one expected instant success. You began as an apprentice and worked for several years in that role. Then you worked for several more years as a journeyman and finally achieved the status, respect, and compensation of a "master." Moreover, while you were an apprentice or journeyman you could feel good about your status and your progress. This is not so easy now. Today's pace and the fact that a few individuals have made hundreds of millions of dollars while in their twenties and thirties give us yet another benchmark. "Not only should I be more," some people think, "but I should have been more earlier!"

These varied and powerful forces have an enormous impact on people as a whole and can have an enormous impact on us as individuals. Powerful as they are, they can be subtle and insidious, difficult to identify—let alone to combat. Our goal in this section was to help you become more aware of those factors that have the most effect on you and thus better able to fight back. Having done that, we want to turn now to the equally varied, powerful, subtle, and insidious effects of living with a negative self-image.

CONSEQUENCES OF THE
NEGATIVE SELF-IMAGE

It is worthwhile to consider the consequences of a negative self-image in terms of its effect on the individual and on the organizations where people work or are otherwise closely associated.

Individual Consequences

A negative self-image can contribute to the difficulties that come with any of the twelve Achilles' heels described in Part I. But it is without question the dominant factor at work in the acrophobe ("Never Feeling Good Enough") and the coulda-been ("When No Job Is Good Enough"). It plays a part in the making of the rebel ("Rebel Looking for a Cause") and the pessimist/worrier ("When Fear Is in the Driver's Seat") as well, and sometimes in the peacekeeper ("Avoiding Conflict at Any Cost").

Beyond contributing to the behavior patterns that can hold one's career back (described in Part I), a negative self-image can have additional effects on the individual as well. First, where one's negative self-image either is the result of depression or has a strong enough impact on the person that negative feelings are apparent, other people may react to these outward signs of negativity in a way that perpetuates the feeling and poor self-image. In other words, if you are depressed and *look* depressed, others may be less likely to approach you for the very casual conversation that might make you feel a bit better. Likewise, if your negative self-image is focused on a verbal tic or on a lack of athleticism, others may see you avoid activities that would display the "flaw" and react to you gingerly, sensing your vulnerability in this area. Patrick, the client we mentioned earlier who was sensitive about his height, not infrequently presented himself to people in such a way that they couldn't help noticing not only his height, but his feelings of inadequacy about it, and they reacted accordingly.

A negative self-image almost always causes a person to hold back from doing things that expose—or even *might* expose—the self-perceived inadequacy. The result, again almost inevitably, is less success than the person might otherwise have enjoyed. Put simply, if you are expending some of your psychic energy "on guard duty," you will be less successful. Similarly, if you are not taking opportunities or chances because "if I do *this*, they may ask me to do *that*, and that would mean I'd have to give a presentation, and I go blank any time I have to give a presentation"—or whatever your personal scenario is—you will be less successful. Which brings to the fore another effect of the negative self-image: Each time you hold yourself back from doing something, each time you go home saying, "I wish I had . . ." or "Why didn't I just . . . ?" your self-image tends to worsen even further.

Consequences at Work

At work, when an employee suffers from a negative self-image, he or she is less willing to take risks that could precipitate the shame of revealing that flaw. That may translate to not risking telling the boss that he or she is wrong, not putting forward an idea for a new way to do things, not taking on a new job with more responsibilities, or any number of other "nots." People in vulnerable positions don't take risks; they can't afford to. The damage from this loss of initiative is typically not confined to the person with a self-image problem. That individual's frustration can be "projected" onto the organization, affecting fellow workers.

Suppose an employee with a negative self-image externalizes the cause of the problem, blaming the organization ("*I'm* not the one holding back my creativity and risk taking, the company [or my boss] punishes anyone with new ideas"). If this individual is able to promulgate that idea among other employees, you have the seed of cultural cynicism and a decline in morale. "Top management doesn't care about what we think" is a notion that finds fertile soil among all those who have trouble dealing with authority, and the person with a negative self-image can provide the seed, water, and sunlight. This can result in serious problems for the company. Cynicism is a disease that is difficult to fight once it has taken hold.

Because a negative self-image stems from not feeling oneself to be an adequate, good enough person, it is painful to think about, and most people would rather avoid it. To do so, however, is perilous. Identifying the facts and roots of those distortions in your internal mirror is the critical first step to changing them. Next we want to present several means of accomplishing this task.

PERSONAL "FLAWS"

By "flaws" we mean those elements of who you are that contribute to your negative self-image. It is the fact that *you* consider them to be flaws that makes them relevant, not whether your perception is accurate or whether other people consider them to be flaws. It may help as you go through these exercises to imagine that you are actually two people: you, and your own "executive coach." There are two benefits to this approach: It may help you to be objective; and it will allow you to create a "psychological distance" between you (the coach carrying out the analysis) and the points of personal inadequacy felt by you (the client). Do these exercises when you have some time and when you have privacy. It may be a good idea to make brief notes as you go along.

We encourage that people preparing for job interviews observe themselves as they look at their résumés and work histories and notice those things that elicit the response "I hope they don't ask me about . . ." or "I hope they don't bring up . . ." In this exercise we want you to do the same thing. In your role as coach ask yourself, "What parts of yourself do you try to hide? Is there any pattern to the types of things you don't want other people to see?" Encourage yourself to "think back over the past year (then over the past five years and then prior to that), and remember those instances when you've felt most embarrassed or ashamed. What precipitated the feelings? Who was present? What things are you most critical of yourself about? Are they internal or external, past or present?" Ask yourself, "What things do you avoid doing out of fear of looking foolish? In the past year/five years/previous years what opportunities have you passed up because you were afraid of failing, looking bad or inept, and feeling embarrassed?"

What about the things you couldn't avoid but delayed? In our experience people procrastinate for one reason only: because they anticipate being judged and found wanting. Procrastination is a way of delaying the "trial" and inevitable judgment (although, of course, the act of procrastination itself leads to yet another element of negative self-image: "I'm a procrastinator, I can't even get my own work done"). Ask yourself, "In the past year/five years/previous years what have you procrastinated about doing until the threat of the deadline loomed larger than the threat of the judgment? Are there things that you always avoid? Things that you always put off?"

Do not do these exercises all at once. Our tolerance for feelings of shame and the memory of shame is small; after relatively brief exposure we tend to "shut down" defensively. Focus on an initial memory until you remember the circumstances as vividly as possible. Stay with the image, resisting the mind's defensive tendency to wander away to other thoughts. When you're doing the exercise, let yourself become aware of the actual feeling that is evoked. Stay with the feeling, "holding" it in your attention, even if only for fifteen or twenty seconds. This feeling is shame itself, the very thing that causes you to hide, avoid, procrastinate, or feel depressed without knowing why. When you consciously stay with this feeling, you are in fact staring down an inner enemy. No heroics are necessary, no rationalizations, no analysis, no need for deep insights. The simple act of feeling the shame generates understanding and is therapeutic in and of itself. Remember, this exercise is to be done a little bit at a time. Write down notes from each exercise experience and then set them, and the exercise, aside.

Return to this exercise as many times as you need to build a comprehensive list of the aspects of your self or your history that you try to hide (and hide from), tasks and challenges that you have avoided, and situations where you have procrastinated. Make sure that you spend those difficult seconds experiencing the shame itself. When your list seems reasonably complete, step back and look for the major themes. These may include topics such as feelings about your physical appearance, athletic ability, social poise, education, or family background. Notice as well the real-life circumstances that are most likely to evoke feelings of shame about these self-perceived flaws. The point of this exercise is to learn with your feelings as well as with your analytical intellect.

Consider how large a role this issue of negative self-image plays in your life. How prone to negative self-image are you in general? In the absence of feedback, what kind do you create? When you don't know how someone feels about you or how they evaluate your competence, how do you imagine they feel? What do you imagine they think? Are you often relieved and pleasantly surprised to find that people feel as positively about you as they do? The more often you imagine the negative, the more often you're pleasantly surprised, the more significant the issue of negative distortions in your self-image.

What, then, can you do about any distortions to your self-image that are having a major impact on your life and success? The exercises that we just recommended are themselves the first step in the healing process. By deliberately returning to feelings of shame with your full attention, you begin the subtle process of building "shame tolerance." Rather than suppressing the feelings and "shutting down" (whatever your style of shutting down might be: not taking initiative, avoiding social risks, procrastinating, becoming depressed, and so on), you are staying awake and experiencing the shame as a *feeling* rather than as who you *are*. You are building distance between the feeling and your basic sense of self. You are becoming more shame tolerant, better able to experience shame without damaging "internalization" (making it into the "who you are") the next time you actually experience it in your day-to-day life. This tolerance is your greatest resource for being able to act and be effective in circumstances where previously you would have become emotionally overwhelmed (whether you were aware of it or not). Returning to these exercises regularly is thus an important therapeutic regimen. Each time you do so you gain a little more ground from the enemy, those inner voices of shame and self-doubt.

It is often important to include other people in this process. Sometimes we simply cannot get the distance we need from shameful memories. No one can do for us the work of building our shame tolerance, but trusted and insightful confidants can help us to see things more objectively. When as adults we remember an emotion-laden event that took place when we were fourteen years old, we reexperience it from that same fourteen-year-old's perspective. Talking the situation through with someone close to you can provide the objectivity necessary to release you from the shame associated with the memory. It is possible to forgive yourself for those things you've *done* (and which carry guilt); those things that you *are* (for which you feel shame) can best—and perhaps only—be forgiven and accepted when you see that others don't condemn or shun you for them. It goes without saying that you would first want to expose the inadequacy that feeds into your negative self-image to someone close to you who is notably nonjudgmental in his or her dealings with people. Later, as you are stronger, you can move on to more difficult "audiences." If you have identified three things that contribute to your negative self-image, you should take on the *least* potent of the three first. After bringing that aspect of yourself out of the psychic box in which you have kept it locked away, showing it to other people, and eventually embracing it, you will then be in a stronger position to do likewise with the next most potent aspect and so forth.

The building of shame tolerance is the core process of healing a negative self-image. It is a process that takes time and must be worked at consistently. Some aspects of your self-image that need to be changed may be intractable or simply too painful to handle on your own. If you find that to be the case, consider getting help from a professional counselor to work on these issues. Even if it were possible to present in book form a comprehensive approach to changing the persistent elements of a negative self-image, such an approach would be far beyond the scope of this book. Fortunately, help from skilled counselors is generally readily available. You may know several people who have gone through counseling or therapy and would be comfortable talking about it. If *you* feel comfortable, tell these friends that you're thinking about getting some counseling and ask them if they could tell you a little about the counselor they worked with, his or her approach, credentials, age, fees, and general "feel." How did they find their person to begin with? Was the therapist very active in the session? Did he or she give advice or mostly listen and reflect the feelings? You could ask your doctor, minister, priest, rabbi, or other spiritual adviser for a recommendation. Alternately, you might call the counseling center of a nearby college or university and ask for a list of their staff members who work privately. If your city or town has a community mental health center, you might be able to see someone there for a relatively low fee.

When you have the name of someone who seems to be a likely possibility, call that person and ask if she could tell you a little bit about her general approach to the process of counseling. Tell her a bit about why you're calling and ask whether she has experience with those issues. Find out how many years he's been in practice. Ask about his fees. While you're doing all this, try to get a feel for the person. Do you find yourself liking him or her? Does the counselor seem to be the kind of person you could talk with easily?

This is a lot to do, and one further suggestion we have is that you do *not* get a list of three or four counselors and call each of them in turn. In our experience, when people call several counselors they are trying to decide among, they *may* eliminate one. Usually if they've done a reasonably good job of composing the list, though, after four calls they still have four people to choose among, all of whom seem quite fine—because they all would *be* quite fine. The choice, then, is no easier, and in some ways it's even more difficult. This is a decision tailor-made for obsessing over. When we are asked for referrals we listen to the person, then make *one* referral. We say that if for any reason this doesn't turn out to be a good match, the individual should call us back and we will then use that information (why it didn't work out with Counselor A) to make a better referral to someone else. We recommend, then, that you ask your doctor (or other knowledgeable source of referrals) for one name, try that person for a session or two, and then decide to stay on or go back for another (singular) referral.

Change in self-image can never be accomplished by a program of muscular skill building. It is not possible to eliminate feelings of shame that surround some flaw or inadequacy—real or imagined—by building a wall of strength around it, by eliminating the flaw itself. In the end, the process of healing negative self-images is a process of acceptance: accepting our own particular shortcomings, accepting and honoring our unique personal history, accepting our poor judgments and other errors that have caused pain to ourselves and to others. This ability to see honestly and feel fully, and then to accept and forgive ourselves, is a central challenge of mature adulthood. The goal is not to be a person who is invincibly self-confident, but rather to be able to act effectively and find satisfaction despite inevitable disappointments and failures, in others *and* in ourselves.

EPILOGUE

TAKING CARE OF YOUR CAREER

THE PERFECT CAREER DOESN'T EXIST ANY MORE THAN "perfect health." Being in good, or even excellent, health doesn't mean that you never come down with a cold, that you can run marathons every other day, that you never get scrapes and bruises. It just means that you're healthy now and that you are generally not sick very often, probably due to some combination of who you are (genetically speaking), a little luck, your previous health history, and what you do to take care of yourself. The same holds true for a healthy career. You can't change who you are, you can't change luck or the past, but you can recognize, understand, and then take action to change patterns of behavior that threaten the health of your career. This book has been about this process of recognition, insight, and change.

People whose careers are in "excellent health" are rarely just lucky or so talented that success comes to them effortlessly. Typically they work proactively to take care of their careers. Consider the cases of two individuals whom we know quite well, both senior executives in the financial services industry. Both are very successful, not just in terms of wealth and status, but in terms of their management abilities, leadership, vision, and personal integrity. Both have accurate and positive self-images, use power effectively, are able to understand things from other people's perspectives, and have successfully come to terms with the issue of authority. Yet both continue to struggle with behavior patterns that, after all, remain rooted in their fundamental personality structures. There is both good and bad news to be taken from this when it comes to behavior change.

The bad news is that there may never be a complete and total "cure" for any of the twelve behavior patterns that we have described. Just as sober alcoholics describe themselves as "recovering alcoholics" (sober but still alcoholics), you may have to continue struggling with those aspects of your personality that keep you from your full potential.

The good news is that this struggle, pursued with intelligence and renewed effort, is in itself good enough. Perfect and total "cure" is not necessary. If you are alert to the signs and symptoms of the patterns that cause you trouble; if you are willing to recognize them for what they are (rather than use any of the psychological defenses at your disposal to deny them or make them someone else's problem); and if you are willing to work hard to keep yourself from falling into the old familiar behaviors—then over time your struggle with self-defeating behaviors will become less difficult and you will be increasingly successful in your efforts. People define success in very different and intensely personal ways, and in our view it is not best measured simply in terms of the absolute level of financial reward or other signs of achievement a person has attained. In this book we have argued for another measure of success: the difference between what each of us has been given (in terms of our talents and hang-ups, our promise and limitations) and what, through insight and effort, we fashion from it.

TAKEAWAYS

A CHECKLIST FOR CHANGE

SYMPTOMS

General *symptoms* of career Achilles' heels (the inner feelings and sensations you have, but that other people may not be able to perceive about you):

- Feeling as if you have not sustained career traction or direction.
- Feeling that you start and stop, engage and disengage in your job and overall career.
- Feeling that you don't belong in the position you hold.
- Feeling that your performance doesn't match your potential.

SIGNS

Observable *signs* that someone under you suffers from one or more career Achilles' heels:

- Performance is erratic, especially if there is a discernable pattern of what, where, when, and/or with whom.

- The person doesn't seem to be working to his or her potential.

- You find that you spend a lot of time thinking about, worrying about, and/or "cleaning up" after the person.

- Other people complain about him or her, or express other concerns (such as worry).

- The individual manages down and/or across and/or up well, but fails dramatically in one of the three.

- As the person's manager you feel pressed into a parental role even more than usual.

TIPS

General tips for curing your Achilles' heel(s):

- Decide: Do you really want to change? (Be honest!)

- If you answer is yes: Do it *now*.

- Employ careful self-observation—of your actions, thoughts, and feelings. Be as concrete and specific as you can.

- Get a "buddy" to help monitor your behavior at work and give you feedback (to ensure that you're changing—but not overdoing it; and to tell you about eruptions of your problem pattern).

- Remember: Don't punish the messenger—even a little—or he/she won't tell you the truth.

- Take on the role of anthropologist in your company and study its customs.

- "Read" the culture of the organization and specific work group before joining.

- Look to stars as role models—both within your organization and outside.

- Decide what is "good enough." Make the definition as clear as possible and *stick by* it.

- In making that decision, remember the 80–20 rule: Often the first

20 percent of your effort gets you 80 percent of the benefit, with the last 20 percent requiring a whopping 80 percent of your effort.

- Remember that accepting rules isn't the same as bowing to them—if you're on a controlled-access highway, you readily accept the fact that you can take only certain exits, for example.

- Likewise, remember that knee-jerk rebellion is just as predictable and reflexive as knee-jerk acceptance.

- The *use* of power is not the *abuse* of power. Put another way, power is not a four-letter word.

- Practice interpersonal literacy: Learn to read other people—empathy is a skill, not a weakness.

- Or, as Machiavelli put it, "All men will see what you seem to be; only a few will know what you are." Be one of those few who know what (and who) other people really are.

- Make a "book" on the significant people in your work life: what motivates and interests them; what their hot buttons (positive and negative) are; what their short-term and long-term goals are; how much they need affiliation, achievement, and power.

- Beware the Sirens' songs of money, fame, and instant gratification.

- Look behind you in line as well as ahead. When you still have a long way to go, it helps to see how far you've come.

- Set aside some time for introspection about the causes of your Achilles' heel(s)—and *use* it.

- Acknowledge your fears—without letting them rule you.

- Learn your internal symptoms (e.g., clenched jaw or buttocks, grinding of teeth, loss of concentration, specific thoughts) that accompany your Achilles' heel(s).

- In formulating an action plan for changing, have one or at most two overarching goals; develop small steps that will take you toward each goal. Go from easiest to hardest.

- A little success goes a long way—so go for early victories and payoffs.

- Script, rehearse alone, and role-play with someone else—then repeat until you've "got it."
- Always bear in mind the distinction between being right and being effective.
- Decide whether you want to be an individual contributor or a manager. They're both good things to do but are *very* different from one another.
- Practice "normalizing" relationships after a confrontation or argument.
- Use reminders (for example, on your screen saver and on your mirror at home)—and change them often, so you don't come to ignore them.
- Be quick to say "I'm sorry" when you're wrong or have blown something—and *mean* it.
- Sometimes other people fight dirty—you have to know when and how to fight back.

General tips for helping cure the Achilles' heels of people you manage:

- Decide whether you are invested in helping the person. Is he or she worth your time and energy?
- If the answer is yes, make sure you're not *too* invested. If the person is having serious problems, you have to be prepared to terminate him or her if necessary.
- Then decide whether you're the right person to help. Do you have the competence and confidence, and feel comfortable acting as the person's coach? Or would that present an uncomfortable dual relationship? Are you and the person in question often involved in personal conflicts?
- Make careful observations (and take notes) before talking to the person. This will make it difficult for him or her to deny what you're saying, and will provide vivid, "live" data for your discussion.
- Plan the meeting carefully: Allow enough time, and be clear about

how you're going to open the conversation and what you want to achieve. Schedule a follow-up meeting for soon afterward.

- In discussing the issue, offer concrete examples and alternative modes of handling situations.

- A little success goes a long way—go for early victories and payoffs in your suggestions.

- Avoid a tug-of-war by using psychological judo. If the person takes a contrary position, jump over to that side and "absolutely agree" with it. A tug-of-war requires people holding on to both ends of the rope—don't grab hold of your end.

- One way to avoid those struggles is to use double binding as an opening move—"I have something to tell you, Jack, and I *know* you're going to disagree and not even want to *hear* it" (thus ensuring that he *has* to listen in order to prove you wrong).

- If it's appropriate, offer the choice: Does the person want to be on a management track or be an individual contributor?

- Offer to help them script and role-play discussions they need to have that are likely to be difficult.

- Set your own expectations and those of the person you're working with. Let him or her know that you don't expect perfection.

- Be sure to "normalize" your relationship after the discussion.

- Meet regularly and frequently to follow up. Remember, you're trying to help change the course of an ocean liner—it doesn't happen with one quick turn of the wheel.

- When you have subsequent observations to share with the person, do it as soon as possible, so the experience is as "fresh" as possible.

- Remember that as long as you're a manager you're *always* in a parental role—whether you're aware of it (or want it) or not.

APPENDIX

USING JUNG'S PERSONALITY THEORY TO ANALYZE WORKING MODE

SWISS PSYCHOLOGIST CARL JUNG DEVELOPED A NOW WIDELY used road map of human consciousness that can be helpful for us in considering the different types of information we must gather about ourselves if our career decisions are to be based on our deepest yearnings. His model is just that—a map or tool to guide our thinking. It is not definitive, it is somewhat simplistic, and it too is an abstraction, so we must be careful not to be concrete about its categories and explanations (as has been the case with its use in many settings). Basically, Jung offered the proposition that there are two major dimensions of human consciousness, a *judgment* dimension and a *perception* dimension. The judgment dimension has to do with the actual function of decision making. Jung said that there are two ways in which we can make decisions: either we predominantly use a thinking/analytic function to decide between alternatives; or we use a feeling/valuing function to decide.

This dimension has nothing to do with intelligence. Thinking decision makers are not "brighter thinkers." When faced with a decision, however, they tend to step back and attempt to become "objective," removing as much as possible the personal, feeling reactions to the decision situation. They weigh the pros and cons carefully. Feeling decision makers tend to deliberately factor the personal dimension into their decision making. They place the value aspects of the situation at the forefront of their choice. They are aware of how the emotional and valuing aspect of the human world plays into the ultimate appropriateness and success of choosing one option over another. Neither of these styles is preferred or inherently more valuable, but Jung did assert two things about the use of one over the other.

First, he said that one or the other of these two functions is dominant for us, essentially from birth. We come into the world, according to Jung, with an innate proclivity to make decisions in a certain way. We will, at least on the practical day-to-day level, make better decisions more of the time if we use our dominant judgment function. His second major point, however, was that we need access to both judgment aspects of consciousness if we are to know ourselves fully and act accordingly. We all need both functions to know what we want, but like "handedness," we have a strong bias toward using one over the other. This bias helps us in most superficial aspects of life but develops a blind spot when the issue is the needs and longings of our deepest being. Strong thinking types tend to undervalue and underutilize their feeling world, but that world is there and has its needs and demands on our being. When we come to big decisions in life we must, if we are to do justice to the realization of our full potential, consider that realm of our self that is accessed by both the feeling and thinking aspects of judgment consciousness.

The perception dimension is concerned with the way in which we take in information about the world. The two poles of this dimension are known as the "intuitive function" and the "sensing function." Again, a predilection toward the dominant use of one perception function over the other is inherent for each person. Those with a strong sensing orientation focus their attention on the details of the world. The sights, sounds, and smells of a place are important. The contact with the physical world provides a primary orientation. The sensing-dominant person focuses on what is present in the environment from which facts and practical realities may be ascertained. Emphasis is placed on fact and detail in the learning process.

The intuitive-dominant person does not typically start from observations in the physical world in arriving at conclusions about the nature of what is real or important. What is not present is typically given more weight: possibilities, organizing principles, the unseen connections between phenomena, and what things seem to be "tending toward." The highly intuitive person relies on hunches, intuitions, and fill-in-the-gap guesses to get at the unseen underpinnings of the phenomenal world. This realm of idea and tendency comprises, for the intuitive-dominant individual, the greater part of what is "real," or at least the greater part of what is worthy of focusing on when coming to terms with reality. Those with a highly developed intuitive function tend to discount the importance of detail and the immediate surroundings, while individuals with a more highly developed sensing function tend to discount the credibility of lines of thought and conclusions that have no apparent support in the world of available facts.

As we mentioned earlier, in Jung's view we come into the world with a tendency toward dominance of one or the other function on each of these dimensions. This proclivity develops further as we build the habit over the years of taking in information and making decisions in one way or another. It is useful for day-to-day effectiveness that we develop a strong, sure, and instinctive way of perceiving and deciding. There is a problem for our development, though, in the fact that the less developed function on each dimension allows us poorer access to vital parts of our being. The thinking-dominant individual needs the richness of a feeling connection to the world as much as the feeling-dominant person needs to think through deeply and objectively. The intuitive-dominant individual lives in the physical world and needs a connection to the immediate environment just as the sensing-dominant person needs to creatively break the bonds of immediate details to participate in the broader sweep of the currents of life. When it comes to decisions of any type, including career decisions, we tend to go with our developed channels of knowing and choosing. We also tend to ignore or undervalue data from the other parts of our being that will beg to have a voice in our new situation, but whose needs may not have been taken into account while making the decision. Before we take a look at some examples of the psychological blind spots associated with different patterns of function dominance, you should do the next exercise to get a rough sense of your own dominant function on both the judging and perception dimensions.

A QUICK LOOK AT YOUR FUNCTION DOMINANCE

The Judgment Dimension

Preference for Thinking

▲ Like to step back, be "objective," and keep emotional responses at a distance when faced with a difficult decision
▲ Tend to understand the world through intellectual analysis
▲ Rely on problem-solving ability when faced with challenges
▲ Often adopt a scientific perspective on the world and its workings

Preference for Feeling

▲ Deliberately factor in your personal feeling response to a situation when faced with a difficult decision
▲ Tend to look at situations in terms of the people involved
▲ See relationships as a major resource in solving life problems
▲ Are known to be empathic and skilled in understanding other people

We all rely on both the feeling and thinking functions to make decisions, we are all "some of both," but after reading the above descriptions, what is your dominant judgment function, thinking or feeling? (Use your first instinctive response.)

The Perception Dimension

Preference for Intuition

▲ Are always more interested in the "big picture"
▲ Rely on your "gut feel" to understand what is going on

▲ Like to theorize, project, and guess and will act based on these assumptions
▲ Tend to skip the details in your hurry to see what's next
▲ Love the new, the unexplored, the unknown

Preference for Sensing

▲ Are known as someone who pays attention to details
▲ Are seen as someone who is practical and "has your feet on the ground"
▲ Prefer facts to speculation and hunches when making a decision
▲ More interested in what is actually going on than in imagining possibilities

We all rely on both the intuition and the sensing functions to understand our world, we are all of "some of both," but after reading the above descriptions, what is your dominant perception function, intuition, or sensing? (Use your first instinctive response.) You may also want to ask a few friends or family members to read the description above and give their assessment.

In addition to the judgment dimension (thinking versus feeling orientation) and the perception dimension (sensing versus intuition orientation), Jung described a third dimension that he called the "attitude dimension."

Jung's attitude dimension concerns an individual's experience of his or her most immediate reality. The two poles of this dimension are *introversion* and *extroversion*. The extrovert derives his or her sense of being alive essentially through a connection with the immediate environment, with the people and ongoing circumstances of his or her surroundings. This is what is "real" for the extrovert, and when access to people and immediate activity in the world is somehow constrained, the extrovert feels cut off from his or her very being. In work settings, extroverts seek a high level of interaction with other people and tasks that call for daily practical and tangible accomplishment. They are pragmatic doers and see "real work" as that which calls for such an attitude.

For introverts, reality resides in the subjective experience of existence.

It is not what is happening but how what is happening changes personal experience that is important. The realms of ideas, the past, and psychological reality are placed in the forefront by an introverted orientation. The intentions and character of another person are as important as his or her behavior. The antecedents and consequences of a fact or an event are as important as the immediate manifestation of that event. The introvert is more attuned to "hidden" realities, whether they are in the realm of poetry or mathematics, whereas the extrovert is oriented toward action in response to the physical givens of the immediate situation. Introverts often prefer work situations that call for skill in apprehending "hidden" realities, whether these are found in the creation of computer algorithms or understanding the interpersonal dynamics of group.

Jung says that we are all, to some degree, both extroverted and introverted. We all respond in a direct and practical way to the immediate circumstances as they present themselves. We also have an abiding introverted sense of an inner "self" that guides us in our decision making. Jung also says, however, that we each have a primary orientation toward dominance by either introverted attitude or extroverted attitude that is present essentially from birth. This primary orientation will influence to a considerable degree the type of work that we find most valuable and "real." There is, of course, no value judgment attached to either orientation. Both are essential approaches to grasping reality. Below you will find a quick and preliminary exercise for analyzing your, or a colleague's, primary attitude orientation. Please do that exercise now. After you have completed that exercise, combine the results with the exercise you completed concerning the perception dimension to arrive at your particular combination of preferences on each of these dimensions.

A QUICK LOOK AT YOUR
JUNGIAN ATTITUDE ORIENTATION

The Extroverted *Attitude*

▲ Prefer workdays that are "interpersonally busy" with give-and-take with many people

▲ You are seen as more action oriented than reflective

▲ Have a wide circle of friends and recover from stress best by spending time with others

▲ Have a practical, fact-oriented approach to problem solving

The Introverted *Attitude*

▲ Prefer a work environment that allows for concentration and depth of focus

▲ Rely on the realm of ideas and imagination to guide you

▲ Tend to have a small number of close friends rather than a large social circle

▲ Others may sense that your "inner world" is just as active as what you do with or say to others

▲ Typically rely on some quiet time alone to recover from stress

We all have some aspects of introversion and extroversion. We are all "some of both," but after reading the above descriptions, what is your primary attitude orientation, extroversion or introversion? (Use your first instinctive response.) You may also want to ask a few friends or family members to read the description above and give their assessment.

In analyzing a person's work mode, we use only two of Jung's three dimensions, the perception dimension and the attitude dimension. There are four possible combinations of perception and attitude orientation: extroverted sensing, extroverted intuition, introverted intuition, and introverted sensing. These four combinations are what we refer to as "work modes." Individuals who have the combination of dominant orientations represented by each of these combinations tend to approach work, or even define what work is, in generally predictable ways. By knowing an individual's work mode, you will be better able to appreciate how he or she approaches a business situation and have a better sense, as well, of the types of tasks necessary for the success of a project that will be most appealing to him or her. Please return to Chapter 13 to read the discussion of each of the different work modes.

INDEX

INDEX

excellence in, 27, 39–40, 55
insecurity about, 7, 10–11, 22
egotism, 33, 87, 113, 210–14
Einstein, Albert, 15
Eisenhower, Dwight D., 84, 268
Elkind, David, 171
Ellis, Charles, 121
emotionally tone-deaf, 33, 149–64, 274
  breaking pattern of, 160–64
  emotions remote to, 150–56
  fundamental truths seen by, 150–51
  inability to take perspective in, 152–53
  indifference and rudeness ascribed to, 150, 152, 159
  introverts vs. extroverts and, 153
  organizational and personal impact of, 154–57, 158–60
  origins of, 157–58
emotions
  consideration of, 21, 215–17, 232–33
  disregard of, 29, 33, 38–39
  repression of, 64–76, 298–99
empathy, 84–85, 97–98, 152, 162
employees
  assessment and testing of, xiv-xv, xviii
  grooming of, xiii
  "high maintenance," xiii, 35, 108–9
  promotion of, xv, 6, 11, 15, 18, 26, 29, 54
  termination of, xii, xv, xvii, xxii, 13, 29, 48, 49, 73, 76, 92, 111
  underutilizing of, 30
  see also personality
entrepreneurship, 117–18, 125–27
Erikson, Erik, 287–90
externalization, 207–10

failure
  avoiding mistakes leading to, xiii, xv, xvii
  fear of, 122, 166, 171–72, 173
  focus on, xv–xvii
  of talented people, xi–xiv, xv–xvii, xx–xxi, 26–30
Farber, Seth, 207–8
fear, 154
  of confrontation and anger, 64–76, 80–81
  of failure, 122, 166, 171–72, 173
  of not belonging, 7–8, 10–11, 12, 13, 20
  overcoming of, 10, 15, 274
  of power, 17–18, 270–74
  of ridicule, 20
  of risk taking, 132–48, 168–69

Federal Express, 109
flexibility, xiii
Fortune, xv, 109, 122, 127, 262
four psychological issues, xxi, xxii, 5, 33–34, 223–25
  combinations of, 5, 223
  coming to terms with authority, 248–61
  examining self-image, 283–301
  taking others' perspectives, 224, 226–47
  using power, 262–82
Freud, Sigmund, 250, 251, 273

Gandhi, M. K., 250, 268
Gates, Bill, 122, 125–26, 127, 130, 268, 275
General Managers, The (Kotter), 127
Genghis Khan, 54
Gentile, Mary, 139
Germany, Nazi, 80–81, 84, 85
"good-enough mother," 177–78
Greek mythology, 17–18, 49, 123–24, 250, 276
guilt, 17–18, 286

Hallowell, Edward, 184
Harvard University, 7, 27, 33, 36, 122
  MBA Career Development Program at, xiii, xiv
health care, 27, 126–27
Helmsley, Leona, 83
heroes, xix, 47–63, 223, 254
  breaking patterns of, 60–63
  burnout of, 48, 51, 53, 55, 198
  compulsive goal setting by, 47–50, 53, 55–56, 58–60
  as driving others too hard, 48, 49, 50–55, 60
  highs and lows experienced by, 59–60
  loner sensibility of, 54–55
  as managers, 49, 51–53, 56, 58, 61
  organizational impact of, 52–58
  origins of, 58–60
  overscheduling by, 49–51
  perfectionism of, 48, 50, 52, 56
  personal relationships of, 50–51
Hillman, James, 206, 265, 276
Hitler, Adolf, 85
home run hitters, 117–31, 254
  breaking pattern of, 127–29
  financial overextension of, 119, 120, 123

ABOUT THE AUTHORS

JAMES WALDROOP, PH.D., and TIMOTHY BUTLER, PH.D., are directors of MBA career development at the Harvard Business School and developers of the Internet-based career self-assessment and management program CareerLeader, currently used by more than 100 corporations and MBA programs worldwide. They are the founders of Peregrine Partners, a consulting firm in Brookline, Massachusetts, specializing in executive development and employee retention. They are the authors of *Discovering Your Career in Business* as well as articles that have appeared in the *Harvard Business Review* and *Fortune*. They can be contacted via their Website (www.careerdiscovery.com).